Tony Fletcher is a̶...
and one novel. His bestselling biography of drummer
Keith Moon, *Dear Boy*, has been named in many a Best
Music Book list, and his biography of R.E.M. has been
published in several languages. His most recent biography,
A Light That Never Goes Out: The Enduring Saga of The Smiths, was
published in 2012. Born in Yorkshire and raised in South
London, Fletcher now lives with his family in the
Catskill Mountains of New York State. He can be found
at www.ijamming.net and www.boyabouttown.net, and
on Twitter @tonyfletcher.

ALSO BY TONY FLETCHER

FICTION
Hedonism: A Novel

NON-FICTION
Never Stop: The Echo & the Bunnymen Story
R.E.M. Perfect Circle
Dear Boy: The Life of Keith Moon
The Clash: The Music That Matters
All Hopped Up and Ready to Go:
Music from the Streets of New York, 1927-77
A Light That Never Goes Out:
The Enduring Saga of The Smiths

Praise for Boy About Town

'An open hearted love letter to the boundless power of music and youth, Boy About Town brims over with infectious passion. This wonderful book will remind you just how much your favourite band matters.'

Russ Litten, author of Scream If You Want To Go Faster

'Reading this I was transported back to the days when everything seemed to matter more – music, fashion, football, girls, life! Evocative, entrancing and entertaining.'

Buddy Ascott, The Chords

'[A] charming coming of age tale . . . An innocent's story, engagingly told.'

Mojo

'[An] excellent memoir of adolescent angst and musical obsession . . . it is surprisingly candid, wryly funny, occasionally harrowing, yet always honest in its descriptions . . . brilliantly written.'

All Mod Icon

'Autobiography is rarely this can-do and candid.'

David Quantick, author of Grumpy Old Men

'[A] gripping account of the post-punk period . . . one of the most essential accounts of this tumultuous yet highly productive period of British music . . . Required reading for anyone who wishes to know more about the late 1970s music scene.'

Louder Than War

'In this memoir of his formative years, covering the years 1972 to 1980, [Fletcher] conveys the thrill of how it was to be a schoolkid who grew up loving and eventually becoming part of the scene . . . It's very funny, fascinating, and at times quite moving.'

The Bookbag

'It reads the way that great cult film 24 *Hour Party People* plays in the memory, and warrants constant re-viewing.'

Woodstock Times

'Fletcher is a powerful writer . . . A touching personal document and a propulsive historic record of England on the edge.'

Chronogram magazine

Praise for *A Light That Never Goes Out: The Enduring Saga of The Smiths*

'[A] meticulous biography. This exhaustive, well-researched account brings fresh detail and thought to the party.'

Sunday Times

'The story itself is riveting and Fletcher tells it lucidly and fairly.'

Irish Times

'Reveals new details and brings new depths to the story of Morrissey, Marr, Rourke, Joyce and the birth of the band.'

Mojo

Boy About Town

TONY FLETCHER

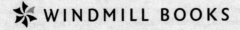
WINDMILL BOOKS

Published by Windmill Books 2014

2 4 6 8 10 9 7 5 3 1

Copyright © Tony Fletcher 2013

First published in Great Britain in 2013 by William Heinemann

Windmill Books
The Random House Group Limited
20 Vauxhall Bridge Road, London SW1V 2SA

Addresses for companies within The Random House Group Limited can
be found at: www.randomhouse.co.uk/offices.htm

The Random House Group Limited Reg. No. 954009

www.randomhouse.co.uk

A CIP catalogue record for this book
is available from the British Library

ISBN 9780099558552

The Random House Group Limited supports the Forest Stewardship
Council® (FSC®), the leading international forest-certification
organisation. Our books carrying the FSC label are printed on
FSC®-certified paper. FSC is the only forest-certification
scheme supported by the leading environmental organisations, including
Greenpeace. Our paper procurement policy can be found at:
www.randomhouse.co.uk/environment

Typeset in Goudy by Palimpsest Book Production Ltd, Falkirk, Stirlingshire
Printed and bound by CPI Group (UK) Ltd, Croydon, CR0 4YY

For Ruth,
For everything

Number 50:
COULD IT BE FOREVER

D avid was my first love. Not David Bowie, though it was Bowie's single 'Starman' that brought my eight-year-old self, my eleven-year-old brother and our thirty-something mum to this place in time: Counterpoint Records in Crystal Palace, a Saturday in summer, 1972. My brother Nic had watched *Top of the Pops* two nights earlier and been transfixed by the sight of Bowie, sporting orange hair, an amazing Technicolor jumpsuit and a blue guitar, throwing his arms around a guitarist whose gold lamé two-piece suit matched the colour of his own considerable mane. The visual impact, and perhaps even the music, had sent him running to our mum, begging her to buy him a copy. It was the first time he'd ever asked for a record of his own.

I'd already pestered our parents into buying me a couple of singles over the years: 'Back Home' by the 1970 England World Cup Squad – because what self-respecting six-year-old football fan could possibly go without? – and, much to my dad's dismay, 'Something's Burning' by Kenny Rogers, which I'd fallen for on one of the few occasions I'd been allowed to watch *Top of The Pops*. Dad, the head of music for the Inner London Education Authority, had always frowned on pop. We'd been brought up learning the cello (me), violin (Nic), piano (both), and taught to read music almost as soon as we had learned the alphabet. My brother spent his Saturdays in Pimlico, at the music-school-within-a-school that Dad had recently founded in the comprehensive there; I was expected to follow imminently.

Still, when he'd left home a few months earlier, the culmination of incompatible parental tensions evident even to a small kid like me, Dad also left behind his collection of late-sixties Beatles albums that appeared to provide the exception to his musical rule. I'd enjoyed isolating them from the symphonies and operas that otherwise dominated the record cabinet, singing along to those songs which made sense to me: 'Maxwell's Silver Hammer', 'Piggies', 'When I'm Sixty-Four' and 'Your Mother Should Know'. The pop bug was something I'd surely been born with. It was just that, until now, I'd been prevented from tending to it.

But with Dad having moved over the river, the mood around the house suddenly changed. It wasn't all for the good: Mum told us that he wasn't paying his share, so she worked a couple of evenings a week at the Youth Club at Norwood Girls School, after already working there all day, teaching English to kids who didn't speak it the way they did on the BBC. And Nic and I had to spend alternate weekends at Dad's posh new flat in Pimlico, the very notion of which brought on migraines for me if some sense of continued bonding for my older brother. Still, freed from Dad commandeering the living room every other night to rehearse the teenage male prodigy violinists he was grooming for his London Schools Symphony Orchestra, we found we could suddenly start behaving like kids were meant to behave – and that Mum could act like a mum was meant to act around kids. Allowing us to watch *Top of the Pops* – and watching it with us – was a major first step. So was taking us to the record store. Mum even got her own single at Counterpoint that day: 'Walkin' In The Rain (With The One I Love)' by Love Unlimited, which came complete with watery sound effects, a high-pitched female chorus and the sound of a man talking to his woman on the telephone in the deepest voice you'd ever heard. Her choice, I figured, was influenced by the teenage girls at Norwood: it wasn't exactly like the music she sang with *her* group, the Bach Society.

Now, as we stood there by the record counter, she invited

me to choose a single as well. But, my interest in pop music having previously been denied, I had no idea what to get. I stared at the racks of 45s, most of which were in plain paper sleeves. They meant nothing to me. I studied the list of the current Top Thirty, laid out in moveable white letters on a black board near the counter. I didn't recognize any of their names. So I did what seemed natural for an eight-year-old. I asked my big brother for advice.

He examined the ranks, as cagily as I had. Just because he'd watched *Top of the Pops* the other night didn't make him an authority. All Nic knew was that by cuddling with his guitarist while singing about a starman who 'thinks he'll blow our minds', David Bowie had made history – and that all the kids in his class wanted to be, or buy, a part of it. Finally, he fingered through the rack of half-price singles – records that had recently fallen off the charts – and pulled out the only one that came with a picture sleeve. It was called 'Could It Be Forever'.

'You should get David Cassidy,' he said, with evident relief, showing me a round feminine face that filled the whole of the cover in colour. 'All the girls love him.'

I was not a girl, but that wasn't the point. He recommended David Cassidy because he thought it was the limit of my expectations. As if to prove him right, I took him up on it. The next I knew, singles in hand, we were walking back to wherever Mum had parked the Hillman Imp and heading down Gipsy Hill towards home – a modern 'Wates' estate of narrow terraced three-story houses called Little Bornes, sandwiched in between the expensive homes of West Dulwich's Alleyn Park and Sydenham's massive Kingswood Estate. Low garden fences separated us from our posh neighbours to the front, a twelve-foot fence from the poorer estate to the back. England could be funny like that.

When I finally got to hear it in full, at home, 'Could It Be Forever' was sugary sweet almost to the point of sickliness, nothing like the alien sounds of David Bowie's 'Starman'. But once I convinced myself that I liked it anyway, then David

Cassidy's feminine face revealed itself as deeply handsome, a fragile symbol of male tenderness. I tried to assure myself that his shoulder-length hair mirrored my own bowl-like cut, even though his was dark and mine was blond. If David Cassidy could look so girly and yet be so popular, then one day, I figured, so could I. And with that, the idea of being a pop star suddenly seemed as worthy a goal in life as any – especially for a kid like me, who was precocious beyond all acceptable limits and who craved the attention that came with it, a kid who thought nothing of heading out alone on his bicycle all over the surrounding neighbourhoods and yet who clung too close to his mother's apron for either's benefit, who worshipped footballers and wished he could be one himself and yet who was overweight and emotionally unstable, as evidenced in easily provoked and alarmingly frequent crying fits. I played the record again and I was convinced. Yes, David, I swore of my first love, it *will* be forever.

I had a stamp collection that filled three books already, and several tins full of old (and, I hoped, rare) coins. I'd started copying out the phone book over the school holidays one year because it seemed like an important project. And I wrote down football attendances in a scrapbook because someone had to keep track of these things. It only made sense then that, having chosen David Cassidy as my pop star, I should collect everything about and by him, and *now*. Setting about my task with a vengeance, I learned that David belonged to something called the Partridge Family, who released their own records, and even had their own TV show. I learned too that he had competition: Donny Osmond, who *also* sang in a family group that had their own TV show. Donny Osmond's 'Puppy Love' was number one in the charts; now that I started paying attention to these things, it was obvious that you couldn't escape it. It was equally obvious that it was a soppy piece of rubbish; 'Could It Be Forever' was far more grown-up than that.

And so, over the next few weeks, I convinced Mum to take me on repeat visits to Counterpoint, as well as to the record store in West Norwood, near her school, so I could find more David Cassidy singles. She didn't seem any more convinced of my taste in David Cassidy than my dad had been over Kenny Rogers, but at least she didn't stop me indulging in my new obsession. Soon I had two 7"s by the Partridge Family to join the one by David Cassidy. I had the makings of a collection.

Singles were great fun. They were inexpensive, they were instant, and they didn't last long enough to lose interest in them. But I knew from the Beatles already that LPs were more important, that they were the mark of proper musicians, as well as the adults who appreciated them. So, one Saturday, about five minutes after receiving my pocket money, I rode my bike over to West Norwood, parked it outside the record shop, walked up to the counter, took a deep breath . . . and asked the manager if he could tell me the names of all the LPs by the Partridge Family and David Cassidy. He studied me closely, as if to assure himself I was not wasting his time; presumably satisfied by my earnest expression, he pulled out a big reference book he kept behind the counter, scrolled through it until he found the right page, and read out a short list of LPs. I then asked which of these LPs had been released first and, after again checking that I was not having him on, he told me: the debut – I loved that word, 'debut' – album by the Partridge Family was called *The Partridge Family Album*.

The cover to *The Partridge Family Album* had a treble clef stave with stick figures of the various Family members across it, designed to look like what I knew to be crotchets and quavers. In the bottom corner, David Cassidy had signed his autograph. (So had Shirley Jones, his mother, though I couldn't understand how, if they were both part of the Partridge Family, they had two different last names.) It wasn't a match for the *Sgt. Peppers* album cover, but if I was to be a real pop music fan, a dedicated follower of Cassidy, I had to start my own LP collection here, at the beginning.

But I didn't have enough money on me. I only had fifty pence. And I was worried that if I tried to save up for the album the record shop might sell it in the meantime and then I would *never* own it. I explained my situation to the manager and he suggested I make what he called a 'down payment'. I could give him 50p now, come back later with another 50p, and when I'd paid the full price of the album, I could take it home with me. Until then, he'd keep it behind a counter so that nobody else could buy it.

I gave him my fifty-pence piece. In return, I got a slip of paper confirming that I had made a down payment on a – no, on *the* – *Partridge Family Album*. My collection could now begin in earnest.

But I hadn't bet on my mother. When I told her about the deal she appeared aghast. She retrieved the deposit the next day. Whether she thought the store was taking advantage of me, or just that I had appalling taste in music, she never made clear.

Number 49:
HELLO HOORAY

Alice was a boy who named himself after a girl. He looked like something that had crawled from the gutter. We were introduced on holiday, in the south of France, only a few weeks after I'd pledged my allegiance to David. I was on a campsite in the Dordogne Valley, where thunder clouds had become trapped by the surrounding mountains and were pelting us – me, my brother and my mum – with such relentless rain that one of the only joys to be found was in the portable radio we'd brought with us.

And that's how I discovered Alice Cooper. I tuned into Radio Luxembourg one day – because I had to find *some* way of staying connected with this new love of mine called pop music – and I heard his single, 'School's Out'. It opened with a screaming guitar riff that cut through the miserable weather like a guillotine. That riff gave way to a sneering verse, and the sneering verse to a rousing chorus. There was a crazy guitar solo in the middle of it all and when the song ended, it did so by grinding to a halt, like someone had turned the record player off – only to suddenly speed up again like a UFO taking off into the distance. The whole thing was dangerously loud: you could tell as much even through the crackle of medium wave on a portable radio in a foreign campsite in the rain. And as soon as I heard it, there was no turning back. From that moment on, David Cassidy was history.

It was partly David's own fault. He seemed so insecure. 'Could It Be Forever' had been followed that summer by 'How Can I Be Sure'. One of the Partridge Family singles I'd picked up was called 'I Think I Love You'. Not 'I *Know* I Love You', or even just 'I *Love* You', but 'I *Think* I Love You', as if he couldn't be sure it could be forever. The other Partridge Family single, 'Breaking Up Is Hard to Do', suggested that even *that* part of this thing called love was laced with doubt.

I had no concept of love – other than for my mum, my cat and my football team. But I knew this much already: breaking up was *not* hard to do. Breaking up was really easy. You just stopped seeing someone. You didn't even have to tell them. So I dropped David – just like that – and pledged myself to Alice, instead.

Alice didn't sing about soppy things like love. And he wasn't unsure about himself, either. Alice sang in statements. 'School's Out' was number one in England for three weeks during the holidays that summer, only dropping off the top spot in time for us to return to school after the August bank holiday. By the time we did so, I owned my very own copy of *School's Out* – and not the single, I was proud to say, but the LP of the same name. We'd gone to stay with my godmother in Beverley, the Yorkshire town where I'd been born, to make up for the disastrous camping holiday, which we had finally cut short due to the endless rain. The record store in Beverley, opposite the marketplace, had a copy of the *School's Out* LP in the window. I stared at that cover daily – hourly, even – and I knew: I had to own it. Not in the way I'd thought I had to own *The Partridge Family Album*. No, this time the longing was real.

Of course, I still didn't have enough money for an LP. So this time I set about it the old-fashioned way: I begged. I made such a case for ownership that my godmother, generous to a fault, decided to treat me. She packed me off to the store with the additional pound I still needed to buy my very first LP.

School's Out came in a sleeve that folded out into a school desk, the top with the group members' initials scratched into it, the inside with a photograph of its contents – catapults, flick knives, a cartoon about someone called Liberace and a picture of the Alice Cooper group sitting on rubbish bins smoking and drinking. If my godmother was horrified at the very sight of this, especially in the hands of an eight-year-old she was still dragging to Sunday School at every opportunity, she was kind enough not to show it. She may have just been counting her blessings: *School's Out* came with the strict instruction that it be played on a stereo record player *only* and hers, an old hinge-top portable, was mono. I had to wait until we were back in London before I could hear songs like 'Street Fight' and 'Public Animal'.

And when I did, it was like being beamed onto a different planet. The *School's Out* LP was not just loud, like the single, it was obnoxious as well, and though it was funny at times, it didn't invite you to snicker along. My dad, I knew, would have hated it.

I set about following Alice with a passion I'd barely hinted at with David. The singles 'Elected', 'Hello Hooray' and 'No More Mr Nice Guy', each on a distinctive green label carrying the same instantly recognisable Warner Brothers logo, made it into my growing collection of 45s. So did Alice Cooper's previous LP, *Killer*, which I bought at Counterpoint, despite the sales person's evident concern that I might be too young: the cover, after all, had a snake on the front and it opened up into a fold-out sleeve of Alice Cooper hanging from a noose. I knew from occasionally reading *Disco 45*, the fortnightly bible for under-age pop fans like myself, that this was all part of Alice's stage act, as was the cutting up of baby dolls and other gory stunts. Sure enough, when I got the album home and played it on the living-room record player, Mum found 'Dead Babies' as funny as I did. She was definitely loosening up.

And so, for my ninth birthday, she gave me what I wanted: Alice Cooper's new LP, *Billion Dollar Babies*. *Disco 45* said that the sleeve was the most expensive ever made, and I had no reason to doubt them. It came in a gatefold jacket with a pocket for a giant-size billion-dollar bank note; a wall of perforated cards to cut out and keep; and an inner sleeve with the lyrics on one side and, on the other, a full-colour photo of the group, in front of what looked like a billion bank notes, ominously cuddling live laboratory rabbits along with a chubby baby sporting Alice Cooper's distinctive eye make-up. The music was no less over the top, 'Elected' and 'Hello Hooray' and 'No More Mr Nice Guy' (all of which I now owned twice) joined by the likes of 'Raped and Freezin'', 'Sick Things' and the grand finale, 'I Love the Dead'.

I read and memorised the lyrics to each of these songs, but I didn't try to decipher them. I viewed 'I Love the Dead' much as I did those Dracula films I'd occasionally be allowed to stay up and watch. It seemed harmless enough. Alice, I figured, was a cartoon hero, like Desperate Dan perhaps, which made his band the equivalent of the Bash Street Kids. The music they made was mad, and I didn't doubt that they were genuinely tough, and I knew that nobody mistook them for the Osmonds, but surely I didn't have to understand the word 'raped' to sing along to them, did I?

But while I loved Alice Cooper more than anyone else, I didn't love him – them? – exclusively. I loved everyone associated with this music they were calling 'glam rock'. And why not? It was obvious that this was a unique time to be eight, nine, ten years old and yet, just as my brother hadn't been able to explain his hunger for 'Starman', only his need, I couldn't tell why I now read *Disco 45* cover to cover, studied the logos on the labels of every single I owned, even memorised the credits underneath the song titles. It seemed more than just useful information. It seemed essential.

Most kids at my primary school, Langbourne – situated on the Kingswood Estate, just a short walk through the grounds of Kingsdale, the local comprehensive – liked Sweet *or* Slade. I loved them both. I loved Sweet for Brian Connolly's shoulder-length blond hair and for Steve Priest's girly winks at the *Top of the Pops* camera, and especially for the thrill of 'Teenage Rampage', which sounded almost as rebellious as Alice Cooper. And I loved Slade for Noddy Holder's hoarse roar, Dave Hill's endless array of platform heels and ludicrously loud clothes, and the group's wonderfully misspelled song titles, silly lyrics and repetitive choruses. I liked Gary Glitter *and* Alvin Stardust; I knew that they'd both been making music since before I was born, that they were old enough to be my dad, but it didn't seem to matter. It was pop music. Who cared about IRA bombs going off elsewhere in London, the three-day work week, the endless strikes by the miners and dockers and railway workers and the rest, or the fact that there were routine power cuts and we had to have dinner by candlelight a couple of nights a week? It was 'I Love You Love Me Love' and 'Good Love Can Never Die'. It was a fantastic time to be alive.

I picked up Suzi Quatro's number one single 'Can the Can'. *Disco 45* said that she was friends with Alice Cooper (they both came from a place in America called Detroit), plus she had the Chapman-Chinn songwriting credit underneath the song title on the RAK label, and if those names were good enough for Sweet, they were good enough for me. Besides, everyone said Suzi Quatro was sexy and it was difficult to argue, given that she was just about the only girl (dressed like a boy) in a scene that otherwise consisted almost entirely of boys (dressed suspiciously like girls).

And I didn't stop at glam. Together, Mum and I collected the novelty hit instrumentals: the squiggly synthesisers of 'Popcorn' by Hot Butter, the pub piano of 'Mouldy Old Dough' by Lieutenant Pigeon, and the foreign yodelling of 'Hocus Pocus' by Focus. I had a soft spot for both the high-pitched ballad that was the Bee Gees' 'Run to Me', and the weepy deathbed poem that was Terry Jacks' 'Seasons in the Sun'. I bought 'Snoopy Versus the Red Baron' by the Hotshots and 'Too Busy Thinking About My Baby' by Mardi Gras because they each had a similar infectious jerky rhythm to them. I bought 'Happy Xmas (War Is Over)' by John Lennon. And I got a copy of Albert Hammond's 'The Free Electric Band' because I loved the message, the idea that the singer would throw everything – school, job, love – away for music.

These songs did more than just entertain me. With the

exception of Lieutenant Pigeon, who appeared on *Top of the Pops* with an old lady on piano who looked like everyone's granny, they suggested that there was a bigger world out there, one that extended far beyond the streets of South London, the fields of Yorkshire, even the campsites of southern France. On 'Be My Lover', Alice Cooper sang, 'I told her that I came from Detroit City, and I played guitar in a long-haired rock 'n' roll band,' and made it sound like the greatest job in the world. On 'Cum on Feel the Noize', Slade's Noddy Holder sang, 'So you think my singing's out of time, well it makes me money,' and the song went to number one, which proved his point. But it was Albert Hammond who put it best when he sang, 'Just give me bread and water, put a guitar in my hand . . .'

I didn't have a guitar yet, just a beaten-up grand piano in the living room that Dad had diverted from the school system's scrap heap, and an equally beat-up school cello, but that didn't stop me dreaming of my own free electric band. In the meantime, I filed my singles alphabetically in their own bookshelf in my bedroom, where I was donated the old cabinet record player once Mum finally had the money to get a new 'hi-fi'. I put the singles that had come in plain white paper sleeves into proper cardboard covers that had polythene inners, writing the title and artist in neat felt tip on the outside. And I gave my most treasured singles a silver or gold star the same way the teachers at Langbourne awarded us silver or gold stars for schoolwork.

Langbourne took in kids from both the council estate and the posher local streets, and we wouldn't have known it was unusual if we didn't occasionally hear our parents talking about it. We were too busy being loud and unruly. Our deputy head, who was also my class teacher, and much loved by everyone, watched these energy levels grow steadily more frenetic the closer it got to the weekend, and made the brave decision to do away with classes on Friday afternoon. He added an extra assembly instead – to be run by the kids. They were an immediate hit, with most pupils seizing the opportunity to read their own silver-starred short stories, show off their latest paintings, explain the results of some successful science experiment and the like.

Me, I sang the latest glam rock hits. Unaccompanied, I'd stand at the front of the hall, facing some 200 or more of my fellow Juniors sat cross-legged on the floor, and I'd break into the current chart-topper by one of the glam rock regulars. If there was a guitar riff, I'd sing it; if there was a backing vocal, I'd sing it; if there was a high-pitched scream during the third and final chorus, as there was on every Slade single, I'd sing it. If there was a distinct move that 'belonged' to a certain artist, I'd copy it. I even took a white secondary school shirt from my brother, ladled the back of it with glue in the shape of a star, spread several tubes of coloured glitter on top, and then wrote, in bold felt-tip pen above and beneath this star, the words 'It's Only Rock 'n Roll'. This was the title of a single by a group called the Rolling Stones, and though I hadn't yet heard it, that didn't mean I didn't *get* it. Wearing that shirt, singing to the entire school assembly, I felt like a pop star. Like I was on *Top of the Pops*. I saw it as training for the real thing.

Other kids soon followed suit. Singing the hits of the day became a regular part of the Friday assembly. All of a sudden, I was no longer unique. Most of the kids had better voices than me. Many had a better build than me. And, I hated to admit it, but some of them were more popular than me. Fortunately, there was only so much time allotted for singing, and it wasn't enough time for everyone. So, towards the end of the school year, four of us teamed up, commandeered the singing time, and presented our own version of the Eurovision Song Contest. We wrote out the lyrics of our chosen songs in different colours according to who would sing which lines, and we practised dance routines. We learned six songs in all, and we sang one each Friday afternoon for six weeks in a row. And then, on the seventh week, we were given the entire assembly to ourselves. We sang all six songs again, one after another, and then we took a vote by a show of hands. The ten- and eleven-year-olds split their choice between the various glam songs. The eight- and nine-year-olds voted en masse for 'The Funky Gibbon' by the Goodies, whose TV show was the funniest thing in the world (for that age group). 'The Funky Gibbon' was the runaway winner. And so, just like on the real Eurovision Song Contest, we sang our winning song again, and the whole hall cheered and laughed and sang along with us. We didn't say as much to each other, but we surely all sensed it: life would probably never get any better than this.

Number 48:
MAKE ME SMILE (COME UP AND SEE ME)

Dean was the best-looking kid in our year at Langbourne: even at the age of ten, we understood that kind of thing. Plus, he was smart, and he was tough. He was captain of the school football team. He'd taught me my first swearword – 'bloody', as in, 'the other team bloody fouled our Terry' – and I'd immediately got into trouble for repeating it at home. And then, at some point in our fourth and final year, he came up to me in the playground at lunch and asked if I masturbated. This was a big word and he knew it.

'Maybe,' I replied, hedging my bets.

'You should,' he hit back. 'It's great.'

As it happened, I already knew as much. The previous summer, Nic and I had gone to Canada, where our dad had recently taken a job as music professor at the main university in Nova Scotia. We spent a week in Cape Breton, staying with a friend of Dad's who had kids more or less our age, ten and thirteen, and one evening when we were all alone in the family barn, the older of the host's kids brought out a copy of a magazine called *Playboy*. It had full colour pictures of naked women, all with bronzed bodies, big breasts, and bushes of tangled hair between their legs that seemed to be hiding some greater mystery, and me and the other younger brother gasped in amazement at the sight of it. Nic though, seemed unimpressed, like he'd seen that and much more. As if to prove as much, he offered to show us all what he could do with his willy.

First, he fished around for some tissue paper, like it was an important part of whatever came next. Next, he took down his jeans and pulled out his penis. This was odd enough behaviour in itself, but then, while staring at the pictures of the naked women, he played with it and teased it so that it grew hard. Then he wrapped his wrist around it and, still looking over the pictures in *Playboy*, jerked back and forth furiously as the three of us watched, confused and scared but equally amazed and impressed. After a couple of minutes he began moaning – was he hurting himself? – as whitish goo came gushing out the end in a sequence of erratic spurts, almost all of which he caught in the tissue paper held an inch or so away from his penis. A bizarre series of facial grimaces accompanied this action, until he let out a deep sigh . . . after which he wiped himself clean, smiled victoriously and pulled up his trousers.

Back in London, in his room up at the top of the house, Nic introduced me to the treasure trove under his bed: dozens of magazines that made *Playboy* look like the *Daily Telegraph*. Where he got them from I had no idea; they were all marked 'Not to be sold to persons under the age of 18' and though Nic was thirteen already, he wasn't yet passing for anyone's idea of an adult. But it didn't matter. His magazines had names like *Men Only*, *Mayfair*, *Fiesta* and *Knave*, and they showed women's naked bodies in much greater detail than the Canadian *Playboy*. Nic talked about parts of the women's body while he turned the pages, and I was even more impressed. I hadn't a clue.

Next time I was alone in the house, I borrowed one of the magazines and brought it down to my own room, where I laid it out on the bed and played with myself as I had seen my brother do in Canada. I pulled at my willy repeatedly and sure enough, without too much provocation, it grew erect in front of me. My penis didn't look threatening the way his had; it looked like a little dagger poking out from under my belly button. But when I played with it, electric currents pulsed through me. I turned to the readers' letters with their graphic descriptions of wild sexual encounters and wondered if I was feeling what they felt when they 'did it'.

And as I went through what I hoped were the correct motions, I found something welling up inside of me. The sensation caught me by surprise, but it was far too pleasurable to stop. Instead, I kept pulling away at myself until the strange feeling washed over me in a series of intensely ecstatic waves, causing me to shake involuntarily and emit a small gasp of pleasure. I was surprised, as much by my reaction as the sensation itself; in failing to control my emotions, it was as if I had discovered something more powerful than my own being. I knew that from now on life would never, *could* never be the same again.

There was only one problem. I hadn't produced any of the white goo that my brother had unleashed in Canada. I wondered if that meant that there was something wrong with me. That evening, in his room, I asked Nic about it while he was poring over the latest *Fiesta*.

'You're not old enough to ejaculate,' he informed me authoritatively.

'Old enough to have an orgasm,' I challenged proudly.

'You are?' He seemed incredulous. 'Are you sure?'

'Sure I'm sure. Great, isn't it?'

'I didn't know you could have one without the other,' he said, shaking his head in surprise. 'You'd better make the most of it.'

I needed no more encouragement. With Nic off early to secondary school at Pimlico, and Mum out equally early to teach at Norwood, I was the last to leave our house in the mornings and trusted to lock the door behind me. I'd use the extra time I had after breakfast to go back to bed, surround myself with pictures of naked women and masturbate. Naturally, I was soon addicted.

. . . So I should have just agreed with Dean in the playground that day. I should have said, 'Yeah, it *is* great, isn't it?'

But I wasn't sure if it was OK to admit to it. It didn't seem the type of thing you discussed in public, let alone in the playground. So, that evening, in the privacy of his bedroom and while we studied the curves on *Mayfair*'s Miss June, I again sought out my brother's advice. 'Does *everybody* masturbate?'

'Of course,' he replied, looking at me in astonishment. 'Everyone. From puberty onwards. Even grown men do it. Anyone who denies it is a liar.'

With that endorsement – and from an expert, no less – I doubled my schedule. I'd masturbate at night as well as in the morning. I could keep quiet doing it and there was still no mess to clean up. It was the greatest hobby in the world. I even began to imagine what it would be like with girls. Not the girls at Langbourne, who were all flat-chested, but with real women. I understood their attraction now, and I had a relatively good idea what sex was about. I couldn't wait to start trying it.

And then I went to an all boys' school.

It was my own choice. I could have gone to Kingsdale, where most of my primary-school friends from the Kingswood Estate were going as a matter of course, including the flat-chested girls who would soon start growing breasts. But it was never on the cards. Kingsdale, which took in thousands of pupils from as far away as Brixton and Peckham, was one of the toughest comprehensives in London.

This reputation, long-rumoured, was confirmed for all to see the day I'd come running out to the playground from the lunch room at Langbourne, only to find a fight taking place in the street that ran between our two schools. And not a normal school fight, between two teenagers. No, this was a fight between two *armies* of teenagers, like you'd see on television when it took place at a major football match. Two schools of kids were charging each other, swinging fists and boots whenever they thought they could make contact, throwing bottles and even the occasional brick. We found out later, after the fight had been reported on television and in the newspapers, that kids from Tulse Hill School had marched across South London that lunchtime, to fight Kingsdale over some girls. We also heard that Kingsdale had 'won'. It was something to boast about, our local comprehensive being that tough, but it didn't mean I wanted to spend at least the next five years of my life in the place.

My dad always said that if every kid, rich or poor, dumb or smart, weak or tough, went to his or her local comprehensive, the schools would get better overnight. I suspected that he was right, but like many people who wanted to make decisions on other people's behalf, he'd had no experience of what he was talking about. He'd grown up in the countryside, been sent to boarding school, gone to Cambridge University. Besides, he'd set up that music-school-within-a-school at Pimlico, so that kids like my brother could choose a comprehensive that wasn't their own. In the meantime, I wasn't willing to be the Kingsdale boys' daily mincemeat just to prove his point.

There was talk of applying for a 'scholarship' at Dulwich College, one of the oldest and biggest – and richest – schools in London. But I had no intention of doing so. The people I admired in life already – footballers and pop stars – didn't come from schools like that. I knew as surely as I had a picture of Alice Cooper hanging from a noose on my wall that I would not be caught dead at Dulwich College.

I opted for Archbishop Tenison's Grammar School for Boys, opposite the world-famous Oval cricket ground at Kennington. It seemed like a sensible middle ground between Kingsdale and Dulwich College, even if it was considerably further away. There was a point during the planning process when my mum asked me what I'd do about its lack of girls when I got older. I thought such a question was rude and invasive – what did she know I knew about them? – and it wasn't a deciding factor. It wasn't as if we talked much about girls at Langbourne.

Little did I know. On our first day at Tenison's, as we got to know each other in the classroom and the playground, trying to find ways to distinguish ourselves (we were all wearing identical brand-new blue blazers with the Tenison's crest across the pocket, our school ties done up tightly to our top button, our black shoes freshly polished), everyone wanted to know who had a girlfriend and how far he'd 'got' with them. This kid Adrian, who'd boarded the number 3 bus to Kennington at the stop after mine – not that I'd dared talk to him on the inward journey – let on that at camp towards the end of primary school, he'd been 'locked' in a cupboard with a girl for a full forty-five minutes, and when we pressed him for details, he declined to elaborate, and smiled instead, like James Bond in the face of similar enquiries from Miss Moneypenny. Adrian had blond hair, like I did. He was shorter than me. If he could talk a girl into a cupboard for half an hour, I figured, then maybe, and perhaps with his help, I could as well. I decided to stick close to him. That afternoon, we rode the bus home together and got talking. Soon we were best friends. It didn't take long to notice that Adrian didn't have a girlfriend any more than I did. He did have two teenage sisters, though, and that was the next best thing. I made a point of stopping in at his house on our way home almost every day, hoping to see them, smell them, simply be near them.

A few weeks into our first term, while we were all still working to impress each other, I brought a copy of Men Only into school with me. That would show them, I figured, and I wasn't wrong. Other than a handful of swots, every kid in class swarmed over me to get a look at it. Most of them obviously hadn't seen pictures of totally naked women before. I noticed a couple of boys' faces turn bright red, their pupils enlarging in front of me. As they grappled for a closer look, one kid offered to buy it from me, there and then. I couldn't see why not – it wasn't like my brother would notice one less magazine under his bed – and I went home that evening twenty pence richer.

I reckoned I was in business. At the rate my brother was stocking up on men's magazines he would probably never find out I was selling them on, and if he did, I could always cut him in. That night, as I climaxed to the perfectly rounded breasts of Fiesta's Miss November, I figured I had found my route to easy wealth.

But then the boy who'd bought the Men Only from me tired of the pictures and resold it to another kid for fifteen pence. He in turn resold it for ten. Within days I had lost track of the magazine and before I could bring a new one in and relaunch the process, the last kid in the chain was dumb enough to leave it in his briefcase, where his mother found it while looking for his homework and called our school to complain that her eleven-year-old son had only been at grammar school for a few weeks and was already bringing home 'pornography'.

Our form teacher launched an investigation. The boy who'd been caught by his mum told on the person he'd bought the magazine from. That person in turn fingered someone else. And so it went, our teacher following a paper trail of embarrassed eleven-year-olds who didn't yet know not to grass on each other until it ended, fairly and squarely, with me. The whole process took him less than half a day. I was told to stay behind after school and report to him.

It was widely rumoured I'd be getting the cane, a weapon used just sparingly enough at Tenison's to sow fear. But it was too early in the school year for last resorts. Before letting me go home, my form teacher delivered a lecture on morals and depravity, the inappropriateness of eleven-year-olds reading *Men Only* during lunchtime – or any time, for that matter – and, in case I thought he wasn't taking it seriously enough, the threat of serious punishment, *painful* punishment, if I ever brought a magazine like this into school again. I hung my head low, said 'Yes, sir' and 'No, sir' and 'It won't happen again, sir' in all the right places, and promised to be a good boy from now on.

But when I raised my head to finally meet his gaze, he was struggling to contain a grin.

Number 47:
DOING ALRIGHT WITH THE BOYS

Jeffries was one of the kids who played on our estate. He was three years older than me, born the same month as my brother, and the two of them were close friends, at first. But for all my brother's fascination with girls (or, at least, with girlie magazines), Nic lost interest in pop music almost as quickly as he'd found it, and he never followed football to begin with. Jeffries, like me – like surely any normal kid – was obsessed with both. As his friendship with Nic slowly ground to a halt due to lack of common interests, his friendship with me grew steadily stronger for the same reason. Along the way, he replaced Nic in my life. Jeffries became my big brother.

Jeffries didn't look particularly tough. And because he lived in a posh house on Alleyn Park, the garden of which backed on to our Wates estate, you didn't expect it from him, either. But he could punch his way out of an argument all the same and people soon learned not to mess with him. I found I could rely on Jeffries to protect me if we went into Kingsdale at weekends and joined a football match with the bigger kids from the Kingswood Estate.

Eventually I came to rely on him for the real thing. We were both, already, Crystal Palace fans. I'd got there through hero-worshipping bigger and better teams: Chelsea, Arsenal, Manchester United and Tottenham, the ones who won the trophies. I'd even talked my mum into taking me over the river a couple of times to Chelsea's ground, Stamford Bridge. But there'd be 55,000 people there and we could never see a thing. (Mum couldn't afford seats and I knew all the action was on the terraces anyway – though neither of us realised that kids were meant to bring crates to stand on and have dads to make space for them.) Most of the time we went to Selhurst Park instead, when one of the big clubs was visiting Crystal Palace – like the day we saw Manchester United, with Denis Law, George Best and Bobby Charlton, three of the greatest players in the world. We stood among the thousands of away fans that day, and walked back up Whitehorse Lane with the victorious supporters afterwards; Palace had been beaten, of course. One long-haired lad, in a V-neck star jumper and massive flared trousers and bovver boots, sat on the shoulders of a couple of other fans, and called out the players' names, one by one, and everyone called the names back at him. It was like he was their pop star and their team captain rolled into one and I was amazed that anyone who wasn't on television could have that much power . . . Still, after a few visits to Selhurst Park, I realised that I was becoming less interested in the fortunes of the famous visitors than those of the home side. I was growing steadily familiar with the Palace players, their strengths and, more typically, their weaknesses. Slowly but surely, I was turning into a fan.

Mum took me to the Palace as often as possible, but after picking up a bad cold standing on an uncovered terrace in the rain for three hours one midweek night, she said that if I was *that* keen on following the team, I should go on my own. So I did. Every other Saturday, for the home game, Mum would drive me up to the Whitehorse Lane end – the 'family' end – a full ninety minutes before kick-off, giving me plenty of time to claim pole position at the front of the terrace, right behind the goal, from where I could bang along on the advertising hoardings to the Palace theme song, 'Glad All Over'. I'd eat my packed lunch, read the programme from cover to cover, watch the match through the Whitehorse Lane goal net, and walk the three miles home, alone. I rarely spoke to a single person throughout. Other than the result, I was happy as could be.

The first year I started going to the Palace on my own, the

team was relegated to the Second Division. The next year, to the Third. The thought of switching allegiance to another, better team never occurred to me. If anything, my devotion only increased, in part because Palace acquired a new manager, Malcolm Allison, who decided to clean house. Out went the old colours of claret and light blue; in came bold red and blue stripes stolen right off the shirts of Barcelona. Out went the Victorian-era nickname the Glaziers; in came the high-flying Eagles. Out went most of the old team, including our veteran goalkeeper and club hero John Jackson; in came cocky local teenagers with names like Swindlehurst and Hinshelwood. And in the process, out went the image of Palace as a drab old place where ageing stars from greater teams were put out to pasture, and in came its reputation as a youthful club where anything might happen – and frequently did, including the brief introduction of American-style cheerleaders on the pitch and the regular appearance of the *Sun*'s Page 3 model Fiona Richmond in the players' bath (and the following day's newspaper). Palace may not have been much good on the football field, but they were suddenly among the most entertaining clubs in the league. Why would we want to follow anyone else?

Jeffries watched these changes not from the Whitehorse Lane terrace like me, but from the opposite end, the Holmesdale Road terrace, alongside those who led the singing, the pushing, and occasionally, the fighting. It seemed an odd place for him, given that his dad was a director of the club. But then lots of things about Jeffries were odd. He attended Dulwich College's Preparatory School, located just the other side of Kingsdale along Alleyn Park, even though his dad was also a famous trade union leader and therefore, supposedly, a man of the people. And from Dulwich Prep, Jeffries had gone on to the posh, private Westminster school, opposite the Houses of Parliament. To make things stranger, Harold Wilson, the Labour prime minister, awarded Jeffries' dad a seat in the House of Lords, alongside all the landed gentry who were born to the title and wore white wigs when they attended Parliament and hated trade unions and their leaders with a vengeance. Jeffries' dad, who'd been born poor in South London and had clawed his way up the Union ladder from his teenage days as an apprentice, accepted the lordship but rarely showed up for 'work', writing a pamphlet called *Abolish the House of Lords!* instead. Yet still Jeffries attended this expensive, exclusive private school. When I asked him about it, he said it wasn't his dad's idea. It was his mum's. And his mum didn't live with his dad. But then nor did mine. Jeffries and I had that in common, too.

As I left Langbourne behind for Tenison's, Jeffries encouraged me to leave the Whitehorse Lane behind as well, join him and his mates on the Holmesdale. They were all at least fourteen, this 'crew', seasoned teenagers to my eyes, yet they never looked down on me; instead, they took me on as if I was some sort of mascot, educating me in the ways of the terraces while shielding me from its worst dangers. We started travelling to away matches together – sometimes me and Jeffries in the car with his mum, and occasionally his dad, but more often a group of us on a supporters' coach or train – and they'd take me into the opposing team's home end with them, yet somehow protect me from the fight that inevitably followed our invasion. Maybe they just recognised me as a younger version of themselves, because Jeffries' mates all had names like Piers, Toby and Giles and, if not Westminster, they mostly attended either Dulwich College or Alleyn's, the very schools I'd refused to even apply to for fear I'd have to leave my love of rock music and football behind at the gates. All of them were rebelling against their privileged backgrounds. And so, in my own way, was I. All my short middle-class life, I'd been told I was 'gifted' and 'bright', and everyone expected great things from me, all the time. At the Palace, I could lower my sights, act out, and copy my older Dulwich friends in learning how to be 'normal', like the tough kids from Croydon, Thornton Heath and other working-class areas. At the very least, nobody expected great things from me. And I liked that.

Number 46:
THE SEEKER

L ed Zeppelin were the biggest band in the world. So when Jeffries called me at home one afternoon during my last weeks at Langbourne, to say he had a spare ticket to see them in concert, at Earls Court, *that very night*, and he'd be happy to take me, I was ecstatic.

But my mum wouldn't let me go. Money wasn't the issue; the show was only a pound, barely the price of a 7-inch. But it was a school night and there was no point even pretending I would be home and in bed by 10 p.m. Jeffries raved the next time I saw him about John Bonham's thirty-minute drum solo on 'Moby Dick'. I told him I was jealous.

My music tastes were changing. Everyone's tastes were changing. Glam was on the way out, that much was obvious. Slade had made a film intended to 'break America' and started spelling their song titles in proper English. Sweet had sacked Chapman and Chinn and started writing their own music. Both moves led to a great single – 'Far Far Away' by Slade, 'Fox on the Run' by Sweet – but the groups soon vanished from the Top Ten anyway. Alice Cooper, meanwhile, split from his band – or his band split from him – and the hits dried up for both. We still occasionally sang 'Come on come on come on *come on!*' at opposing fans on the terraces, from Gary Glitter's 'I'm the Leader of the Gang', but when it came to his music, or that of Alvin Stardust or Suzi Quatro, I left them behind at primary school, where they belonged.

But what to replace them with? 10cc and Cockney Rebel were all well and good – 'I'm Not in Love' and 'Make Me Smile

(Come Up and See Me)' were proper, adult number ones – but it was hard to get excited about them as bands worth 'following'. Unlike many of the first-year swots at Tenison's, I wasn't impressed by Abba, however much I fancied the two girls. I didn't 'get' Bob Marley and the Wailers the same way that Jeffries 'got' them. Similarly, while Jeffries was enthusing about something called 'Philly Soul', I could only really identify with 'Kung Fu Fighting', which, he informed me, wasn't the same thing. Big 'disco' hits like 'Rock the Boat', 'Rock Your Baby' and 'Ms Grace' didn't touch me emotionally, and I didn't understand the new music by David Bowie and Roxy Music, who had escaped glam to make something called 'white soul', and whose followers were called 'soul boys'. You saw more and more of these 'soul boys' on the terraces, with 'wedge' haircuts that fell off their foreheads at strange angles. My hair was straight as an arrow; the thought of it forming anything as interesting as a 'wedge' was beyond comprehension.

So I became a rock fan, plain and simple. I stopped watching *Top of the Pops*, and started following the bands that didn't appear on the show anyway. Like Led Zeppelin, who supposedly had never even released a single, which hadn't stopped everyone in the world agreeing that 'Stairway to Heaven' was the greatest song ever made. And like Pink Floyd, whose *The Dark Side of the Moon* showed up in our home as it did in every middle-class household, like it had been delivered with the phone book. Before my first term at Tenison's was over, it was joined by their new album, *Wish You Were Here* – and by my brother showing an interest of his own in rock just long enough to purchase *A Nice Pair*. A 'reissue' of the group's first two albums from the sixties, the title *A Nice Pair* was further explained by a picture of a pair of tits on the front cover (and, for good measure, on the back as well). That was good enough reason to like the album, but truth was that I liked *everything* about Pink Floyd: the early musical nursery rhymes 'Bike' and 'The Scarecrow', written by someone called Syd Barrett; the drawn-out instrumentals 'Astronomy Domine' and 'A Saucerful of

Secrets'; 'Time' and 'Money' from *The Dark Side of the Moon*; and *Wish You Were Here*'s nine-part centrepiece, 'Shine on You Crazy Diamond', supposedly about Syd Barrett himself, who had left Pink Floyd after the first album and promptly gone mad. The thought that making music could drive you insane somehow made it seem more noble.

I liked Deep Purple, too, because they were listed in my *Guinness Book of Records* as the world's loudest band. I bought their 1970 'classic' *In Rock* from an older kid at Tenison's who had tired of it and soon found myself playing the first side's closing epic, 'Child in Time', at home, repeatedly, imagining that I too might one day play in the world's loudest band, though I knew that I would never be capable of screaming like Ian Gillan – at least not in tune.

I thought I liked Yes because I thought everybody liked Yes; posters of their science-fiction-painting album covers were on the wall of every (male) teenager's bedroom, or at least those bedrooms I got to see inside. Besides, their latest double LP, *Tales from Topographic Oceans*, included just four pieces of music, one per side, and what more proof did you need of serious musicianship than that? And I figured I should like Genesis because their front man Peter Gabriel was featured every other week in fancy dress on the cover of *Melody Maker*, the weekly music paper I occasionally saved up to buy but more frequently read while at the newsagent on Gipsy Road on Saturdays, waiting for the *Evening Standard* to come in with all the football reports. I wasn't sure Peter Gabriel was being *entirely* serious about his costumes, but it was art, all the same, and that was close enough.

I didn't want to give up buying singles entirely, so I paid close attention to those rock bands that still released them, like Bad Company and Nazareth. They seemed a bit ordinary, these groups, but I liked them all the same, and being fond of the underdog – I was a Crystal Palace fan, after all – I decided that I preferred them to everyone else's favourite ordinary rock band, Status Quo.

I still wasn't sure about the Rolling Stones. They hadn't

released anything since that single 'It's Only Rock and Roll', and they weren't the topic of much discussion among my friends, anyway. Among those groups from the 1960s whose names began with 'the', my friends at the Palace all followed The Who.

Naturally, it was Jeffries who turned me on to them. He had played me *Quadrophenia* at some point in 1974, while schooling me in 'proper' rock music. *Quadrophenia*, he told me, was an opera – not that it sounded anything like the operas my mum listened to. The cover to the double album featured a teenager sat on a motorbike (of sorts), the word 'Who' painted on the back of his army 'parka'; pictures of what Jeffries told me were the four members of the group were reflected in the bike's four mirrors. On the back cover, the same bike was shown drowning in a grey sea that met, off in the distance, an equally grey horizon. How the bike got from its front cover glory to its back cover demise was explained in part by the music, in part by a short story inside the album cover full of sex and swearwords, and in part by a massive book of album-sized black and white pictures, some of which were set in the streets around Battersea Power Station, the most recognisable sight on the South London skyline other than the BBC transmitter at the top of Crystal Palace.

The *Quadrophenia* story was set in the 1960s, around the year I was born, and it involved the journey of its central character – the kid on the bike – through something called 'mod'. I was immediately hooked on the idea that there had been another movement of music and fashion before the glam rockers and the hippies. I was particularly taken by the pictures showing mod kids turning over a car on the Battersea streets and smashing the windows. So was Jeffries. His favourite song on the record was 'The Punk and the Godfather', the one that started with a BBC news report about mods and rockers fighting on the beaches of Brighton. He often told me he wished he could have been there – fighting for the mods, of course.

Jeffries may have tutored me on *Quadrophenia*, but he also knew that, musically, it was beyond me. He recommended that

I start my Who collection with *Meaty Beaty Big and Bouncy*, the compilation of their early singles. Knowing that I could trust him, I did. Still, it was a shock. Here I was, just getting used to all this 'progressive' rock, with its idea that longer was better, that multiple key changes and time signatures and, especially, complex solos were all a good thing – and that singles were some form of sell-out and that lyrics were not necessarily there to be understood. But from the opening chords of 'I Can't Explain' to the last chorus of 'I'm A Boy', *Meaty Beaty Big and Bouncy* was simplicity itself. The songs were two, three minutes long, hit singles every one of them. The melodies were easy to sing along with. The lyrics were relatively obvious. They came with bright harmonies. And the arrangements were never so complicated that you couldn't hear everything that was going on: Roger Daltrey's proud vocals, Pete Townshend's singular guitar riffs, John Entwistle's thunderous bass lines and Keith Moon's epileptic drums. The result was a racket, all right, but it was a reassuringly straight-ahead racket, one that a ten- or eleven-year-old could easily identify with. And even if I didn't fully get the gist of 'Pictures of Lily', I understood that 'The Kids Are Alright' spoke to . . . well, the kids. Like me. Glam rock had had some of this sense of fun and adventure, but glam had hidden behind make-up and dressed in silly clothes. There was no such sense of pretence about The Who. They seemed absolutely *real*.

So *this* was what the 1960s sounded like? No wonder they'd gone back to the era on *Quadrophenia*: it all seemed so much bloody fun. It was not a coincidence that the only song on *Meaty Beaty Big and Bouncy* that wasn't from the 1960s, 'The Seeker', was the only one that I didn't really love. I still identified with the lyrics: I felt like I was on my own spiritual journey to discover the perfect music. Now it seemed as if I'd found it – and yet the fact that these Who songs were all (but one) from the previous decade put the band's appeal at a frustrating distance. The more I listened to them, the more I studied up on them, and the more I fell in love with them, the more I figured I had missed out on them. What I wouldn't have given to have been in the audience at the Railway Hotel or the Marquee when The Who had taken up residency at those London clubs in 1964 and '65, smashing up their equipment every night.

To compensate, I got hold of *The Who Live At Leeds*. The sleeve was designed to look like one of those illegal 'bootlegs' that some of my older friends kept talking about. It came with an insert package of record company rejection notices, lists of hotel damages and the like. This only furthered my view of the group as worthy hooligans – and yet the music on *Live At Leeds* stood at odds to (some of) the (same) songs on *Meaty Beaty Big and Bouncy*. As recorded on stage *way* back in 1970, The Who drew 'Magic Bus' out to seven-plus minutes and 'My Generation' to double that. But, if anything, *Live At Leeds* was that much more direct, that much more aggressive than the original recordings. There were no overdubs, just the sound of the three musicians and the singer in unison, as one, at full volume. I couldn't imagine anything greater than seeing The Who in concert like that – other than being *in* The Who. So I took from the *Live At Leeds* package the souvenir picture of Pete Townshend on stage at Woodstock, photographed from behind, leaping in the air wearing a white boiler suit, his Gibson SG held high above his head like he was wielding a scalp, and I placed it on my bedroom wall, above my desk, from where I could pretend I was Pete.

Then The Who released a new album and it seemed like I might not have missed out on them after all. As befitted their no-nonsense image, *The Who By Numbers* stood out from all the other rock music my posh friends talked about on the terraces. The artwork didn't even run to full colour – it was just a black and white join-the-dots cartoon of the band drawn by the bass player. The song titles were handwritten on the sleeve, much as they had been on *Live At Leeds*, and the music barely filled two sides, just eleven songs of straight-ahead rock. Capital Radio, London's brand-new 'independent' radio station – broadcasting in FM stereo, which was more than Radio 1 could boast, and more than most transistor radios could deal with anyway – got behind 'Squeeze Box'. Me, though, once I'd saved up and bought a copy, I gravitated straight to songs like 'How Many Friends' and 'However Much I Booze', on which Pete Townshend seemed to question the meaning of life – or at least the part of it that involved being a rock star – with chord changes in the middle eight sections that seemed impossibly perfect. My acoustic guitar, which my dad had kindly paid for and which I hadn't been kind enough to thank him for (in part because I rarely saw him any more), was no longer good enough for me; I desperately needed an electric.

Jeffries got one first, a Woolworths Fender Stratocaster copy. The very day he brought it home, he asked me to come round and show him how to play it. He had started writing a rock opera of his own already, about someone called Che Guevara, and he needed help with the melodies. I was honoured. I had no real idea who Che Guevara was, though when Jeffries showed me the set design he had drawn for the stage, I recognised the face from T-shirts all over town.

Jeffries talked me through the opening song. The curtain, he explained, would come up to reveal Guevara's face, his eyes backlit. Accordingly, the opera's first words would be: 'Che, the light shines through your eyes.' I read the rest of the lyrics and tried to think of a chord pattern that would go along with them. Most of all though, I tried to figure out how to use the tremolo arm that came with all Stratocasters, even Woolworths' copies, and which seemed to be a vital tool for the likes of Eric Clapton and Pink Floyd's David Gilmour. After strumming an initial open D chord, I pulled the bar as far back as it would go. It came right off in my hands.

Jeffries' parents took the guitar back to Woolworths the next day, and though he got a replacement and I occasionally still came round to play it, he soon lost interest in the idea of a rock opera, stopped talking about forming a band. It was obvious that he didn't need it in his life. Me, though, I did. Desperately.

Number 45:
MAMMA MIA

Nicky Horne was a DJ on Capital Radio with a late evening rock show called *Your Mother Wouldn't Like It*. Not my mother, though. She liked all of it. Everything I was into, she was into. Following the Palace, for one thing, which wasn't so bad, now that she was attending matches with Jeffries' mother. But liking my music, that was something else.

She heard me playing *Meaty Beaty Big and Bouncy* every day after school and started coming into my room to sing along to 'I'm A Boy' and 'Happy Jack' and, especially, 'Boris the Spider'. All right, so these were funny songs and I could see their universal appeal, but The Who weren't the Goodies or Lieutenant Pigeon. *Meaty Beaty Big and Bouncy* also included the original 'My Generation', with its warning to the old people – 'Why don't you all just f-f-fade away' – the stutter always making me think that Roger Daltrey had intended to sing 'fuck off' but changed his mind at the last moment. I had barely been born at the point that The Who had released 'My Generation' and I wasn't quite sure I had the right to claim it as my own, but I had more right to it than my mum, that was for sure. (She had been over thirty when it came out. Thirty!)

Mum's refusal to let me see Led Zeppelin had felt like a rare parental crackdown, something I wasn't used to, what with having no dad around the house to keep me in line and having my own key to the back door and a general understanding that I went to the football matches on my own and would often stop round Adrian's house after school without telling her. So when one of the Dulwich College kids – Bof, short for Boffin, though I suspected this might not be his real name – announced on the terraces that he was selling his ticket for Queen at the Hammersmith Odeon, I was round his house on my bike for it before he could change his mind or my mother could tell me otherwise.

Of all the bands in Britain, only Queen had successfully straddled the glam rock of my primary years with the hard rock to which I was now, so I assured myself, devoted. They released singles, and those singles charted, big time. And yet they weren't an obvious pop band. There was something theatrical about them, what with the flowing capes and jumpsuits, but there was also something intellectual, nearly classical, about their arrangements. They were slightly pompous, singer Freddie Mercury given to falsetto vocals and guitarist Brian May to wild guitar solos, but the music was, like The Who's, laden with good humour, like you didn't have to take everything too seriously. All of this was evident in 'Bohemian Rhapsody', number one in the charts the very week I got my ticket (and showing very little sign of dropping off in a hurry). An opera rolled into six minutes, 'Bohemian Rhapsody' was so ludicrously over the top that you couldn't help singing along. As Abba, whose popularity at Tenison's was starting to really worry me, put it in their own single that same month: 'Mamma Mia.'

When I waved the Queen ticket at my mother, she demanded to know where I got it. But she wasn't angry with me. No, she too had been swept up in all the fuss about 'Bohemian Rhapsody', and as a choir singer herself loved its operatic vocals. She wanted to come with me.

'Too late,' I told her. 'It's sold out. All five nights.'

'You can't get me a ticket?'

'No. There was just the one. But you can take me if you like.' The Hammersmith Odeon was on the other side of London, after all, and I didn't know that part of town.

Gamely, understanding that my love of rock music was not going to go away, she agreed to drive me to Hammersmith – and wait around until the show finished. Only once inside did I discover that my ticket was for the very back row of the balcony, pretty much the last seat off in the corner: so *that's* why Bof had wanted to sell it. Still, it was a concert, and it was the Hammersmith Odeon, and it was for the biggest group in the land right now and I wasn't about to complain. Standing on my seat, trying to peer over the heads of everybody in front of me, I saw Freddie Mercury, dressed all in white, playing a white piano during 'The Prophet's Song', a highlight from their new LP (called, but of course, A *Night at the Opera*). I could hear Brian May applying tricks to a lengthy guitar solo that overdubbed itself many times. I heard 'Bohemian Rhapsody' broken into two or more sections, which was a little strange, and I heard all their previous big hits, including 'Now I'm Here' and 'Killer Queen' and the one that first made them famous, back at the peak of glam, 'Seven Seas of Rhye'. The show ended as did every night on the BBC, with the national anthem. But it was Queen's version, from A *Night at the Opera*, and that made it OK. Funny, almost.

I bounced down the stairs, eager to tell my mum every detail, fully expecting to see her waiting for me out on the street. I found her in the lobby instead. Turned out that she'd quickly got bored of walking the local streets and couldn't find a decent pub either, and had returned early to the Odeon, where a security man had taken pity on her situation and allowed her to watch the remainder of the show from the back of the stalls. She'd had a much better view of the stage than me.

'Weren't they great?' she asked, genuinely.

'Yes they were,' I admitted, putting on a smile. But inside, I fumed.

We came up with a different plan of action for the Great British Music Festival, held at Kensington Olympia a few weeks later, at the start of January 1976, and headlined by Bad Company and Nazareth, my two favourite regular rock bands. Mum had bought me the ticket for Christmas, and this time, given that the event started in daylight, she agreed that I could make my own way there. I took a train to Victoria (which I was used to doing), a tube to Earls Court (which I was not), and then another tube to the Olympia station, which only opened for special events like this. At Olympia, I was met by a queue that looked a mile long. There seemed nothing unusual about this. A few days earlier, I had queued for an hour to get into Aldershot's football ground: they weren't used to followings like the Palace. And I'd queued just as long, also over the holidays, to see the hit film *Jaws*. Why should I not expect to queue for an event for which I already had a ticket?

The hall itself was vast, like an aircraft hangar. The area in front of the stage was unseated, and I was able to wander around, look at the sound desk and the lighting board at the back of the floor, take up position in front of the stage if I wanted. But I felt more comfortable choosing one of the many seats that ringed the stage and floor in a vast oval. I found a nice couple that seemed impressed – or just surprised – that I was attending on my own, and said I could leave my bag and my anorak with them any time I wanted to go down the front. I did so during the Pretty Things who, so I'd read, had recorded the very first rock opera, a few months ahead of The Who and their double album *Tommy* – which had recently been made into a film that I wasn't allowed to see because I was only eleven. Older than everyone else on the bill, the Pretty Things weren't the sort of group I'd figured for a rock opera. There was something of the underdog about them and when I went down to the floor, I shook myself a little bit, like I was dancing. Like I was a grown-up.

I was uncertain which of the next two bands was Ronnie Lane's Slim Chance and which was Be-Bop Deluxe, and almost bought a Ronnie Lane poster, until I realised that the bearded, gypsy-like man in the middle of it could not possibly have been the same singer and lead guitarist who had just coaxed beautiful sounds from an equally gorgeous orange Gibson Les Paul. That would have been Bill Nelson of Be-Bop Deluxe who, like Queen, had traces of glam left over, but were ambitious, anthemic, certainly artistic. I was impressed. Properly so.

There was no such confusion about Bad Company and Nazareth, even though both were hard-rocking, very loud, had singers who screamed a lot, and lead guitarists whose solos were more in line with Pete Townshend than Jimmy Page. If I was disappointed that Nazareth didn't play their latest, 'Holy Roller', which I'd recently bought on 7-inch, at least Bad Company played all theirs: they started with 'Good Lovin' Gone Bad', finished with 'Feel Like Makin' Love' and encored with 'Can't Get Enough'. They might have played a second encore too, but I couldn't stay: part of the deal with my mother was that she would meet me in the West End afterwards – where she would treat me to a late-night dinner at the Hard Rock Cafe.

The Hard Rock served hamburgers – not the flat tasteless things you got at a Wimpy Bar, but big, fat, juicy American ones, and I'd been to Canada already, so I knew the difference. Plus, it was well known that rock stars themselves hung out there. No wonder we had to queue to get in. For forty-five minutes. In the cold January night air.

We weren't served our hamburgers until after midnight. Mum said hers was undercooked, and she sent it back. She was in a bad mood. She'd got into London far too early and had ended up killing time at Victoria station for so long that someone had apparently tried to 'solicit' her, whatever that meant. She wasn't happy about having to queue for a restaurant, so late at night. Was not amused by being served a raw burger. And she was even less happy when it came back, and it was still undercooked. And now her chips were cold, too. She gave the waiters a piece of her mind, and refused to leave a tip, even though the waiter said it was the normal thing to do at an American-style restaurant. (She reminded him we weren't *in* America.) We didn't get home until almost two in the morning. The later the better as far as I was concerned. I'd always wanted to stay up past midnight. I'd always wanted to go to the Hard Rock Cafe. And, especially, I'd always wanted to go to a rock festival. I'd managed all three in the same day. And best of all, my mother didn't like it.

Number 44:
JOIN TOGETHER

Charlton Athletic were the third South London football team. They weren't as well supported as Crystal Palace, and those supporters weren't as menacing as Millwall's – who we'd faced on the terraces three times in one frightening week before Christmas, learning the pecking order of football crews in no uncertain terms – but they had the biggest terrace in the country, and that was a good enough reason for The Who to play there. I'd already stood on that East Terrace with Jeffries, to watch Palace (lose, of course). And The Who had already played Charlton, in 1974, before I'd started going to concerts. Now, two years later, they had announced a return visit, for Whit Monday, and the thought of seeing them in concert, at a football ground, was more excitement than I could bear. There was no way I going to miss out. I just had to make sure I bought tickets while they were still on sale.

I got my chance when my dad came back to the UK for a visit, and offered to take me into town just before my twelfth birthday, in April. We hadn't seen each other since the previous summer's repeat journey to Canada. It had been a disaster. Dad had been recovering from a bout of typhoid he'd caught in Mexico, and mainly left us in the hands of some woman – not his girlfriend – who I flatly refused to take orders from on the basis that she wasn't my mum. My brother promptly seized on the absence of authority figures to bully me relentlessly. We went back up to Cape Breton and visited the same family as before and went camping with them, and I spent a whole night in my tent sobbing that I wanted to go home. There were no shared evenings over *Playboy*.

As always, Dad didn't know what to do with me when we met at the Oval tube station, just down the road from school. I did, though. I knew exactly what he could do with me. He could help me get a ticket to see The Who. He took me to Leicester Square and then we set off down Shaftesbury Avenue, where all the big ticket agencies were located. (And all the instrument stores, too.) The first of them was sold out of Who tickets. So was the second. And the third, the fourth and the fifth. My dad kept telling me I should give up, that I'd have to accept that I couldn't have everything I wanted. But he didn't understand. I was used to getting everything I wanted.

Finally, we walked down Great Newport Street, near Leicester Square, and found one more tiny little agency. It had tickets! They were £4, plus 50p 'agent's fee', and my dad thought that was astronomical for a rock concert. I assured him otherwise. There were six groups. It would go on for eight or ten hours. And it was The Who! Besides, I had £2.50 on me already. I wasn't asking for the whole ticket. He eventually contributed the other £2 as my birthday present. Then he took me to a Wimpy Bar at Victoria station for dinner. We had to eat quickly because he was going to a concert himself that night, a classical one. He hadn't invited me; we both knew I wasn't interested. Instead, he dropped me at the bus stop, and I made my own way home while he went on to the Festival Hall. My mum was furious that he hadn't driven me back through South London, but it was fine by me. I'd got what I wanted from the encounter.

. . . And just in time. Like Third Division Palace on their epic FA Cup run that had just ended at Stamford Bridge, a semi-final short of a Wembley appearance, everyone was now talking about The Who playing Charlton. Even the Rolling Stones. They'd finally come back with a new album, called *Black and Blue*, and they were playing a full week of shows at

Earls Court Arena to promote it – during the very week leading up to Charlton. Mick Jagger claimed that the Stones had received a million applications for tickets for these concerts. The Rolling Stones, he insisted, were the greatest rock 'n' roll band in the world.

I knew otherwise. So did all my fellow Who fans. The Who weren't poncing about with shows in *arenas*. They were playing football grounds. Three of them. One in England. One in Wales. One in Scotland. 'The Who Put the Boot in', it was called, like they were proper hooligans.

Just like at the Great British Music Festival, I went up to Charlton in plenty of time to see all six groups, and just like at Olympia, I found a great big queue waiting for me, so long that it tailed back to a street full of semi-detached houses. So I did what came naturally to me: I joined it. Unlike at Olympia though, this queue didn't move. At all. An hour after I joined it, we were all still standing there, in exactly the same spot. Word came down that there were thousands of forged tickets around, that's why it was taking so long. I looked at mine again. I'd bought it from a ticket agency, so I knew it was good. Then we heard Widowmaker, the opening band, start up – so loud it was as if we were inside the Hammersmith Odeon – and people started getting restless. Two young men, long-haired and in jeans like everyone, walked past us, strolled up to the one house on the street that was boarded up – and broke in. For the next ten minutes, above the noise of the band on stage, we heard them destroying anything they could lay their hands on, like they were Keith Moon and Pete Townshend setting about their instruments at the end of a Who show. Glass, furniture, chairs . . . none of us really knew because none of us followed them in. Finally they came back out, to a round of applause, took a bow – and carried on walking down the street towards the ground as if it was the most normal thing in the world.

A few minutes later, like a giant flock of birds acting in unison, everyone suddenly turned to face a different direction. And again, without instructions or comment, everyone started walking, then jogging, and then some of us running, and the next thing I knew, I was actually at the ground – and there were turnstiles, and they were open, and if we just queued a little more, we could get through them and into the concert. I got to the turnstile, handed over my ticket. The man behind the gate looked at it, held it up to a light he had beside him, examined it closely, and then turned to look at me again. He let out a long sigh.

'Where'd you get your ticket, son?'

'A ticket agency,' I stammered.

'Where?'

'Leicester Square. A little road off the side. I paid the agency fee and everything.'

I was never good at lying. It was, oddly, the one thing that kept me out of trouble. The man behind the turnstile must have figured as much. He shook his head, let out another sigh . . . and clicked the turnstile.

I was in. I didn't care that I was on my own. (Jeffries was coming later in the day, after going to the pub for lunch, and it wasn't that he hadn't invited me along as that I didn't want to miss anything.) I didn't care that it would be several hours till The Who were on. It didn't even bother me that it started to rain, and carried on raining, and that only one stand at Charlton – other than the one that contained the vast stage – had any kind of cover, and it wasn't the enormous East Terrace. I was willing to get wet for The Who. So were tens of thousands of others. Fifty thousand? Sixty thousand? Seventy? Nobody seemed to know. It was obvious, though, that there were too many people for comfort – and that the crowd was living up to the location. It was a football crowd. I suspected that many of them were drunk. (My mum had introduced me to Pomagne while Palace had been on their Cup run, so I knew what it felt like. It felt good.) I *knew* they were drunk when they started hurling bottles at each other. I saw people getting carried out to first-aid tents and it was obvious that it was getting out of hand. A football match, at

least, was over in ninety minutes. This crowd was going to be
here all day.

The afternoon wore on with the appearance of two long-
haired American bands, the Outlaws and Little Feat, neither
of whom did anything for me. The Sensational Alex Harvey
Band, who were from Scotland, made up for it. Harvey spent
a song parading around the stage as Hitler. Afterwards he
told us, 'In case you get the wrong impression, Adolf Hitler
was a bastard, and don't let any fascist cunt tell you otherwise.'
It didn't really occur to me that there were any 'fascist cunts'
around these days; surely my granddad had fought in two
world wars to prevent that ever happening again?

The rain kept coming down and I worried that my poster
and my programme were getting wet. The programme was called
Bellboy – after the song on *Quadrophenia*, the one that Keith
Moon sang as his 'theme' – and it was based on *Playboy*. Moon
was on the cover, in a bellboy uniform, shown entering a hotel
room, carrying a tray of drinks, a look of surprise on his face
as if, perhaps, there was a naked woman on the bed waiting
for him. Sure enough, Moon filled the centre spread, too, as
'Baggage of the Month'. In this picture he was entirely naked,
though his legs were carefully positioned to avoid any rude
content. It was genius.

When The Who finally came on stage, Roger Daltrey slid
his way across it, announcing, 'The 'Oo on ice.' Pete Townshend
followed behind – and immediately slipped on his arse. They
hadn't even played a note yet, and already they had proven
what I'd always suspected: that they were real.

But once they started playing, I realised that I couldn't see
anything from the East Terrace. And I knew I couldn't possibly
make it down to the front, not when I saw how many people
were being lifted out from the crash barriers, several of them
unconscious. So I found some space just in front of the terrace,
on the grass, the width of a football pitch from the stage. I
stood there, jumping up and down, delighted but frustrated.
I wanted to be able to see the whites of Townshend's eyes, to

watch what chords he was playing. I wanted to be able to count the number of Keith Moon's tom-toms.

I settled for the music. The Who played some of their early hits, and they played much of *Tommy*. They skipped most of *Quadrophenia*, played only a few songs from *The Who By Numbers* – which was weird given that it was their new LP – and played the extended version of their teenage anthem, 'My Generation', including part of an old single 'Join Together' that I'd grown to love after hearing Jeffries' copy but couldn't find in any shop anywhere. (And it wasn't on any album, either. It was almost like it no longer existed. Music could be funny like that.)

The night ended with their adult anthem, 'Won't Get Fooled Again'. As with the finale to *Tommy*, earlier, green lasers went off above our heads, bouncing from the stage to the floodlights and then off around all four corners of the ground. It was cosmic, to use David Bowie's choice of word from 'Starman'. But there was no smashing up of the instruments. Apparently they'd grown out of all that.

I made it home on my own, a train back in to Charing Cross and the last number 3 from Trafalgar Square. I walked in the house around midnight. The next morning, me and Mum got up early to go to our caravan for the rest of the Whitsun Week. The caravan site was set above a little village on the South Devon coast, near where my dad's dad and his sister had lived, in a remote field, where cows grazed in the grass until the farmers took them in for milking. It was the perfect destination, allowing Mum to escape London and the tension of her schools for short bursts of time without spending unnecessary (or unavailable) money on hotels, boats, planes or leaky tents. She looked forward to it more than anything, and wasn't thrilled that we were delaying three days of this holiday just so I could see The Who at Charlton. It was bad enough that Easter and summer holiday and various half-term breaks were all arranged around Crystal Palace games.

I read my copy of *Bellboy* on the drive, much of it out loud. There were individual articles on each member of The Who.

Pete Townshend proclaimed, 'When I was a kid, a guitar was all I had,' and I imagined that was me. John Entwistle observed, 'I've got four cars but I don't drive,' and I hoped that would be me. Roger Daltrey said of his bandmates, 'They've always hated my guts, mate,' and I hoped that would *not* be me, even though I loved the idea that a band like The Who hated each other's guts.

The profile on Keith Moon capped them all, though. It read like a greatest hits of his destructive episodes, involving various amounts of nudity, cherry bombs, piranha fish, Lincoln convertibles sinking into hotel swimming pools and the remarkable ability to carve through an entire hotel wall with a paper knife. It ended with a quote from Keith himself: 'I don't give a damn about a Holiday Inn room,' he said. 'There's ten million of them exactly the same. I book it and it's my home for the time I stay there. If I smash it to smithereens, I'll pay for it. When people ask me if I act like it at home, the answer is yes.'

How I wished that was me. But I knew it never would be. I didn't have the guts.

Number 43:
I'M A BOY

C hris Boyle was the oldest kid in our class. Always. From that first day at school, when we worked so hard to one-up each other with stories about non-existent girlfriends, Chris acted the adult. His parents were working-class intellectuals whose involvement in local left-wing politics (dad a Labour councillor, mum at the Brixton Advice Centre) allowed Chris and his older brother John to grow up unchecked in the heart of South London. They grew up fast. And they grew up big.

During our first year at Tenison's, Chris took up the drums. It was the ideal instrument for his physique, and it turned out he had a natural sense of rhythm. Chris was into soul and reggae, black music mainly, but he played like a rocker, our very own Keith Moon. He would frequently spend lunchtimes in one of the music practice rooms, pounding away on a school kit that, judging by the crowds of fourth and fifth years who gathered in the hallway to watch, had never taken such a beating in its life.

That Christmas, Chris's parents bought him a kit of his own. A Premier. The real deal. This was a serious development. I still had only the acoustic guitar. I knew I couldn't afford a Fender Stratocaster or a Gibson Les Paul; they cost several hundred pounds. I'd set my sights instead on the 'copies', which began at £50 – hoping that if I could ever save up as much, mine would prove more reliable than the one Jeffries had got from Woolworths.

Physically, I was fearful of Chris. But in his drumming I saw a chance to pursue my dreams of rock stardom, and given that

I was the only kid in our class who could play guitar, let alone cello and piano as well, he saw in me a similarly promising prospect. We decided to team up. It happened during an art class, in early December. We'd all of us quickly grasped that our school was not the place of fine learning it had advertised itself as being. It was antiquated, slowly falling apart. The art teacher was (barely) living testimony to this. Approaching the end of his career, he had long ago stopped trying to actually teach; he would just tell us what to do for the lesson then leave us to it while he snoozed at his desk. I could barely draw and lamented that the teacher wouldn't do anything to help me improve. Chris, though, could draw 'from his head' and as soon as we made the commitment to music that day, he used the materials at hand to paint a picture of us in a band together. It was a four-piece band, and two of the people were nobodies, figments of his imagination. But at the back of the picture, on the drums, Chris drew himself – and at the front of the stage, on lead guitar and vocals, he drew me. I had imagined the scenario many times before, but this was the first time I had ever seen it. It looked like The Who: it looked real.

We didn't know anyone else our age who could play any other instrument and round out the group, fill in those two figments of our imagination. We just assured ourselves that it would come together eventually and every now and then, when Chris used the drum room, I'd borrow the school's acoustic guitar and play along with him. Nobody could hear me, of course, but it still felt worthwhile, like we were actually practising. Getting somewhere.

In the second year, Chris started going out with girls. Every Monday, he'd arrive in the classroom, sit on his desk, and promptly offer some update on his love life. No one put such activity past him, but there were never any witnesses either. Not until the day that Chris brought a photo into school, a black and white print of a teenage girl sitting naked on the floor, her hands around her shins, pulling her legs towards her chest. Her breasts were almost fully grown but her crotch, which was entirely visible due to the angle of the camera, had only the slightest tangle of hair on it and we could clearly see the crack between her legs. There was a leer on her face, aimed straight at the camera. Across the photo, in felt tip, were the words, 'To Chris, come and do me sometime, love Suzie.' It had been given to him over the weekend by one of Suzie's friends, he said.

Everyone wanted to see that photo. Even kids in the top years heard about it and came round our classroom at lunchtime to take a look. My brother's girlie mags were nothing compared to a nude self-portrait by a genuine South London slag.

Chris lived off Denmark Hill, in an area sandwiched between Brixton, Camberwell and Herne Hill, and occasionally I'd come back with him after school. Unlike Adrian, he didn't have big sisters to admire, but he did have that drum kit. I always hoped he'd sit down to play on it and we could write songs together, but Chris preferred to just hang out, listen to the radio, drink tea and watch TV. If we could find any, we'd smoke a fag or two as well. It didn't seem that big a deal; everyone smoked. It was part of growing up.

One afternoon, while hanging out like this at his house, no one else on the premises, the phone rang. Chris picked it up, smiled, started chatting, and then nodded to me to pick up the extension in the living room. There were two girls on the other end. This was new to me. Girls didn't phone me, especially out of the blue, particularly two of them at once. I was nervous even at the thought of it, but having the phone line between us provided some security, and I was able to engage in a little bravado. They seemed to find me funny. They even asked what I looked like. Blond hair, I said. Blue eyes. They sounded excited. 'Got any earrings?' 'No,' I confessed. Now they sounded disappointed. Chris had one in the left ear. He called it a stud.

After fifteen minutes, Chris suggested we all meet up in

Ruskin Park. The girls agreed, and we hung up. Chris told me which one he fancied, and that I could have the other. They sounded identical to me, all dropped aitches and exaggerated swearing, but what really confused me was what he meant by 'have'. Have? For what? For a walk in the park? A snog? Or a shag back at his house? What was familiar territory for Chris and these girls? How far was too far?

We met them a few minutes later. They were totally average, all white blouses and grey skirts, badly applied make-up and cheap jewellery. Exactly the type of girls I'd decided to avoid until I could become a rock star and have my pick of the opposite sex. (The fact that I showed absolutely no signs of progressing towards puberty had plenty to do with my reticence, too.) But still, *they* had called *us*, and that made me feel like a rock star already. Besides, Chris hadn't given me much choice in the matter. So I played my part as best I could as we circled the park together, smoking No. 6s, telling rude jokes, moaning about our schools, and swearing for the sake of it. I wasn't half as funny or confident in person as I had been on the phone, but I was getting by. Given some practice, I thought, I might even be able to do this on my own sometime.

Towards the end of our first circuit we came across Chris's brother John, hanging out with a couple of friends his own age. They looked menacing. Even Chris broke his confident step for a moment. But then he resumed it: this was his brother, after all, there was nothing to fear. So we said our hellos and circled the park again. When we came back around John and his mates were still there, looking our way while talking to another kid closer to our own age. Chris didn't seem bothered by this. But my coward's antenna picked up a warning signal. That or it sent out one of its own announcing myself as a soft target. Sure enough, this kid peeled away from the older teens and walked towards us. He ignored Chris and came straight up to me.

'You,' he said, sticking his face right in mine. A harsh, spotty face, but it was a lot tougher than mine, and we both knew it. 'Didn't you beat up my brother?'

Sure it was a cliché. You'd have laughed if you saw it on the telly. But it was being used on me for real, by a truly tough kid, and there was nothing I could say in response that would have any positive effect. Still, I tried.

'Your brother? I don't know any . . .'

The punch hit me so hard I almost fell over. My nose went numb and I put my hand to it. It came back red. The girls gasped. Chris just stood there.

'You cunt. Why d'ya beat up my brother?' This time the punch caught me in the eye. I covered my face with both hands and started crying. I wasn't used to this. I didn't know how to handle it. I was in someone else's park, in some other part of South London, and I didn't want to be here. I hadn't come to fight. I hadn't even come to pick up a girl. I just wanted to make music.

'Fuckin' cry-baby, are we? Didn't mind beating up my brother though, did ya?' He gave me another punch and I fell over. I heard John Boyle snort from a few feet away. 'All right mate, that's enough.'

A few seconds passed. No more blows came my way. I uncovered my face. Through the tears and the pain and the blood from my nose that was now all over my hands, I could see, on my left side, Chris and the two girls, in shock, stock-still, uncertain how to react; and on my right, John and the other boys, sniggering. My attacker put out his hand to me and I flinched. He laughed.

'It's all right, mate,' he said. 'Come on, get up.' He pulled me to my feet. 'Testing you, know what I mean? You gotta fight back next time.'

Like that would have helped me, I thought. But I didn't say anything.

'You're not from round 'ere, are ya?'

'No,' I said. 'I'm from Dulwich.'

'That figures. 'Ere. 'Ave a fag.' I took the cigarette, though given my pounding head and bleeding nose, smoking was the last thing I wanted to do. He showed the pack to Chris and the two girls and they all took one as well. They still hadn't said a word since the whole thing had started.

'What school d'ya go to?'

'Tenison's.'

'Kennington,' he said. 'We could 'ave you lot any day of the week.' Rumour had it that they recently had done. A vicious unprovoked attack on our school playground one lunchtime by just a handful of non-uniformed kids had been credited to that school.

'Well, see ya round, mate,' he said, and he gave me his name, like we were friends now and we'd meet again for a repeat performance the next night. And then he wandered off.

As the boy turned his back on us, John nodded at Chris, acknowledging him for the first time since the attack, and then set off in a different direction with his own mates. I dropped the cigarette, stubbed it out under my feet quickly, pretending I'd already smoked it. My head was throbbing as if Chris was playing the drums on it. I wanted to go home. But saying so would mean admitting further defeat. So I stood there, saying nothing, trying to dry my tears without drawing attention to them.

One of the girls eventually broke the silence. 'It's time for our tea.'

It was only five o'clock. But we didn't argue. The mood was too sour for us to think of being boys and girls, that we had got together as part of the courting ritual and had all figured we might end up kissing or doing something more. They went their way and Chris and I walked back to his house, where I washed my face, collected my school bag and headed straight out to the bus stop. Chris came down the street with me, searching for the right words.

'Come on,' he said. 'It made you look good. You got in a fight. That always impresses the birds.'

Yeah, right, I thought, as a number 68 came along and I opted to sit on the lower deck, with the old biddies, rather than the upper deck, where every self-respecting schoolkid normally sat. Those two were *definitely* impressed.

Number 42:
SOMETHING BETTER CHANGE

John Matthews was one of the only other kids in my year who cared about rock. He bought the three weekly music papers, rotating *Melody Maker* with *Sounds* and *New Musical Express*. He bought albums. When I was going to see Queen, he offered to make me a tape of their album *Sheer Heart Attack*, and he was good to his word: he put the record on his stereo, placed a portable cassette player on his desk, and hit the 'record' button. Occasionally his parents walked into his room and talked over it, and at one point I could hear him singing along, but that was OK: it made it more like a bootleg, like my own personalised copy.

But why was he so excited this Thursday morning? I hadn't even made it across the playground before he cornered me.

'Did you see it last night? Did you see it?'

Did I see *what*? It had to be something to do with music – that was the one thing we had in common – yet *Top of the Pops* hadn't been on last night. Nor had *The Old Grey Whistle Test*, the one show that had rock bands perform live in the studio, though it was on too late at night for most of us. I pushed for more information.

'On ITV, the *Today* show . . . This group swore at Bill Grundy. The Sex Pistols, they're called. It was brilliant. It's all over the *Mirror* today. You must have seen *that*?'

But I hadn't. We didn't read the *Daily Mirror* at our house. I had tried buying the *Sun* for a while at the caravan. The football coverage was easier to read, and it had more pictures. But my mother put a stop to that. She didn't want the lady at the village post office to get the wrong impression about us. And we didn't watch ITV either. We got our early evening news from the BBC; if the TV stayed on beyond that, it was for *Nationwide*, not the *Today* show. I'd never even heard of Bill Grundy.

By lunchtime, my family's middle-class habits had put me thoroughly in the minority. It seemed like half the school had spent their tea-time watching this band called the 'Sex Pistols', with a singer named Johnny 'Rotten' (of all things), saying the word 'fuck' several times on live television. And John was right again: the *Daily Mirror* had plastered the incident all over its front cover under the headline 'The Filth and the Fury!' To prove how outraged it was, the paper reprinted the entire interview, asterisked-out swearword for asterisked-out swearword.

I was gutted. Events like this didn't happen in Britain. Sure, there were outrageous chants on the football terraces, and *Monty Python* used rude words on their albums, and Nicky Horne, when he had DJed at The Who concert at Charlton, had said the word 'Starfucker' over the PA . . . But nobody ever said 'fuck' on live TV. Not in Britain. At least not until now. And I had missed it.

For the next few weeks, leading up to Christmas, 'punk rock' was rarely off the front pages of the tabloids. The Sex Pistols embarked on a tour to promote their single 'Anarchy in the UK' on EMI, Britain's oldest and most prestigious record label, and yet they were banned from playing almost every show, the local councillors and clergy clearly convinced that, if allowed to get on a stage, the band would . . . Well, nobody was entirely sure what they might do, given that they didn't seem to be given the chance. Puke over everybody, as was rumoured? Spit on the audience? Smash up their instruments? Swear at people like they had on TV? Whatever it was, we – the British youth – evidently needed protecting from it.

It wasn't just the political and religious establishment that was outraged and opposed. There was talk that other acts on EMI, people like Paul McCartney and Pink Floyd, didn't want to share a record label with the Sex Pistols. Sure enough, early in the New Year, EMI 'dropped' the Sex Pistols – and the group disappeared with it.

Punk rock, though, did not. More and more bands started getting mentioned in the music papers. More singles were released. Albums even. It appeared to be something of a movement.

I wasn't yet thirteen. My concert experience had been confined to arenas, football grounds and the Hammersmith Odeon. I couldn't begin to understand how entirely new forms of music emerged. But I'd had a vague sense that something was going on, even before this whole business with the Sex Pistols. Back in March, I'd been to Jeffries' fifteenth birthday party. I didn't stay long: the crowd was different than I'd expected (there were some serious long-hairs in attendance, looking for trouble, and my mum had dressed me in my best clothes and even sent me off with a neatly wrapped present so I felt totally out of place) and so was the music. Before I left, before the party descended into something of a riot and the neighbours called the police, I got to ask Jeffries about the LP that everyone was singing along with.

'Dr. Feelgood,' he said. 'Ace, isn't it?' He said it in a way like he thought I knew about them already, but I didn't. And I wasn't sure I liked it, either. There was something primitive about this band, something old-fashioned, like it was a throwback to 1950s rock 'n' roll, and it caught me off guard. I figured my friends were into more complex music than that.

And then, when the new football season had started, I found some of the Dulwich crew – Piers, especially – raving about an American band called the Ramones, who they'd seen play in England over the summer. Apparently they had a song that went, 'Beat on the brat with a baseball bat.' I had figured them for a joke at first, a novelty. Now I understood that *they* were a punk band, too. This music had somehow crossed the Atlantic before I'd even realised it existed.

Other than John Matthews, the only other kid in our year

who had any real interest in rock music was Lawrence Weaver, whose dad worked for a firm of concert bouncers and got free records and tickets as a result. Lawrence was seriously into hard rock – his taste began with The Who and worked from there out towards Led Zeppelin and Deep Purple – and he started and ended any conversation about punk rock with the insistence that because the bands didn't care about playing their instruments properly, we shouldn't care about the bands. As a classically trained musician who was (still) taking regular cello lessons, I couldn't fault his logic.

And that's why, come the spring, 1977, I was thrilled to see Pink Floyd play live at Wembley Empire Pool. I'd worked far too hard at developing good taste in rock music to let it go simply because of a couple of front covers about punk rock in the *Daily Mirror*. Pink Floyd were, I knew, the opposite end of rock music from The Who, but the more albums we added to the household collection – *Ummagumma* and *Meddle* had recently helped fill in some of the early gaps – the more I came to admire them. Their musicianship didn't seem to be tied into fashion; it was beyond that. And yet they had somehow changed constantly over the years, from their first, 'psychedelic' album in 1967 to the new one, *Animals*, ten years later. *Animals* had a picture of Battersea Power Station on the front cover, the same South London landmark that had featured prominently on the *Quadrophenia* sleeve, and that was neat. I liked, too, that the actual song 'Pigs' (the eleven-minute version in the middle of the album, as opposed to 'Part 1', which opened the record, and 'Part 2', which closed it) took a poke at Mary Whitehouse, the self-appointed guardian of public morals who'd always had it in for Alice Cooper and who had given her name (though not her permission) to a *truly* pornographic magazine I occasionally found under my brother's bed. Pink Floyd were finally getting political. Right on.

I went to Wembley on my own. Of course. I had gone to every concert so far on my own. (Though because Wembley was so far from home, I stayed overnight with my uncle and aunt, who lived in the area.) The Empire Pool was much like Olympia in terms of size and layout, and my seat was up and way back and far off to the side. When Pink Floyd took to the stage, without a support act, they played the whole of the *Animals* album. Then they took a break, and when they came back they played the whole of *Wish You Were Here*. For encores they played a song off *The Dark Side of the Moon*. None of the four members spoke to the audience throughout. None of them even moved as far as I could tell from my distant seat. I could have stayed at home and played the albums on my stereo for all that there was anything personal about it. But then I wouldn't have seen the giant inflatable pig float across the hall – and after all, wasn't that half the fun of attending?

I stood a little bit taller my next day back at school – and I figured I would do so my next time out on the terraces, too. After all, I wasn't yet thirteen and I'd seen both The Who *and* Pink Floyd. I had serious rock credentials. And yet all of a sudden, it wasn't totally evident that they were still the right ones. The Who part of it was OK: the Sex Pistols, so I read somewhere, covered 'Substitute', and were on record as saying that The Who had been the punks of their day. But one of the Sex Pistols had also been photographed wearing a T-shirt that read 'I Hate Pink Floyd'. This seemed childish to me, like he was jealous of their success and their skill, but apparently the Sex Pistols weren't the only ones. I started hearing how bands like Pink Floyd, with their eleven-minute songs, their refusal to release singles, and their lack of communication or movement in concert – concerts that only took place in arenas or, as The Who were also being criticised for, at football grounds – represented everything that had gone wrong with rock music. They were 'boring old farts'. On *Your Mother Wouldn't Like It*, Nicky Horne had begun peppering the likes of Pink Floyd and The Who with more and more of what he carefully called 'new wave' – a term used to distinguish the idea of good new music from the less favourable aspects of punk rock – and I figured

57

that it was my musical duty to see what I could get out of it.

I didn't get to hear the Sex Pistols. 'Anarchy in the UK' had been banned from the airwaves immediately after the Bill Grundy incident, and once the group were dropped from EMI, quickly became a rarity. Even if anyone I knew had a copy, they weren't looking to loan it. Of the other major bands connected to the 'new wave', it seemed OK to like the Stranglers because they were proper musicians who'd 'paid their dues'. Their vocals were rough, but the keyboard player evidently had some talent. It was all right, too, to like Eddie and the Hot Rods, who were connected to Dr. Feelgood by the fact that both came from Southend and were part of some sort of 'pub rock' 'back-to-basics' movement that I might have known more about if I'd ever got into a pub. (John Matthews loaned me his copy of the Hot Rods' *Live at the Marquee* EP. He said he'd been there the night it was recorded. I was jealous as anything; I had no idea anyone at school was going to club gigs, let alone the legendary Marquee.) I wasn't so sure about the Clash. They seemed to be the most notorious 'punk' group after the Sex Pistols, but there was something genuinely scary about them. They looked like thugs, and they sounded like terrorists. There was also a group called the Damned, who were something of a cartoon band that no one took seriously – least of all, so it seemed, themselves.

That left only one other new wave band with an album out. They sounded discordant, unruly, dishevelled and, as much as anything, ugly. When I heard them on Nicky Horne I had to turn the radio down, I disliked them so much. They were the boil on the abscess of punk rock as far as I could make out and I vowed to steer clear of them. They were called The Jam.

Number 41:
WHEN I NEED YOU

C indy was beautiful: tall and powerful with long black curly hair, strong thighs, big breasts and lips of steel. At least that's how she looked to a newly christened teenager still awaiting his first proper kiss: like a woman among girls. I had my eyes on her all night long.

Adrian had invited Cindy and some of her friends to my thirteenth birthday party – and they had actually showed up. This was, truly, a surprise: up until now, almost two years into our friendship, I'd yet to see any real evidence of his expertise with the opposite sex. We had a little 'gang' going now: me and Adrian, his mate Christopher, who lived on Alleyn Road, and his cousin Danny, who lived on Rommany Road, just off Gipsy Road. (Yes, there was a Rommany Road off Gipsy Road. What were our town planners trying to tell us?) Danny and Christopher were just as obsessed with sex as Adrian and me, and we all shared our knowledge of the subject by showing each other what we could do to ourselves – much like my brother had in Canada. Occasionally, we even had 'wank' fests round someone's house. We all kind of knew we'd be hitting puberty soon and be embarrassed by what we were doing right now, and so we might as well make the most of it while we could.

During school holidays and, occasionally, on non-football Saturdays, Adrian, Christopher, Danny and myself would take off on Red Bus Rovers, travelling all over London for thirty pence or less. On one of these trips, on a bus heading for Epping Forest, as far away from home as our Rover could take us, we embarked on a contest to see who could come first. The bus conductor knew that we were up to something: he kept running upstairs to try and catch us in the act. But we were keeping our own eye out on him via the wide-angled mirror at the top of the stairs and never gave him the satisfaction of seeing us with our willies out. I won that day. I didn't have any proof, but then it wasn't something to lie about: why would I want to miss out on the fun of getting there?

Eventually though, we accepted that while playing with ourselves was all well and good, it was time to start playing with girls. Adrian led the way. He convinced us to go to a youth disco one night. The very idea of a disco – or of anywhere that we were expected to chat up girls – filled me with terror, but Adrian offered a strong incentive: his big sisters would help us get ready. Round at their house early that evening, one of them – she was at least fifteen – sat me down and ran gel through my hair and then blow-dried it; in the process she brushed her bra against my neck, giving me an instant hard-on that I tried to hide. (It wasn't difficult; there wasn't much to obscure.) Then, after the two of them had finished with our hair and doused us in after-shave, the older sister – she was sixteen or seventeen now – looked at us with great satisfaction.

'I wish we'd had boys like you when we were your age,' she said.

We blushed. A woman of the world had paid us a compliment!

(But they weren't women of the world. At his insistence, Adrian had borrowed a copy of *Whitehouse* from me one day, for the picture of a bloke lying back on a bed, naked, his erect dick filling the whole page; with me as his witness, Adrian showed it to his big sisters and they almost ran out of the room in horror. We were equally disgusted: our willies looked nothing like this trunk of muscular flesh, and we couldn't imagine what any girl would ever see in something so ugly. Did they *really* like to put *that* in their mouths?)

The disco was all the way over in Beckenham. We had to get one bus up to Crystal Palace and another one down the other side. When we finally reached our destination, at a community hall on a council estate, we paid our money, and entered a room with a small dancefloor. At one end was a DJ with lights on top of his speakers that flashed to the beat of the music: all that 'disco'-style stuff that I couldn't understand. We went up to the bar and ordered ourselves Coca-Colas and then sat in a corner waiting for girls to show up. For an hour. When they did, they were all that much older than us – or at least, they looked it. Eventually, a group of about four girls started dancing, and Adrian, being fearless, quickly got up from our corner of the room and went over to dance with them. We saw him saying something to one of them and then we heard them telling him to fuck off from where we sat. He didn't act bothered when he came back over. Just called them slags and looked around for another group to show up. About fifteen minutes later, a group of older boys came in – fourth years at least – and immediately started dancing with the same girls. Nobody told *them* to fuck off. I convinced the others that we should give up, and we did. We went home. I had no plans to ever attend a disco again.

But now, tonight, there were girls at my house. On *my* birthday. And even better, one woman was absent: my mother, who had agreed to go to a friend's for the evening, warning me she would return at ten o'clock and expect to see us all still on our best behaviour and ready to call it a night. I found myself with a surprising amount of confidence, more than I had in Ruskin Park that time, for sure. I made an impression on the girls, Cindy especially, and at the end of the evening, we slow-danced together, to Leo Sayer's 'When I Need You'. Adrian kept making comments about how he could 'drive a bus' through us and at one point may have even pretended to do so. But I knew he was just jealous, especially when Cindy took the hint and leaned further into me.

'Do you wanna walk us home?'

I was the envy of the party when I left with Cindy and her two mates. Almost as soon as we stepped out of the house,

Cindy placed her hand in mine. Then she let her two friends get ahead of us, and we lingered behind, heading slowly up Alleyn Park towards the roundabout. I was nervously wondering where this all might lead, until we started walking up the hill from the roundabout – at which point I *really* started wondering where this might lead. I asked where she lived and she told me it was over the back of the Palace Parade. Anerley or something. At least another mile or two.

Oh. Only then did it properly dawn on me that in my enthusiasm for Cindy, I had abandoned my own birthday party, left my house unattended, and with my mum due home in less than an hour. I weighed up the options. I could walk up to the Palace and beyond, and hope for some kind of sexual encounter. Or I could get home before my mum did. There wasn't time for both. I didn't really imagine us having sex or anything, so I told Cindy I'd better get home – and why. She seemed to agree with me.

I said goodnight, and I looked at her, freezing on the spot as I dared myself to go ahead and do something more. It was Cindy who moved first. She leaned down and brought her face against mine, and as she did so she put her arms around my shoulders, drawing me closer. And then she kissed me. It wasn't just lips, either: her tongue pushed its way inside my mouth. I responded as best I figured how, which was to open up my own mouth and try and copy what she was doing. It seemed a peculiar way to get to know each other, licking tongues like this, but as I got into the swing of it, it started to seem perfectly proper, like maybe this was what our tongues were *for*. I rubbed my hands across Cindy's back as she was doing to me, and her friends . . . well, I didn't know what her friends were doing; I had my eyes closed, thinking how brilliant it was to be finally French-kissing someone, especially on my thirteenth birthday, but why were we doing this in the middle of the pavement on a busy street and why did it have to be nine-thirty already?

Eventually we broke free and I rubbed my lips as though they were bruised.

'Good night,' I said.

'See you soon,' she replied. It sounded like a promise.

I turned and ran back home, victorious. The house was still intact. My mum was not yet home. And my mates were all after details.

The next evening Adrian came round, as he often did on a Sunday. He brought with him a note from Cindy. One of her two friends had visited him during the day and asked him to pass it along, he said. Excited to receive my first real love letter, I unfolded it as fast as I could.

I liked being with you last night, it started, promisingly enough. *But I can't go out with someone who won't walk a girl home. Cindy.*

Wow. It looked like I'd been chucked. I had expected this to happen now and then in my love life, but I figured I'd at least get to go steady first. I showed the note to Adrian, and he just nodded.

'You don't want to go out with a girl like that,' he said. I didn't have the heart to say that, actually, with a body like hers and a kiss of molten steel, I most certainly did.

Adrian left a little later. He was hardly out the door when the phone rang. I picked it up before my mum got to it. It was Cindy. She was upset. She said that someone had written a fake note, pretending it was from her, and had I received it yet? I said that I had.

'Then throw it away,' she urged. 'It weren't me what wrote it. One of the other girls last night did. They don't like me. Please ignore it. I promise, I'm really into you. I wanna see you again. Can we go out sometime?'

We chatted for a couple of minutes, and when I put the phone down, I was elated. I had a girlfriend. A real one, a beautiful woman who stood taller than me and who liked me and who had a killer kiss and who I would be totally happy to be seen with in public. I rubbed my lips every few minutes that evening, as if to bring back the sensation of the kiss twenty-four hours earlier – and later at night, under the safety of the covers, I had a wank as well, thinking of Cindy and what might lie between her legs. Perhaps soon, I thought, as I ejaculated the smallest drops of semen, I'd no longer be a virgin.

The next day I got home from school to find a letter on my front doormat. It had my name on the envelope and that name was embroidered with a heart. Wow, I thought. She must be *really* keen. I ripped open the envelope and read it before I even threw down my school bag.

Please please please ignore the letter you got yesterday, it said. *I promise I didn't write it. I really like you and want to see you again. Call me later. Love Cindy.*

She finished it by putting a flourish of 'x's next to her name, as if to signify her passion. There was only one problem: the letter had exactly the same handwriting as the one I'd already received.

I decided I wasn't yet ready for all this boy-girl stuff. I didn't call Cindy. I never even saw her again.

Number 40:
ALL AROUND THE WORLD

Queen Elizabeth was our monarch. As far as we were led to believe, she was good at the job and the rest of the world envied us for having her. So Adrian and I were disappointed to miss out on the peak of her Silver Jubilee, when the whole country paused for a week to celebrate her twenty-five-year reign with a series of carefully orchestrated street parties. We were in France, instead, among a handful of second years on the school's annual exchange trip to Nantes. The odd timing was drilled home as our coach made its way out to the M3 via Fulham, where countless brick walls had been painted with 'God bless ya, M'am' messages of loyalty. Still, we promptly forgot about the Queen – and everything else going on back in Britain – the moment we boarded the ferry in Southampton. Spending two whole weeks in another country, living with another family, represented a new frontier, one that we hoped would be marked by successful encounters with alcohol and the opposite sex.

Perhaps because we couldn't get our hands on the first of these items as easily as we hoped, we failed to get our hands on the second as well. There was a distinct language barrier with the French girls. And though there were actual females alongside us on the trip, from the all-girls Charles Edward Brooke school, just down the Camberwell New Road from Tenison's, it turned out to be no easier to chat them up either; we just weren't used to being around girls. There was this one from CEB that I kept taking the mickey out of, until we eventually decided to become friends and made plans to 'go out' with each other once we got back to London. But almost as soon as we did so, I realised that being seen with her acne would make me a laughing stock. All in all, the trip seemed like it was more fun for the older kids – mainly fourth years, as the third and fifth forms were busy with exams. Adrian and I made a promise to go again two years later, when we would have seniority and be free to run riot.

Back in London, there was still Jubilee fever, so when the Queen's tour of the UK came to Kennington, we decided to stay after school to see her do her act. Adrian and I waited forever on Kennington Park Road, in our bright blue blazers, at the front of a crowd about ten people deep, petrified to move from our spot for fear of missing her. Finally, at about six o'clock, we heard the cheers from further up the road. Along came the motorcade: police bikes, police cars and then a very posh black car – a Daimler or a Bentley – with the Queen waving regally at us as she passed by. Being loyal subjects, we waved back. The motorcade continued on its way towards Camberwell, and that was that.

The Queen's journey did not take her through Brixton, and for good reason. While riding the bus to school one day, we'd seen the graffiti that had gone up on the train bridge over Brixton Road: 'Stuff the Jubilee', in big white painted letters. We could hear the old people on the bus gasp in shock. The next morning, it had been painted over; life was back to normal. Except that a couple of days after that, there it was again: 'Stuff the Jubilee'. At the same time, handbills started showing up on the local walls, especially around Brixton tube station. They carried a picture up top of 'Queen Elizabeth' who 'earns £1 million a year, tax free'. Underneath was a picture of what looked like a dosser: 'Elizabeth Queen, unemployed, earns £8 a week, including benefits.' The posters had been printed by something called the Socialist Workers Party. The SWP.

There was another political party putting up posters around town, with a statistic of their own: something about how 90 per cent of muggings were by black people, and 90 per cent of their victims were white. The fliers came with an instantly recognisable logo: NF, the two letters joined together as one. The National Front believed in Britain for the British, which meant repatriating all the blacks (and the Asians and anyone else who wasn't white) 'back to where they came from'. My mother taught loads of West Indian and Asian children as she worked her way up through a number of tough South London schools, and never spoke ill of them. Chris Boyle's mum worked on behalf of immigrant families at the Brixton Advice Centre and his dad was a Labour councillor for Lambeth, and they too were supportive. And Adrian told me his parents were 'left of Labour'. All of them made sure we understood that the National Front were, as Alex Harvey had put it at Charlton, 'fascist cunts'. Still, there was a lot of NF graffiti around London. You had a sense that, like the Queen, they weren't going away any time soon.

Nor, it turned out, were the Sex Pistols. They re-emerged after several months' silence on Virgin Records – the label that had made its fortune on teenage prodigy Mike Oldfield and his *Tubular Bells* – with their own contribution to the Jubilee, a single called 'God Save the Queen'. At first people thought it was a cover version of the national anthem, like the group Queen had included on *A Night at the Opera*. But it wasn't. It was something else entirely. It was something that rhymed the title with 'fascist regime'. That called the Queen a 'moron'. A potential H-bomb. Radio stations wouldn't play it. Many record stores wouldn't stock it. Somehow, this didn't stop it rising up the charts until, the very week of her Silver Jubilee, 'God Save the Queen' peaked at number two on the singles charts. (Officially, at least: there were all kinds of rumours that it should have been number one, but that 'they' wouldn't allow it.)

Once again, the Sex Pistols were all over the front pages: if they weren't being arrested for hosting their own anti-Jubilee party on the Thames, they were getting beaten up by right-minded monarchists: Johnny Rotten was attacked by two gangs in just four days, one of them wielding knives. Punk may have seemed like something of a sick joke six months earlier, when the Pistols had sworn on TV and EMI had dropped the band under pressure, but now it looked like this was something serious. The Sex Pistols had lit a fuse.

I didn't get to hear 'God Save the Queen' any more than I'd heard 'Anarchy in the UK' before it. None of my local thirteen-year-old friends had embraced it. And it was summer; there would be no gathering on the football terraces for another month. The only way to hear 'God Save the Queen' was to buy it. Except I didn't really buy singles any more. I was a proper rock fan, wasn't I?

I hadn't counted on my mother. Late in the summer holidays, reading about the Sex Pistols in *The Times* or the *Guardian* or whatever fold-out newspaper we had delivered, she asked if I had heard 'God Save the Queen' and could tell her what all the fuss was about, and I said that I had not and therefore could not. And she said, 'Well, next time you go to the record store, why don't you get a copy? I'll pay for it.'

I really wasn't sure I was going to like the Sex Pistols. But free music was free music. So I took the number 3 up to Crystal Palace, went into Counterpoint, and asked, a little sheepishly, for a copy of 'God Save the Queen'. They didn't have it. It wasn't that they had refused to sell it, like some of the high-street stores; it was that the single was more or less off the charts now, and they weren't ordering any more. They pointed me to the new Sex Pistols single, 'Pretty Vacant', instead. But I didn't want to get 'Pretty Vacant'. It wasn't banned; it wasn't the same thing. I thought about going home and giving my mum back the money. But I figured she'd only say I should have bought something else, that I shouldn't have wasted the trip. I scanned the rest of the charts, looking for inspiration.

Then I stopped. This was . . . what did the French call it? *Déjà vu*? No, it was something more than that. I actually *had* been through this before. Five years ago, I'd stood in this very record store, in precisely the same position, with money in hand to buy a 7-inch single and yet not a clue which record to get. Here I was, only thirteen years old, and my life had already come full circle.

So I decided to take the same course of action as back in 1972: to look through the picture sleeves, hoping that something would appeal to me the way David Cassidy had appealed to my brother on my behalf. There were, at least, more picture sleeves to choose from now. And all of them, I quickly noticed, were for 'new wave' records; it seemed to go with the territory. The sleeves tended towards pictures of the group in menacing street wear, or menacing scenes of street chaos – or both. The band logos and song titles were all laid out in stencils, or newspaper print, or spray paint, or just hand-drawn lettering. I didn't want to admit it, but the whole thing carried about it an air of excitement, the same way an imminent scrap did on the terraces.

Finally, I found myself clutching a copy of 'All Around the World' by The Jam, the punk group I *really* disliked. They were wearing black suits and white shirts, like they were office boys or something. Didn't they realise that kids of today hated uniforms? Then again, their ties were loose at the collar like most of us wore them at Tenison's, and they each had these distinctive black and white shoes that made them look . . . different. And they were standing in front of a bright orange background, with their logo spray-painted behind them, all three staring at the camera with an expression that seemed equal parts pride and contempt. I turned the single sleeve over. Now one of them was in a pink button-down shirt, just like the one I'd refused to wear as a hand-me-down from my brother, and he was holding over his right shoulder a black and white chequered jacket, in exactly the same pattern I'd also refused to wear on a duffel coat my mum had bought me as a little kid. How could they possibly think this stuff was fashionable? The camera had zoomed in on their faces here on the back, and it only made their expressions harder to read. (The one in the middle, who I figured must be the singer, was wearing dark, square shades. Because you couldn't see his eyes, his face was a totally blank canvas.) They looked like yobs – like punks – but they were so well dressed that you could hardly place them in the same camp as the Sex Pistols. I couldn't make them out.

And then, at the bottom of the back cover, there were three words, one under each band member: 'Direction Reaction Creation'. This reminded me of The Who's second single: 'Anyway Anyhow Anywhere'. And there was something else, too: a credit for their hairdresser. No band, no rock star, no pop singer *ever* credited their hairdresser on the back of a single sleeve. Not unless they wanted people to think they were poofs. And I knew, instinctively, The Jam were not poofs. But there it was. 'Hair: Schumi.' And for a scruffy thirteen-year-old like me whose straight blond hair defied all attempts to shape it or style it, I had to admit: their haircuts were ace. They were short, and they were sharp. I needed no more convincing. I bought the single sleeve.

When I got it home, I figured I might as well play the record that came with it. 'All Around the World' was just like I remembered The Jam from *Your Mother Wouldn't Like It*: a nasty assault of brittle voices and ugly guitars. The first word was 'Oi!' of all things, and it was shouted, not even sung. Besides, it was too short. Barely two minutes. That was all right back in the sixties, I figured, but this was 1977. Times had changed.

I turned the single over. 'Carnaby Street' wasn't much better. The vocals were grunted, the harmonies shouted, and the guitars sounded like Pete Townshend playing badly. Really badly. It was a waste of money. (My mum's money, admittedly, but . . .) I played 'All Around the World' once more and again it was finished before I knew it. So I played it once more. Every time it finished, I was still sure I hated it. Except that every time it finished, I felt compelled to play it again.

And the more I played 'All Around the World' the more I grasped what had been missing from the rock music I'd been claiming for myself so earnestly this last couple of years . . . Not just power chords and feedback and gruffly shouted vocals, though that was a part of it. But black and white shoes. Pink shirts. Square glasses with black shades. Haircuts that were neat but spiky. Catchphrases like 'Direction Reaction Creation'. And above all: youth! The Jam may have been older than me but they were so much younger than Pink Floyd, and Bad Company, and Nazareth – and The Who – that they could almost have been my big brothers.

Best of all, 'All Around the World' was singing about the new while saying we couldn't forget the old. That was something I really could identify with. Besides, the more I listened to it, the more that feedback guitar solo in the middle sounded like an update on the same section in 'Anyway Anyhow Anywhere'. Finally, it dawned on me: this was *a punk record made by mods*. Teenage mods. Mods of the 1970s, mods that I hadn't realised until now actually existed, mods that I'd thought were confined to the booklet in *Quadrophenia*. My generation just might have its own Who, after all.

Number 39:
1977

'All Around the World' was barely off my record player for the rest of the holidays. I couldn't wait until school started again so I could talk about my conversion to the cause.

Nor, it seemed, could my schoolfriends. Something happened to us all during those six weeks away. We'd broken up in July talking about the Silver Jubilee and perhaps *The Old Grey Whistle Test*, and returned to school in September enthusing about punk rock, new wave and the joys of watching *Top of the Pops* again. Here we were, newly pronounced teenagers heading into the rebellious stage our parents had long dreaded and suddenly, literally overnight – or at least during the school holidays – the nation's music scene had started supplying us with ready-made anthems for the occasion.

Every week, another group emerged, singing another message of teenage insurgence. Eddie and the Hot Rods shortened their name to the Rods, and encouraged us to 'Do Anything You Wanna Do'. The Stranglers warned that 'Something Better Change'. Generation X sneered at 'Your Generation'. The Sex Pistols taunted our parents for their 'Holidays in the Sun'. The Clash hit out at their record company with 'Complete Control'. That American band the Ramones had a hit single called 'Sheena Is a Punk Rocker'. And the Boomtown Rats from Ireland sang 'Looking After Number One', with a chorus that went 'I-I-I don't wanna be like *you*.' All of us in the third year, stuck in our school uniforms, felt exactly the same way.

Back on the terraces for the new season – in the Second Division again now, newly promoted – Jeffries insisted that the

first Clash album was the best record ever made. Better than
Dr. Feelgood. Better even than the Ramones, who the rest of
the Dulwich crew had firmly adopted as their favourite band,
to the point that they were now wearing the group's uniform
of leather jackets and frayed jeans. *Straight* jeans. Jeffries had
bought the Clash's self-titled album over the summer and, happy
as always to educate me, he made me a tape. Unlike John
Matthews, he remembered to plug his cassette deck in to the
stereo system – but he did so with the recording volume turned
up full, so that it came with a crazy level of distortion. To make
the most of it, and absent a cassette player of my own that
hooked up to any stereo system, I'd take the Clash tape upstairs
to Nic's room when he was out and blast it on his expensive
hi-fi. Compared to Pink Floyd, or even early Who, the sound
was thin, almost weedy, and I couldn't make out a word of the
verses, but it didn't really matter, because the choruses were
essentially just the song titles, shouted as if they were a new
terrace chant. 'White riot, I wanna riot!', 'What's my name!',
'I'm so bored with the USA!'

I was happily singing along at full volume one afternoon
when all the power went out. Ace, I figured; I'd blown the
entire house. Then I heard my brother screaming at me from
downstairs; turned out *he'd* cut the power because, he said, he
could hear *The Clash* from all the way back in Kingsdale's
playground as he took the short cut from Sydenham Hill station.
He sounded like my dad, like anyone's dad moaning about his
kid's taste in music, and so I told him I didn't believe him. He
suggested I go down to Kingsdale and listen for myself, and I
did just that. He turned the power back on in the house, hit
the play button on the tape and . . . He was right. You *could*
hear *The Clash* from the Kingsdale playground. You could hear
it loud and clear. It sounded fucking brilliant too, and I told
him that as soon as he got home again. He took my swearing
as a further mark of my delinquency, and we got into an argument about the Clash song '1977' (a B-side that Jeffries had
tagged on to the tape) and its lyric 'No Elvis, Beatles or

the Rolling Stones'. Without any Elvis, Beatles or Rolling Stones there wouldn't be any punk rock or any Clash, he insisted, and I told him to shut up and took my tape back and went downstairs and put my 7-inch single of 'All Around the World' on my own stereo – at full volume.

He had a point of course, not that he'd hear me admit it within earshot. There were plenty of other contradictions to consider too. Like, was it OK to annoy the neighbours with loud punk music if the stereo you played it on was expensive? Could you form a punk band if you already knew how to play guitar? Could you lay claim to being a punk if you'd seen Pink Floyd in concert that same year – and, more than that, still *liked* Pink Floyd (and, if you were honest about it, Genesis, and Queen)? Could you be a punk in attitude only, not appearance? And, most worrying of all, could you be a punk if you didn't buy all the right punk records? Older kids at school sneered at us third years when we went into the record shop at the top of Brixton Road, conveniently close to the bus stop, and asked for the new Stranglers single 'No More Heroes'. They were buying 999 instead. 'They're from Tulse Hill,' they told us. I wondered if they meant the school. That would have made them extra hard.

Not everyone joined in. Abba remained the most popular group in class 3A: that was what you got for being in the top stream. Chris Boyle wasn't convinced either, though when Bob Marley brought out a single called 'Jamming' with the B-side 'Punky Reggae Party' – a song that name-checked the Damned, The Jam, the Clash (and Dr. Feelgood too) – he softened a little. Lawrence Weaver, meanwhile, had got into an American group called Kiss, and a Canadian band called Rush, and he thought the rest of us had all gone insane.

And Adrian's cousin Danny decided to become a teddy boy. He'd gone through puberty ahead of us and had come out the other side big. Really big. No more wank fests for him. Danny got himself drainpipe jeans and brothel creepers. They made him look old, but that was part of the attraction to him: his dad had been a teddy boy, and he was ready to follow in those footsteps. Danny talked about going up to the King's Road in Chelsea, where the Sex Pistols had formed at manager Malcolm McLaren's clothing store, to fight the punks alongside other teddy boy revivalists. We figured he was joking. Then he talked about meeting up with fellow teddy boys round West Norwood for some Paki-bashing and you could tell by the way he said it that he was most certainly *not* joking. Adrian held on to him for a while but finally had to agree that he wasn't worth it, and we lost sight of him.

Our other mate Christopher Modica, though, he was all for it. He bought the Buzzcocks' single 'Orgasm Addict' – only to have it taken away from him when his mum heard the line 'Johnny wants fucking always and always.' Christopher couldn't see why playing 'Orgasm Addict' up in his bedroom was any worse than his sister walking down Alleyn Road wearing only a black dustbin liner as a punk fashion statement. I thought of his sister and her big tits and hoped she would let us know next time she was thinking of taking a walk like that.

Occasionally, me and Adrian and Christopher would strut around the neighbourhood making our own punk fashion statements: wearing old school shirts that we'd cut open with scissors and then resealed with safety pins. We still put our blazers on to go to school every morning, but we no longer felt guilty about it. After all, The Jam wore uniforms, didn't they?

During October half-term, The Jam released a new single. It was called 'The Modern World'. My mum and I were on holiday at the caravan in Devon when it came out. Woolworths, the only record store in the nearby retirement town of Sidmouth, had the single in stock, which was odd considering it wasn't yet in the charts. I asked if they could play it for me and they said no. I stared at the sleeve for a while – this one was designed in bright DayGlo colours, like it was trying to be 'new wave' rather than 'punk' – and the next day, I came back and bought it regardless.

I counted down the days before we got back to South London

and I could check if the record lived up to expectations. It did. 'The Modern World' was just as brutal and ugly as 'All Around the World'. (It was much the same song, to be honest.) But it spoke to me more directly. 'Even at school I felt quite sure,' sang the vocalist, 'that one day I would be on top, and I'd look down upon the map, the teachers who said I'd be nothing.'

That was me, I believed, derided by teachers who insisted I'd be a failure. In truth, most of my teachers were sending home school reports saying I could excel at anything and everything if only I'd put more effort into it, but I refused to do so. If I could be dedicated enough in my rebellion to prove their faith in me unfounded, I figured, then soon enough, surely, they would lose that faith in me and I would have further reason to rebel. With 'The Modern World', then, I had finally found my voice. It just happened to belong to The Jam.

Number 38:
AWAY FROM THE NUMBERS

P aul was your typically confused teenager. He came from a suburban town south of London, for which he seemed both proud and apologetic. He spat out his anti-authoritarian statements like a true punk yet he wore the Union Jack with pride – he even said he'd be voting Tory at the next election. He was the kind of punk who wouldn't condemn you for waiting in Kennington for two hours to watch the Queen drive by in a limousine when the real action on the South London streets over the summer had been the attack on a National Front march in Lewisham and the pitched street battle that followed. Paul was, in short, the kind of punk that grammar-school boys like us could identify with.

Paul was not, as I'd first thought, the one in the middle of the 'All Around the World' single sleeve, wearing glasses with black square shades. That was Rick Buckler, The Jam's drummer who, like the bassist Bruce Foxton, was twenty-two years old. No, Paul was the one on the left of that sleeve, with the haircut that managed to be both punk and mod at the same time, the one who was so young – just nineteen – that he still had spots on his face, but who looked hard as nails and yet almost pretty with it. Paul Weller was the singer and the songwriter, the guitarist and quite clearly the leader of The Jam, and overnight, he became my idol.

Shortly after buying 'The Modern World', I begged and borrowed (but didn't steal) the money to buy The Jam's first album, *In the City*. The cover showed the three group members in their regulation black jackets, white shirts and loose black ties, but unlike the recent single sleeves, the photograph was printed in black and white – which made sense, given that *In the City* sounded like it had been recorded in monochrome. And yet those same songs I had disliked when I heard them on Capital Radio a few months back carried new meaning now that I had been converted by my two Jam 45s. All of a sudden, I loved the way they were all shouted rather than sung, how the arrangements were encased in walls of guitars and unrelenting drum rolls and cymbal crashes. I appreciated that the lyrics featured so much youthful antagonism towards the older generation 'bastards' (as Weller called them) for building car parks over the remains of the British Empire, and that they came complete with demands for 'truth' and proclamations about 'the street'. A couple of songs even had swearwords in just the right places. ('Why don't you fuck off!' shouted Paul on 'Time for Truth' and it was hard for me not to sing along while doing my homework.) There were a few references to relationships, though mainly about breaking up, and that was fine by me, after my experience with Cindy. And there were two 'cover' versions, which I'd already noticed was a common tendency among the punk and new wave bands, like it had been back in the early days of The Who, before groups like Pink Floyd and Queen and Yes wrote all their songs themselves.

But then, towards the end of side one, there was 'Away from the Numbers'. It was the only slow song on the album, though it still came with that gravelly voice and the regulation power chords. It was also the only number that was longer than four minutes. And it was the only song that spoke not about politics, romance or dancing, but about personality. 'Away from the Numbers' was about declaring your right to individuality, or, as Paul put it, about the link breaking away from the chain.

If the rebel tone of 'The Modern World' merely reflected my wishful thinking, then the confessional style of 'Away from the Numbers' represented my true experience. I was, genuinely, no longer fitting in at school. I was unsure of my friends, and they seemed increasingly unsure of me. I had different aspirations from the other kids in my year: I wanted to be a rock star – a punk rock star, if need be – and yet none of them shared my ambitions; even the increasing number who claimed to be into music seemed more interested in conforming to the expectations of their classmates than in thinking for themselves. I was starting to feel like an outsider. I wanted to believe this was just a product of puberty but if so, it wasn't a product of mine. While all around, voices were starting to break, acne beginning to appear, facial hair sprouting out, I remained all flabby flesh and innate scruff, with a high-pitched whine and not a muscle to my name. Intellectually, I could come top of the year if I put my mind to the work (though I was increasingly disinclined to do so). Emotionally, I could converse with the older teens on the football terraces, and with adults in record stores and music shops. Yet physically, I was the runt of the class and rarely allowed to forget it. I had developed an unfortunate knack of antagonising other kids in my year with my mouth, and they had an equally unfortunate tendency to express their dislike for this with their fists. It was becoming common for me to get a slap or a punch during the school day, and I never dared fight back on the understandable principle that I'd just get hit harder. I had no father at home to help me out in any of this. I rejected the seniority of my own big brother who, besides, was too wrapped up in being sixteen to give a damn about me. And of course, I could hardly talk to my mum about any of this; it would only confirm that I was a mummy's boy.

So I took solace in The Jam. A lot of punk groups spoke to teenagers about their problems: it was at the crux of the movement, this return to lyrics about life on earth as opposed to the dark side of the moon. But most punk rock songs assumed that we had all been hardened by our upbringings, that we could fight our way out of trouble. 'Away from the Numbers' dared to assume otherwise. It suggested that the narrator – and by extension his audience – was used to being on the receiving end. It spoke instead to inner strength. 'Away from the Numbers' promised me I would be all right despite it all. It assured me that I'd get my own back on 'all those fools I thought were my friends', that later in life they'd moan 'how they never had the chance to make good'. It became my personal anthem, my best friend and constant companion. 'Away from the Numbers' gave me the confidence to pursue my own path in life.

Jeffries was *not* a big Jam fan. Like the rest of the Dulwich crew, he saw them as politically immature and musically outdated. The Jam had been part of the Clash's White Riot tour earlier in the year, but pulled out halfway through, upsetting the punk spirit of community. Besides, he was more immediately concerned with trying to find out where the Sex Pistols were playing at Christmas. The group had hardly managed a publicised gig in Great Britain all Jubilee year, and now there was wild rumour of a college show in London before the holidays.

'You know I'll be there,' Jeffries announced at the Palace. 'You know I'll fuckin' be there.'

But he wasn't. He couldn't find out where the show was taking place in time. He didn't have the connections. He came to see The Jam at Hammersmith Odeon with me, instead. It wasn't what he wanted for Christmas, but at least the ticket was free: as an incentive to accompany me, my mum paid for it. I'd only been to one other concert in 1977: Pink Floyd at Wembley nine months earlier. And though I wasn't about to start wearing an 'I Hate Pink Floyd' T-shirt, the excitement I'd felt back then was nothing – literally, nothing – compared to how I felt about seeing The Jam play live. So much so that the day that tickets went on sale, I'd taken a bus or three out to Hammersmith and bought two seats direct from the box office. They were for the fourth row, a damn sight better than being at the back of the balcony. Come the night of the concert, accompanied by Jeffries, I was so excited by the prospect of sitting that close to the stage that I kept examining my ticket all the way across London. When we got to the Odeon, I couldn't find it. I must have left it on the bus.

They let us in anyway. Of all the punks trying to bunk into the Hammersmith Odeon that night, this particular thirteen-year old, wearing his school tie hanging loose and his brother's black school blazer with a safety pin where the crest should have been, was the least of their concerns. And as it turned out, we were still early enough to catch the opening bands. The Jolt, who had a song personally written for them by Paul Weller, were primarily distinguishable from what I expected of The Jam by their Scots accents. The New Hearts were distinguishable by being a four-piece, and for a stand-out song of their own called 'Just Another Teenage Anthem', which lamented how clichés were the only things left to use. I thought that was a highly sophisticated observation and decided to 'follow' them from now on.

Between the bands, the PA pounded out rock songs, like it always did at concerts. I recognised the music instantly: Bad Company. Two years ago, I had been thrilled to see them headline the Great British Music Festival. But that was then. I was different now. I was into punk rock. New wave. Bad Company were part of the old guard. Or so I'd thought. I was confused. Jeffries suggested we go to the bar. He bought me a Coke and himself a beer. He raged about the price of the drinks. I insisted we go back to our seats in case we miss The Jam.

When the lights went down, The Jam took to the stage wearing their black suits, white shirts, skinny black ties and black and white shoes, as I'd expected. They also had their Rickenbacker guitars and Vox amps. They were loud and furious, just as I had hoped they would be. Paul Weller and Bruce Foxton jumped in the air continuously, performing scissor kicks, like Pete Townshend must have done when he was their age. Rick Buckler was obscured behind drums, but you could certainly hear him. The 'old' songs from In the City sounded as good as I'd hoped – especially 'Away from the Numbers', which I sang along to at the top of my unbroken voice. The 'new' songs, from This Is the Modern World, sounded familiar even on first listen; it was impossible that I wouldn't love the album when I opened my Christmas presents in a few days' time. Throughout, The Jam gave it their all; you could tell from the sweat stains on their shirts.

The show was only forty-five minutes long, but I refused to let that bother me. Punk wasn't about two-hour shows. Besides, The Jam must have played twenty songs during their set, almost everything they'd released. There was just one problem. The Jam had the whole of Hammersmith Odeon's stage to run around on; the audience was confined to its seats. Every time anyone tried to move into the aisles, the bouncers pushed them back. Aggressively. The true punks in the audience were pissed off about this, and they let it show. So did Jeffries. He recognised the push and pull from the terraces, with the bouncers in the role of the police, the empty aisles the holding space between rival fans. He egged on a few of the bouncers, eyeing other teens around him to see if they would rise up as one. He was hoping for a full-on ruck, but it didn't happen; the audience, reluctantly but obediently, stayed in their seats. And then, come the encores, the bouncers relented, as if they had planned to do so all along. This didn't help me any; as I took to the aisles, I was swallowed up in a mass of masculinity, dwarfed by those taller than me. I pogoed around as best I could under the circumstances, and then I returned to my row. I tried standing on my seat for a better view, but a bouncer came along and made me sit back down again.

In a break between the encores, the crowd chanted, terrace-style fashion, for 'Art School', the opening track from *In the City*.

'We don't do that song any more,' sneered Paul, without offering further explanation. They played something else from *In the City* instead. Then the house lights came up and Bad Company came over the PA again. Bouncers pushed us to the rear of the Odeon like it was on fire. Jeffries pushed back a little and then he gave up. This, he knew – and now I did too – was the way of big concerts. Just because it was The Jam didn't make it any different.

Number 37:
DO ANYTHING YOU WANNA DO

*S*ounds was the music paper of choice for us third years. Not *Melody Maker*, which seemed to be trying to ride out the new wave by pretending it didn't exist. Not *New Musical Express*, which apart from its entertaining gossip page, 'Thrills', was too intellectual for us. No, it was *Sounds*, which seemed happy to celebrate loud music of any description – heavy metal as well as punk and new wave – and in a language we could understand. They seemed to be having fun with their music, which meant that we didn't have to apologise in turn for liking the Boomtown Rats' 'Mary of the 4th Form'. (If only we could *have* girls in our fourth form.)

Typically, the centre spread in *Sounds* each week was an 'On the Road' exclusive about that week's cover stars, equal parts debauchery and glamour, all of which made me only more determined to get a band together, get on stage and get some of that debauchery and glamour for myself. But before I could do so, *Sounds* broke with its regular format and gave over its centre pages to a piece on 'fanzines' instead. Rather than a large photo of a group concert, there were miniature pictures of home-grown publications, with names like *Sniffin' Glue* (the first and most famous, apparently, from Deptford in South London), *Punkture* and *New Pose*. The writer, Jon Savage – a lot of music journalists seemed to have a punk name like that – talked about how there were dozens, even hundreds, of these self-produced music 'fanzines' being published out of bedrooms all over the country. Most, it seemed, were hammered out on typewriters, though some were handwritten; headlines were composed in Letraset or Magic Marker, and logos made from newsprint cut out from other publications – the 'ransom note' concept that the Sex Pistols had made so popular. The only rule, it appeared, was the lack of them.

I was in a maths lesson when I read this. I found maths itself easy enough, perhaps too easy, given that I was reading *Sounds* under the desk. But it bored me, as did most subjects. I was finding the whole structure of school – from the uniforms to the homework, from the precise timing of the periods to being called by our last names – increasingly stifling. By comparison, the fanzine covers as printed in *Sounds* seemed liberating. My mind wandered from the numbers on the blackboard back to the centre spread under my desk. Could I? Why not? I was good at English. And when it came to music, I knew more than anyone in my class. Well, almost anyone . . . And so, on the way out of the maths lesson, I went up to John Matthews.

'Do you fancy starting one of these fanzine things?' I asked him.

He thought about it for all of five seconds. 'Nah, not really. Why don't you ask Weaver?'

So I did. On the way to the next classroom, I caught up with Lawrence Weaver. All right, so he hated punk, but at least he knew his rock music.

'Hey, Lawrence. Do you fancy starting a fanzine?'

'A what?'

'A fanzine? You know, a music magazine. Do you fancy writing a music magazine with me?'

'Yeah, all right.'

And that was it. We were on our way. There were a few things we'd need to work out – like a title, for one; how to print it, for another; and how to pay for the printing, for a third. Oh, and what we would put in it, too; that might prove important. But all those issues were secondary; they were bound to fall into place. The important thing was that we'd decided to do it.

For the title, I chose *In the City*. Loads of fanzines were named after songs, it seemed, and this was as good as any. And it wasn't dishonest. Even though I lived in Dulwich (and Weaver all the way out in Wimbledon), Tenison's was barely half a mile from the Lambeth Bridge. We were much closer to 'the city' than The Jam's home town of Woking.

Printing did pose something of a problem: photocopying cost about five pence a page, and most fanzines, according to the piece in *Sounds*, only charged ten pence a copy at most. But just by talking about the idea, we found a solution: our form teacher, a good egg among a pretty rotten bunch, suggested we ask about using the school's Roneo machine.

The school office was tucked away under the stairs near the front entrance, next to the headmaster's office. You only tended to go there if you were in trouble. I knocked on the door anyway, and asked the school secretaries if we could use their Roneo machine for a music magazine – and soon enough word came back that we could. We'd have to pay for the stencils, but they weren't expensive. We could probably print about fifty copies of a six-page magazine for £5. If we sold them all, we'd break even. If we sold 100, we'd make money. And Lawrence and I could definitely scrounge up a fiver between us.

That only left the small detail of what to put in there. Lawrence said he would write a history of Led Zeppelin. I offered to help him review the new Genesis live double LP if he'd loan me his copy. And I said I'd review the new Queen album all on my own if Matthews would lend me his. In a sentence each, I reviewed a bunch of new singles (including those by Generation X, Talking Heads and the Damned), all of which I had only heard on the radio, and came up with a gossip page based on the NME's 'Thrills' entitled, with delib-erate similarity, 'Spills'. For the front cover, I hand-drew, directly on the Roneo stencil, stick figures carrying NF banners being attacked by other stick figures whose banner was emblazoned 'Smash the Nazi Front', an interpretation of the riots in Lewisham. In Chris Boyle's hands (who was too busy 'seeing girls' to take it on for me), this would have been art. In mine, it was awful.

The whole thing was awful. And I was aware of its faults even as I handed the Roneo sheets to the school secretaries. But at the same time, I knew that my only real crime was enthusiasm. There was something about the immediacy of the punk ethic that made it a matter of absolute necessity that *In the City* was published before Christmas 1977, so that we – or at least I – could stake a claim to being part of what was widely considered the most exciting year in British music since . . . possibly ever. I also had an excuse for the content. Although I was buying some of the new wave 45s (and taping many more off the radio), and though I had the *In the City* LP, and *The Clash* LP on cassette, my knowledge of punk or new wave was still almost non-existent. I mean, I didn't know any real punks, hadn't been to any punk gigs. Hadn't been to *any* gigs, come to that. Only concerts. I was scared of writing the wrong thing, of coming across as some kind of poser. But I did know about Queen, and Genesis, and other hard rock acts as well, and I figured that people would at least respect me for having built up that knowledge base. Besides, everyone knew I was doing the fanzine with Weaver, the resident hard rock expert; I didn't have that much leeway.

The day we broke up for Christmas, we got fifty copies of *In the City* back from the school secretaries. Our classmates didn't exactly laugh at it – nobody laughed at Weaver – but most of them seemed short of a 10p piece when we asked them to buy a copy. We were lucky if we sold five out of a school of 500. Lawrence took a dozen or so home for the holidays. I got stuck with the rest. I sold a couple to my uncle and aunt, and Jeffries was good enough to buy one and act all enthusiastic, but I didn't dare take it on the terraces for an opinion. By the time we got back to school, we had sold a grand total of twenty-five copies.

Number 36:
JAMMING

T om had a head full of curly hair that he clearly had no intention of spiking up or cutting off. He sported a thin tie hung loose around a shirt with its top button undone, worn underneath a beaten-up jacket with small badges pinned to the lapel. It was the archetypal new wave look, that of the over-grown schoolboy.

Tom was the leader of a band: the Tom Robinson Band, or TRB for short (and street cred). They had a snappy logo: the group's name, in spray-painted stencil letters, around a clenched fist. Tom was into politics. In fact, Tom was gay, and proud of it. This was astonishing. Nobody else on the music scene, not even the weirdest of punk rockers, admitted to being gay. Nobody admitted to being gay almost anywhere. Not if they didn't want to get beaten up for it.

For his bravery, Robinson was celebrated as a hero. The *New Musical Express*'s Tony Parsons and Julie Burchill called him 'the finest thing to come out of punk'. Parsons and Burchill were, if not necessarily the finest, then surely the most famous music journalists to have come out of punk, in part because they got engaged to each other after meeting at the paper, but also because they seemed to be trying to enact their own revolution within music journalism. Everything they wrote was controversial, clearly intended to provoke. They'd been around at the start of the Sex Pistols, had championed The Jam, and during the past summer, Parsons had interviewed the Clash for a vinyl EP that was given away with the *NME* one week.

Like the Clash, Tom Robinson claimed his was a people's band, and like the Clash before him, he figured that the best way to connect with those people was with the help of a major record company. In the summer of 1977, the Tom Robinson Band signed to EMI, the same company that had dropped the Sex Pistols in embarrassment only a few months earlier. This time EMI seemed to know what it was doing, because within a matter of weeks, the Tom Robinson Band had a Top Five hit – something neither The Jam nor the Clash, nor the Damned, Stranglers, Boomtown Rats or Ramones for that matter, could claim to their name. Mind you, there was nothing punk about '2-4-6-8 Motorway'. It was a cheerful pop-rock sing-along, complete with handclaps in the chorus and a couple of old-fashioned guitar solos in the break. The lyrics were all about how much fun you could have driving Britain's M-roads with the radio on, and Britain's radio stations responded in kind by playing the hell out of it.

Among those radio stations was Capital. It wasn't hip to like Capital. In fact, on the same single that had been given away through the NME over the summer, the Clash had included a song called 'Capital Radio', which accused London's only independent music station of 'making all the action stop'. That made it quite amusing that I first heard the Clash's next single, 'Complete Control', on Capital itself. It came blasting out of the radio at a volume – and with a venom – I'd never heard before. Besides the speaker-busting guitar riff, and the anger with which singer Joe Strummer attacked the music business, there was this incredible guitar solo in the middle. Punk was meant to be anti-solos; none of that John Bonham 'Moby Dick' stuff. But the Clash's Mick Jones couldn't help himself. On the group's first LP, on 'Police and Thieves', a Jamaican reggae song that the band stretched out to six whole minutes, he'd taken a sort of non-solo which basically just replicated the melody from the verse, in a decidedly weedy manner, as if inviting every bedroom guitarist to play along. (And I did.) The solo on 'Complete Control' was not especially elaborate either – you'd never confuse Mick Jones with Jimmy Page – but as it went on, and he reached towards the higher end of the guitar neck, Jones bent the guitar string like all hard rock soloists, and Joe Strummer immediately sang-shouted, 'You're my guitar hero . . .' as if mocking his bandmate. This bizarre solo as anti-solo was followed by a third verse attacking their record company, who for some reason had released the song anyway, and then the backing vocalists kept shouting 'c-o-n, control' throughout an extra-long coda while Strummer screamed a bunch of stuff I couldn't understand and the song ended just as loud as it had started out. 'Complete Control' was exhausting. It was probably the best three minutes and ten seconds of music recorded in 1977.

Tom Robinson obviously thought he could handle EMI better than the Clash could deal with CBS, and by having such a big hit with his first single, he was proven right. Still, a lot of people – Parsons and Burchill aside – criticised him. Not so much for signing to EMI, but because they'd expected him to release the song that had made him famous in the music press in the first place, 'Glad to Be Gay'. I first heard 'Glad to Be Gay' when Capital brought TRB in for an exclusive 'session' before the release of 'Motorway'. It had a memorably sarcastic opening line: 'The British police are the best in the world.' And for its chorus, Robinson encouraged listeners to sing along whether they were gay or not. I was not. (At least I didn't think I was.) I sang along anyway. In doing so, I figured, I was offering 'solidarity'.

TRB had several other numbers that appealed to a thirteen-year-old wannabe leftie like myself, all with reassuringly bigger and bolder choruses designed for either the football terrace or the political rally, including 'Up Against the Wall', 'Don't Take No for an Answer' and 'Right on, Sister'. (Jeffries' sister, fourteen years old and as much an aspiring feminist as her brother was a self-proclaimed socialist, took issue with that one. Regardless of whether Robinson was gay, she didn't think women should let men pat them on the back like that. She used the word 'patronising' – and I had to go and look it up.) Tom also had a funny song about a fictional brother called 'Martin', which he sung in a fake cockney accent – to emphasise their rough-and-tumble relationship and to match the upright pub piano that was its only accompaniment – and it was an instant winner with those of us in the third form who heard it, what with its references to 'six of the best' and smoking and stealing and all the other stuff we liked to pretend we were involved in.

TRB published their own 'bulletins' – two-page fanzines that combined information about their upcoming gigs and EMI releases with addresses and phone numbers for various radical causes. You got the bulletins for free if you sent a stamped addressed envelope to an official band address in the centre of London. I liked the idea of getting something free from a group, and I liked the Tom Robinson Band, so I sent in a stamped addressed envelope. And I decided to push my luck while I was at it: I enclosed a personal letter to Tom in which I told him I was starting this magazine called *In the City*, and perhaps I could interview him for it?

I received a typed letter from Tom early in the New Year. It was the first piece of mail I had ever received from any kind of pop star – or rock 'n' roll star, as Tom would have preferred – and I was excited. But I was not especially surprised: Tom had claimed a high moral ground, and I figured he had an obligation to live up to it. He apologised for taking so long to reply, explaining that he had a 'mountain of unanswered mail' that had built up 'while we were on tour' and that he was trying to clear it all out while fitting in rehearsals 'as we're off to Europe for a tour next week'. He didn't have time for an interview right now, he wrote, 'but you could maybe take it up with our manager in a month or two if you're still keen'. And in between all this, he shared the information that 'there's already a very good mag called *In the City* run from somewhere outrageous in Neasden'.

Shit. There was no way my *In the City* could compete with 'a very good mag' from Neasden. But I had no intention of calling it quits. In fact, once I got over the disappointing real-isation that *In the City* had not been an original fanzine title, I felt relieved: changing its name would allow for something of a fresh start. This time I chose a Bob Marley song, one which had been all over the radio on its way to his first Top Ten hit: 'Jamming'. It had a good rhythm to it. It embraced reggae as well as rock. ('Jamming' was the single with the 'Punky Reggae Party' B-side, which I loved. That track had been produced by a Jamaican Rasta called Lee 'Scratch' Perry, who'd also produced 'Complete Control'. I liked the way these things connected.) Anyone who knew about music knew that jamming was a term for getting together to play, without sheet music, just letting the groove take you where it would. In fact, it was the phrase from which The Jam had taken their own name. It occurred to me (how could it not?) that I was throwing out one title that referred to my new favourite group and replacing it with another. But I figured people would see beyond that: they'd know that *Jamming* wasn't really named for The Jam, wouldn't they?

Number 35:
LIFE FROM A WINDOW

*T*his Is the Modern World was the greatest album, ever. The songs on *In the City* had been similar to each other – even 'Away from the Numbers', which was all about being different, still had the same *sound* as everything else on the album – but most of the dozen songs on *This Is the Modern World* occupied their own space, distinct and separate from the others around them. OK, so the front cover was a cliché – the three members of The Jam framed by London tower blocks, a backdrop at odds with their button-down shirts, Union Jack badges, and the sticky-tape black arrows Paul Weller had affixed to his white woolly jumper like he was imitating The Who in what I now knew had been their mid-sixties 'pop art' phase. But the inner sleeve was something else entirely. It featured all the lyrics, laid out in a neat, very non-punk typeface, and surrounded by coloured pen-and-ink drawings that brought the words into cinematic clarity.

One of these drawings showed a kid in a loose tie staring out from a balcony, intended, no doubt, to accompany 'Life from a Window', a song that built up from nowhere, and which lacked a chorus, but had the most amazing middle eight about how people changed their minds on you from one day to the next – especially relevant to a thirteen-year-old like me – and which elevated the conversation with a poetic reference to painting a grey sky 'teenage blue'. And there was another picture, of a young couple standing under the rain, looking beautiful in a combination of punk and mod clothes, as if introducing a fashion that combined the best of the two worlds.

This drawing was surely a reference to 'Tonight At Noon', which started with the familiar English sound of rain, but then introduced acoustic guitars (acoustic guitars! On a new wave record!) picking gently against power chords, as Weller sang, 'You'll feel my body inside you,' about as graphic – and yet heartfelt – a description of sex as I'd ever heard.

Then there was a drawing of a beautiful nude woman, her breasts and pubic hair on show as she walked, in high heels, the opposite way from a crowd of suits, and though this should have appealed to me in the same way as a picture from one of my brother's magazines, I found it artistic instead. Erotic. The woman was hopefully something to do with the song 'I Need You (For Someone)' which laid out the singer's love for his girl in such equally naked tones and terms that it would have been embarrassing if not for the fact that he so clearly meant every single word. And it wasn't simplistic either: 'I Need You' came with an unusual chord progression that I couldn't work out on my acoustic guitar, however hard I tried. Punks weren't meant to be romantic: Johnny Rotten had called sex 'two minutes and fifty-two seconds of squelching noises'. But with 'Tonight At Noon' and 'I Need You', Paul Weller declared himself distinct from all that, away from the numbers if you like. He was in love, and he wasn't ashamed to tell the world.

There wasn't a dud song on *This Is the Modern World*. (At least not among those written by Paul Weller.) But apparently the public didn't agree: word had it that *This Is the Modern World* was a failure. I was unsure how this worked: surely I was a member of the public, and if my copy had been bought and paid for and appreciated, then didn't that constitute some form of public approval? And there were other kids at school who felt similarly positive about *This Is the Modern World* – Richard Heard and Keith Percival, to name two whose musical tastes were awakening with The Jam – and who was to tell them that they were wrong, too?

The *NME*, for starters. Mick Farren, who had some kind of

credibility from being in a long-haired hippie punk band, hated *This Is the Modern World*. So did his wife, or his girlfriend: if they're going to replicate the sixties, he quoted her as saying in his review, why can't they go all the way and do the harmonies like the Beach Boys? Given a chance to reply, us thirteen-year-olds – the ones who were buying The Jam's records – could have said, if his missus was going to write the review for him, why didn't she go the whole way and attach her name to it? We could have complained about the rest of the review, too, a vicious attack on The Jam for supposedly failing to acknowledge their sixties influences, when any fool knew that 'All Around the World' had pointedly asked, 'What's the point in saying destroy?' But the damage was done. The punk backlash had started and The Jam – with their debt to the sixties, their office suits, their love of the Union Jack and that promise to vote Tory in the next election – were the prime targets. *This Is the Modern World* was in and out of the charts in the time it took us to enjoy our Christmas holidays. The single 'The Modern World' didn't even make the Top Thirty. Not knowing any better, I continued to play *This Is the Modern World* almost every single evening when I got home from school. Nobody, not even Paul Weller himself, could tell me the album was anything other than a life-changer.

Still, signs of the group's own self-doubt were evident when they released their new single. It was the third in a row to use the word 'World' in the title. And it was the first to be written by Bruce Foxton, suggesting that perhaps Paul Weller had run out of ideas. You couldn't have blamed him if he had: the single followed just two months after The Jam's second album, itself released just seven months after the first. All the new wave bands were releasing records at a furious rate, as if to take six months off would lead to instant obsolescence, and yet the music was suffering in the process. And so, as if lowering their expectations, The Jam promoted 'News of the World' not with a full tour but with what they called a 'London Blitz': four club shows in four nights. One was at the Nashville in West

Kensington. One was at the 100 Club on Oxford Street. The other two were at the Marquee.

I knew that I could get into the Marquee to see The Jam, despite my age, because I had gone there two weeks beforehand on a trial run, to see the New Hearts, the band I'd promised to 'follow' after they opened for The Jam at the Hammersmith Odeon. There, on Wardour Street, in the heart of Soho, in the very centre of London, the undisputed capital of the music world, I paid my money at a narrow doorway, got my ticket (and one for The Jam show as well), and then walked down a long hallway with a coat check off to the side, my palms sweating with anticipation. At the end of the hallway I found myself in a bar. Through a glass wall on the far side, I could see right through to the stage. It was a great view for those who didn't want to be out on the floor with everyone else, but I couldn't think why anyone in their right mind would want to watch from the bar, separated from the music like that, not when you could walk into a small, dark, square room that came complete with an acrid smell of smoke and beer and the happy ghosts of a thousand late nights, a room where none other than The Who had made their name and where countless new wave bands were now doing the same. A room where, best of all, there wasn't a seat in sight.

The New Hearts came on stage that evening to the theme from the *Andy Pandy* show. Some of the audience immediately threw beer glasses at them. Vocalist Ian Pain responded by mocking the kids pogoing at the front as 'Young Boys', the title of their next song. I didn't get all this. Were the people around me fans? Or foes? Did the band like their audience, or not? Judging by other song titles like 'Revolution, What Revolution?' and 'Here Come the Ordinaries' the New Hearts were trying to distance themselves from punk. They wore brightly coloured suits. And they referred to their music as new wave pop. I spent the whole show in the front row, leaning over the stage, close enough to touch the band if I really wanted to. I felt so mature, being there, especially watching a group that the rest of the world didn't yet know about, a group of my own. Still, I had to leave early. There was no way I could miss the last bus home.

When I returned to the Marquee for The Jam, I figured on taking up exactly the same position, centre front of the stage. To be sure of doing so, I got there when the doors opened, at 7 p.m. I was about the very first person through them. As I came into the bar I saw Bruce Foxton, The Jam's bass player, the one with the perfectly spiked hair, standing there, talking to someone. I went through to the club proper, but there was no one staking claim to the front of the stage, so I came back again and, timidly, approached Foxton, standing by the bar now, and asked for his autograph. I'd been through this routine before, with footballers up at Crystal Palace, often waiting for them on training days during school holidays, and I'd never met a player who didn't have time to scratch his name in an autograph book on the brisk walk to and from his sports car. But musicians were a different matter. I had no idea what to expect from them. Especially people like Bruce Foxton, who had been lumped in with punk rock. Still, he was very polite. He signed my ticket, the only souvenir I had on me, and he smiled and said, 'Cheers.' I said 'cheers' back.

Autograph in pocket, I spent the next two hours pressed against the stage, waiting for The Jam to come on, the weight of bodies behind me steadily pushing down on me. Unlike the New Hearts show, this gig was sold out. Plus, it was a Saturday night, which made that following all the more boisterous. Still, I stuck with it, and eventually the lights dimmed, and Paul Weller's dad – their manager – came on stage to introduce the band in his gruff working man's voice, and the crowd surged forward with such force it was as if a fight had broken out at the back. I was used to this at football matches, where I would dart under a turnstile and escape the worst of it. But here I had nowhere to go. I was being pushed up against what felt like a solid wall and it was painful.

Both Paul Weller and Bruce Foxton recognised as much. They looked at us young kids in the front row (I was pretty sure I was the youngest) and immediately asked the crowd to move back. 'There's some people really getting crushed down 'ere,' said Weller before even playing a song. The crowd obliged, and I figured I might survive the night. But the crush came right on back within moments of them starting up the music. I'd been waiting all my life for this, and now I couldn't focus on anything but getting out alive. So the second time Weller made his plea and the crowd moved back a step or two, I seized my moment, squeezing through the sweaty mass of teenagers and young adults and out to the far side of the club. I wasn't disappointed at vacating my place at the front of the stage. I was just relieved to be able to breathe again.

There were 'flight' cases lined up against the far wall, and people watching the show from on top of them. I hung about hopefully, bouncing up and down, partly pogoing but also as a hint, and eventually one of the bigger kids leaned down and held out his arms to pull me up. Up there I could see the world – or, at least, all of the stage and the entire crowd, which was all that mattered to me at that moment in time. And I could hear the music too, as if my head was inside the speakers – which wasn't far off the truth. Unlike at the Hammersmith Odeon, it felt like we were in this together, just The Jam and their most loyal fans. When the strobe lights went off, it was different than when they'd gone off at the Odeon. The effect was crazy, like I imagined it must be for people who took crazy drugs, like time stopped still every split second. The Jam didn't let up throughout their set, which in just forty-five minutes managed to include three-quarters of the new album, two-thirds of the new EP and a fair amount of In the City as well. They played so quickly I was able to stay for all of it. At the end, after the other fans had jumped down, I leaned back against the side wall and almost slid over, it was so slick and slimy. I'd read about sweat dripping off the walls at gigs, but I always thought it was one of those metaphor thingies. I didn't think you could actually see it.

The Jam at the Marquee was everything I'd ever hoped for from a gig. I raved about it for the first issue of *Jamming*, as I did the New Hearts gig. These reviews were joined by another about the Rich Kids, the band formed by Sex Pistols bassist Glen Matlock after being kicked out of that group to make way for Sid Vicious. The Rich Kids had played at the London College of Printing at the Elephant and Castle, and some of my classmates who lived in that area, John Matthews among them, went along – it was an all-ages show – and got to talk to Matlock beforehand. We printed every word of the two-sentence conversation, as if we had an 'interview'. Matthews, warming to the prospect of a school music fanzine now that it actually existed, also reviewed the new Elvis Costello album, *This Year's Model*. Another classmate figured out a better way to use the school Roneo machines and hand-drew a decent impersonation of the Sex Pistols' new and infamous album cover, changing the title to read 'Never Mind *In the City* Here's *Jamming*'. And I wrote an editorial about 'powerpop', having a go at the *NME* for trying to invent new musical trends when the old ones hadn't yet run their course. Alongside all this, Lawrence Weaver's glowing reviews of Rush and Judas Priest were part of the minority, though a very forceful minority all the same. We dared print 100 copies – and when we got them back from the school secretaries, it looked almost like a proper fanzine. Almost.

Number 34:
WHAT DO I GET?

'What do I Get?' was the Buzzcocks' take on the Ramones' chainsaw guitar sound, yet it was as much pop as punk anthem. It embraced the subject of love even as the singer, Pete Shelley, complained at not getting any. It had a fabulous hook for the verse, a magical chorus (or a twice-repeated middle eight, depending how you viewed these things), and a guitar solo that, like 'Police and Thieves', was simplicity itself. It then provided a fresh vocal refrain for the finale, one that ended on a harmony, an extended 'ooooh' at the end of the word 'you' that would have made Abba shimmer with pride. That harmony faded into the distance just five seconds short of three minutes, which, for those who understood the importance of such things, rendered 'What Do I Get?' the perfect pop song.

As a 7-inch single, it was even better than that, though, because 'What Do I Get?' came with a B-side, 'Oh Shit', that served as its antidote, repeating the title at the start of each line, and every kid I knew – but especially Christopher Modica, after the incident over 'Orgasm Addict' – had to be very careful not to play it when their parents were within listening distance. Packaged in a tantalisingly simplistic two-tone green sleeve, the single was a work of art, the perfect way to start 1978.

'What Do I Get?' was not a hit, however. The week it entered the Top Fifty, *Top of the Pops* chose as its token-new wave-act-not-yet-in-the-Top-Thirty the band formed by the Buzzcocks' previous lead singer, Howard Devoto, instead: Magazine, and their debut single 'Shot by Both Sides'. I thought it odd that the show opted for the darker, longer and less commercial single but I also figured that the BBC was not comfortable announcing the word 'Buzzcocks' to millions of pubescent kids. As it happened, 'Shot by Both Sides' was not a hit either, despite the exposure on *Top of the Pops*; some music just didn't appeal to the show's audience. I studied all this with my usual attention to detail, and concluded that Buzzcocks (*the* Buzzcocks? Nobody seemed quite sure) had been dealt a major disservice.

But there was no time to dwell on their misfortune. Great singles were coming at us no less fast and furious than 'What Do I Get?' itself. The Clash released 'Clash City Rockers', which, like 'Complete Control' before it, seemed somewhat obsessed with the group's own mythology, and I didn't mind that so much, nor the fact that the chord sequence ripped off 'I Can't Explain', as that the emerging bullies of the third year, Raymond and Glover – who had somehow befriended Chris Boyle and, by extension, now hovered close by me and others with good music taste in the top stream, alternately threatening us with violence and threatening us with friendship, and I couldn't be sure which was worse – latched on to it as their introduction to punk and made sure to wave the sleeve, a picture of boot boys on the march, at us as proof.

The Clash were no more welcome on *Top of the Pops* than the Buzzcocks. The BBC preferred the Tom Robinson Band, who followed up their Top Five hit with a live EP that included 'Glad to Be Gay', although it wasn't the lead song: that was the less controversial 'Don't Take No for an Answer'. The BBC also stuck by the Stranglers, despite constant accusations that they were 'sexist'. And they had plenty of time for the Boomtown Rats, whose 'She's So Modern' quickly joined 'Mary of the 4th Form' as a lunchtime sing-along among our age group.

And then there was Blondie, who hailed from New York – over *there* – and who, early in the New Year, had a number two hit, as high as any new wave single had charted, with the effortlessly harmless 'Denis'. It was a cover of an old doo-wop song, so we were told. We didn't know doo-wop from be-bop; all we knew was that overnight, every single British male between the ages of twelve and eighteen developed an immediate crush – make that an instant hard-on – for Debbie Harry, whose beauty I found so godlike I even took a picture of her singing on *Top of the Pops*. When the photos came back from the chemist, a few weeks later, it turned out that by using the flash I'd blanked out the television screen and all I had to show for my efforts was a large blur of white in the middle of the print. But I didn't mind, because by that point I'd got Blondie's newest single, '(I'm Always Touched by Your) Presence, Dear' in limited edition and additionally expensive 12-inch form. The extra inches were there, I figured, to blow Debbie's seductive face up to the maximum possible size on the front cover. They certainly weren't there for the music: the three-track 'EP' took up just eight minutes in total.

A reverse image of Blondie could be found closer to home, in the shape of X-Ray Spex, whose lead singer, Poly Styrene, was short, plump, kind of ugly, with braces on her teeth, and dark-skinned. She treated these potential limitations as advantages, though, introducing her band to the public with the spoken words 'Some people think little girls should be seen and not heard, but I say . . .' before screaming 'Oh Bondage Up Yours!' at the top of her voice almost as tunelessly as her saxophone player (a sax player! In a punk band!) wailed something vaguely impersonating a riff. It seemed like a significant moment, a statement of punk women's lib, if you liked. And then, with the follow-up, 'The Day the World Turned Day-Glo', much more tuneful but no less spirited, X-Ray Spex too had a hit. Unlike Debbie Harry though, who was rumoured to be in her thirties, Poly Styrene had only recently left the tough Brixton comprehensive Stockwell Manor, where my mum now taught, and there was confused talk about my getting a copy of *Jamming* to her. The confusion may have been because I was reluctant to give any away for free.

X-Ray Spex weren't South London's only new wave band.

There was Tulse Hill's 999, who kept releasing singles, none of which charted and none of which I paid special attention to. There was Squeeze, from Deptford off to the east, where Jeffries and his mates often went to party, who had a minor hit with a song called 'Take Me, I'm Yours', which featured what sounded suspiciously like a synthesiser, with a weird semi-spoken vocal. And there was Generation X, from down Bromley way, a little south of Crystal Palace, who named their third single 'Ready Steady Go' for the main music TV show of the swinging sixties; I knew of it because The Who had once released an EP *Ready Steady Who* that was rarity itself. The Generation X single was a throwback to the sixties not just in its lyrics, but in its power chords and harmonies, and that seemed like no bad thing. Singer Billy Idol had great looks, and he had credibility that came with being an early follower of the Sex Pistols, but after 'Ready Steady Go' had run its course, he still didn't have a hit. The charts weren't fair.

Like Debbie Harry with Poly Styrene, Billy Idol had an opposite on the scene: Ian Dury, an older cockney who walked with a limp from polio and, so it turned out, had written the superb singles 'Sex & Drugs & Rock & Roll' and 'Sweet Gene Vincent' in a block of flats just the other side of the cricket ground from our school, in a place called Oval Mansions. (Typically, anything in London that went by the name of 'mansions' was a run-down housing estate that dated back before the war and was now in a state of serious disrepair.) We'd probably passed him in the streets on the way to and from school over the years and clocked him for one of the winos who hung out in the churchyard. Now Dury brought out a single called 'What a Waste' and suddenly he had a Top Ten hit. (So sometimes the charts *were* fair.) He wasn't much of a punk, Ian Dury, but there was something cheerfully, disarmingly rebellious about him that allowed for honorary punk status; his success was like the great revenge of your mad uncle. (I had one of those: my mum's brother, the one who lived up in Wembley, a talented musician who'd given up a potential career as a jazz pianist after the war for the security of the family's chemist business. He hated all pop music after the Andrews Sisters, but he smoked like a chimney, knocked back gin and tonics and whatever else was in stock like it was V-Day, and told a damn good joke or ten. Plus, he had the most beautiful – and loyal – wife in the world, and that offered hope for us all.)

Those who paid attention to the labels in the middle of all these singles knew that Ian Dury was on Stiff Records, the 'independent' label that had released the first UK punk single, by the Damned. Stiff had also given us Elvis Costello and his buddy Nick Lowe, and so it was big news when those two jumped ship with one of Stiff's founders to start up their own Radar label. Radar launched in those same hectic weeks at the start of 1978 with Elvis Costello's inch-perfect *This Year's Model* – home to the hit singles '(I Don't Want to Go to) Chelsea' and the aptly titled 'Pump It Up' – and Nick Lowe's *Jesus of Cool*, which actually had the bigger hit, the easy-going 'I Love the Sound of Breaking Glass', which was quickly followed by one that didn't chart but which I thought was far superior, 'Little Hitler'. Like the song 'Night Rally' that closed *This Year's Model*, 'Little Hitler' was about the rising tide of fascism, evident in the increasing amount of NF graffiti on our neighbourhood streets, and occasionally – despite (or, most likely, *because*) of the growing number of black and Asian kids at our school – on the toilet walls at Tenison's.

Stiff was always good for a novelty or two – its catchphrase was 'If It Ain't Stiff It Ain't Worth a Fuck' – and it responded to the loss of Costello and Lowe by looking to the States, far beyond the New York of Blondie, the Ramones and Talking Heads, and all the way out to Akron, Ohio. We had never heard of Akron. We had no concept of Ohio, come to that – our geography lessons never touched on the USA as anything other than a territory discovered by European explorers – but thanks to Stiff, we now knew that Akron was the rubber capital of the world. At a time when record companies were trying to buy our loyalties by releasing singles in various shapes and sizes and especially in different colours, Stiff went one further. It placed *The Akron Compilation* inside a scratch 'n' sniff cover. Scratch the cover and you inhaled the smell of burning rubber.

I wasn't convinced *The Akron Compilation* was worth buying just to smell the rubber. After all, it didn't even include the one Akron band I was genuinely excited about, Devo, who with their spaceman suits and flowerpot hats and their strange theory of 'devolution' seemed positively alien and therefore totally intriguing. Fortunately, John Matthews came to school with a copy of *The Akron Compilation* and, at a couple of designated times during the day, allowed us all to get a sniff while he scratched.

Quite how Matthews was able to acquire so many records, I couldn't figure out. All these incredible singles and albums were released in a mad assault, over just a few weeks at the start of a new year. Seven-inch singles weren't particularly expensive, and we all got pocket money, but none of us were rich. There was a limit to how many 45s you could buy in any given week.

Eventually, Matthews let us in on his secret. He was nicking them from the HMV store on Oxford Street. Shoplifting, he said, was a doddle. Everyone was at it.

Not me, though. I was going to the Virgin store at the other end of Oxford Street – the Marble Arch end – where I would *pay* for my 7-inch singles. On Saturday trips into town with Adrian and Christopher, I'd also stop off at stores around Denmark Street and ask to hear records I knew I couldn't afford – like the 12-inch mix of 'Ku Klux Klan' by Steel Pulse, who got grouped in with punk partly because they were a reggae band and the two musics went hand in hand, but also because of their political lyrics. A new teacher had shown up at Tenison's who told us he had been to school with them in the area of Birmingham that they had named their album after, *Handsworth Revolution*. This should have made him popular, but we couldn't help taking the piss out of his Brummy accent all the same – besides which, he kept *trying* to get in with us, and that made him as ready a target for ridicule as our hunchbacked, dwarfed and thoroughly unpleasant German teacher. (What did it say about our school that the only female teacher was a hunchbacked dwarf? And what did it say about the school that it took our new teacher, from Birmingham, to inform us that Don Letts, the famous DJ at punk club the Roxy, and a close friend of the Clash, was a former Tenison's pupil? None of the other teachers had ever mentioned him to us. In some ways this made sense: the list of famous 'old boys' imprinted on a plaque near the assembly hall consisted entirely of military figures. Besides, Letts was black.)

I wanted to doubt Matthews's claim, the same way I doubted that he'd seen Eddie and the Hot Rods at the Marquee in 1976. He didn't seem the type to shoplift. He was relatively studious, a little heavy-set. He brought his own toilet paper to school. But maybe the fact that he didn't look the part made him less likely to get caught. Certainly, he lived in a tough corner of South London: the Borough, just off the Elephant and Castle, near Peckham, too close to Millwall for my liking. He had a whole bunch of mates in these neighbourhoods who went to all manner of different schools. And the one thing these friends had in common, so he was sure to tell me, was that they were all regularly shoplifting from HMV.

The next Saturday that Palace weren't at home and I couldn't get to the away game, I went into central London and visited the HMV store for the first time. It was right next to Bond Street station, in the posher part of Oxford Street between Oxford Circus and Marble Arch; Polydor Records, home to The Jam, was just over the road. HMV was enormous, and as Matthews pointed out, there was no one standing guard at the front door. On the second floor, I found crowds gathered around the singles racks. This was not uncommon, given how many incredible records were coming out every week, but it was a much bigger crowd than at Virgin, as if word had got out about the easy pickings.

On Monday morning, I told Matthews I'd been to the HMV,

and he was quick to ask what I'd stolen. And when I told him, 'Nothing,' he seemed disappointed. He pulled from his bag the new Devo single on Stiff Records, the Akron band's weird reggae cover version of the Rolling Stones' 'Satisfaction'. He'd got it that weekend from HMV, he said. Without paying, of course.

'(I Can't Get Me No) Satisfaction' by Devo was exactly the kind of single that was causing me so many problems. In the sense that my life would continue without it, and probably along exactly the same path it had been going, I didn't have to own it. There were other 7-inch singles getting written up in the music papers, getting airplay from Capital Radio or Radio 1's late-night DJ John Peel – whose show I was now listening to for an hour until lights out at 11 p.m. – all of which I was just as keen to own. And yet I was equally certain that my life would be greatly enriched for having my own copy, for being able to play the song whenever I felt like it. Besides, interpretations of the great British bands' mid-sixties hits were few and far between, unless you considered the cover of The Who's 'The Kids Are Alright' by the Pleasers – the group the NME had placed on the cover to herald their so-called 'powerpop' movement – and I certainly didn't.

And so, the next weekend, again on a Saturday afternoon, I went back to HMV. Up on the second floor, I studied the singles closely, like I was thinking hard about what to buy. I took my time about it: I could happily spend all day looking at new releases, trying to gauge what a record sounded like based purely on its picture sleeve. More than once, I pulled out the Devo single and then stepped back, like I was examining the sleeve in the light. Once when I did so, a man in a moustache stood back alongside me, looking at his own choice of record, but I figured he couldn't be a security guard. They wouldn't make it that obvious, would they?

Finally, when the singles section seemed especially crowded, I pulled out the Devo single one more time and, without looking in front of me, beside me or behind, slipped it into a plastic carrier bag I'd wedged between myself and the rack. Nobody said a word. If anyone around me had noticed my theft, chances were, I figured, they were here to do the same thing themselves. I moved out from the mob. I didn't feel especially nervous or insecure or scared: I knew that to do so would mean giving myself away. I walked confidently down the stairs and out of the front door – and I was less than a footstep onto Oxford Street when I was approached from two directions. The man in front of me I'd never seen before. The man behind me was the one with the moustache.

I didn't refuse their request to follow them into a back office. And when we got there, I didn't pretend that I'd bought the Devo single at another store, as they seemed to expect me to. I admitted, immediately, that I'd taken it. And when they asked me why, I told them that as well: everybody was doing it. It was known all over London – well, all over South London or, at least, now I came to think of it, by John Matthews – that it was easy to shoplift from HMV. They then asked me for my home phone number, and I didn't make one up; I was in enough trouble as it was. They kept me in the room for a while, long enough that I started shaking, by which point they could surely tell that I was a loser, a barely-teenager desperately trying to prove himself, as much to himself as to anyone else, and that I was hardly going to make a successful career out of shoplifting. After what felt like an hour left on my own to consider my wrongdoing, I was officially warned never to come near the store again. Then they let me go – after I paid for the Devo single.

They'd called my mother while they'd left me locked up there, I found out when I got home. This would have been embarrassing enough for any middle-class kid who didn't come from a family of career criminals, but it was especially awkward given that my mother had recently become a voluntary magistrate. I didn't advertise her second career at school, given the anti-authoritarian nature of punk rock and fourteen-year-old boys in general, but she was proud of it.

There should, then, have been a scene. I should have been

grounded for months. But I was so ashen-faced when she confronted me about it, so abjectly and forlornly guilty, so apologetic and genuinely truthful in my assurances that I would never try such a thing again, that I was let off without further punishment. The only reason that I hadn't been officially charged with theft, apparently, was because every other member of the HMV security team was already at the local police station dealing with other shoplifters, and they couldn't let the last of them go or they'd have nothing left to sell on Monday morning. My mother was dismayed: did I think I could just steal my way to happiness?

I went to bed early that night, with a headache, and I tried to be useful around the house the next day. I didn't feel proud about shoplifting, but I was especially embarrassed at being caught. Monday morning, at school, Matthews asked how I got on. I told him. I'd been nabbed, I said. Security were all over the store, I told him. The only reason I wasn't prosecuted was because they had been taking so many other people to the police that day.

'All right,' he said. 'Yeah. I figured they'd catch on. That's it, then. No more HMV.'

Number 33:
TITS

Jeff Carrigan was the first person I'd ever spoken to at Tenison's. He'd looked as nervous as myself that September morning back in 1975 when I met him at the school gates. The difference was, he had his mother with him.

'This boy looks nice enough,' I heard her say. With my bowl haircut, tightly knotted school tie, crisp white shirt done up to the top button, newly pressed trousers and freshly polished shoes, there was no question that she was right: I did look nice.

So did Jeff. He had short, curly brown hair, round spectacles, and his uniform was every bit as neat as my own. He was smiling – a permanent habit, I soon came to realise – and he seemed shy. So he let his mother do the talking.

'Are you new here?' she asked me. I thought the question unnecessary: did I look anything other than a new boy? 'Can you be friends with my son?' she then asked. I agreed.

Jeff and I had got on fine that day, and the month or two that followed, but even though I was initially determined to behave well, work hard, and make a good impression all round, I was to no extent the swot that Jeff proved himself to be. Throughout our first two years at school, he sat up front in class, with that perpetually goofy smile, listening attentively to the teachers, copying patiently into his notebooks, acting blissfully ignorant to the hum of chaos behind him as some of us quickly grew bored with the rules of the secondary-school system and found other ways to pass the time. Jeff and I had almost nothing in common, no reason to ever assume we would be closer than we had been that first day at school.

Punk changed that, as it seemed to change everything in our lives, though in Jeff's case, the Sex Pistols had already broken up by the time his desk began moving, slowly but stealthily, towards the back of the class. Jeff decided to start his punk education with the Sex Pistols all the same – but not Johnny Rotten's band that had rocked the establishment to the core through late 1976 and all of 1977. He modelled himself instead on Sid Vicious, who, with Malcolm McLaren still playing the managerial role, replaced Rotten as singer and led the band back into the charts that summer with his punk rendition of Frank Sinatra's 'My Way'. Jeff didn't look much like Sid Vicious and he certainly didn't act like Sid Vicious. There were no broken bottles in the classrooms, no swastika armbands, no use of drugs. But Jeff did start to talk like he reckoned Sid Vicious talked – in short, staccato sentences that typically started and ended with the word 'Wot?' and occasionally extended into the full-blown statement of defiance, 'You think I'm thick. But I'm not.'

Nobody who was thick spent two years of their lives in the front rows of the top stream, but we did think Jeff was stupid to base himself on a cartoon punk. Still, it was impossible to dislike him for it. While the new wavers and the hard rock fans routinely engaged in heated musical arguments, Jeff sailed right though the middle of the two factions, his endearing grin giving apparent lie to the anarchy symbols he began drawing all over his textbooks.

. . . Except Jeff was serious. Anarchy, to him, meant the freedom to do whatever you wanted – and that included being nice to people. It was his own way of dealing with adolescence, of coming to terms with his role in a family that lived in one of the old working-class terraced streets near the Elephant and Castle, with a toilet out back and a senile grandmother upstairs, and yet had a classy weekend home down in Hastings and the ambitions to go with it.

And so, along the way, Jeff and I became friends. Not through any forced introductions, like on that first day at school, but out of a natural bonding. Notably, when everyone else at school was laughing at my stick figure abomination of a race riot on the cover of In the City, he was the one who offered to help out, replicating the Sex Pistols album cover for the first issue of Jamming. And it was Jeff who attended the show by the Rich Kids at the London College of Printing – right at the end of his road – with John Matthews; Jeff who had the nerve to talk to Sid's predecessor in the Sex Pistols, Glen Matlock; Jeff who sat down and wrote it up for that same issue.

And it was Jeff Carrigan who came up to me and Chris Boyle at some point during the third year and confided that his dad had offered to buy him an organ or an electric piano, a reputable instrument for a respectable boy like himself, and there were paid lessons awaiting him if he agreed. However, he admitted conspiratorially, he was leaning more towards getting a bass guitar.

Chris and I had been going in circles as musical partners these last two years, progressing no further than the occasional 'practice' in the school music room or at my house. (After the incident in Ruskin Park, I avoided Chris's place in Denmark Hill like the plague.) Along the way, I had finally acquired a Gibson Les Paul copy, a 'Satellite' guitar that was my pride and joy even if it didn't sound like the real thing, and I even had a little practice amp that I had selected after checking out the options at every single store on Shaftesbury Avenue. Still, there was only so much noise Chris and I could make with guitar and drums, and not much of it was any good.

The opportunity to acquire a third playing member from within our class was, in the words of another Tom Robinson song, too good to be true. As a student of rock mythology, I could already see the interviews and the headlines, could visualise the biographies and documentaries. Lennon and McCartney, teenagers the day they hooked up at a village fete in Liverpool, couldn't match the fact that Jeff and I had met each other on our very first day at school. The Who may have had three members at Acton Grammar, but they never had three members in the *same class*, let alone three who started playing together in the *third year*. I told Jeff to get a bass – or rather, to get his dad to get him a bass – and held my breath until the day he came to school and told us he was the proud owner of a Fender copy.

We now had a band, with its own equipment and, all of a sudden, a rehearsal space too: Chris's mother allowed us to use the Brixton Advice Centre on Sunday mornings. A handful of rooms on a street corner, with dank carpets on the floors and smoke-stained posters on the walls, the Advice Centre offered local residents free information on how to claim benefits, shirk rent, avoid arrest and otherwise fight the system. It was located on the Railton Road, Brixton's official 'front line' with a reputation for drug dealing, gang warfare, and a general disregard for the niceties of English terraced street decorum best typified by the constant playing of reggae music, at full volume, all day and night. (The Advice Centre actually lay at the southern end of the Railton Road, closer to Herne Hill, where the white people had not yet all moved out, and it wasn't unsafe there – but just to be sure, I always approached it from a side-street off Dulwich Road.) In other words, it gave us instant credibility.

All that was left, then, was the music. I knew my way round the guitar. Jeff revealed a natural affinity for the bass. And Chris, we knew already, was a master of the drums. But putting the three instruments together was not so easy. It was like trying to get off with girls. We knew what to do, and when we practised on our own, in the privacy of our bedrooms, we thought we had it down. But then, when the opportunity arose to interact, we were all over the place, fumbling, bumbling and generally making fools of ourselves.

So we started out by playing other people's songs. I had picked up the chords for 'I Can't Explain' from a songbook and shared them with Jeff. Apart from the occasional use of a C-sharp minor that tripped us up every time it came around, it was relatively straightforward. I had also learned 'Substitute' and 'Pinball Wizard' at a family Boxing Day party the previous year, when I'd stumbled upon a good-looking, amiable kid a couple of years older than me who was playing the songs to himself on an acoustic guitar in a bedroom. His name was Guy and he was impressed that I'd seen The Who at Charlton. (He had not.) We formed a friendship that day, even if we never expected to see each other again. But 'Substitute' and 'Pinball Wizard' were far too difficult for Jeff and Chris, and besides, one Who song was enough. For our other covers, we chose the music closest to us: punk rock.

We played 'Pretty Vacant', because what kid with a new electric guitar – whether a six-string or four-string – didn't get off on that simple, mesmerising opening riff? We did 'All Around the World' because it was the song that had changed my life and, according to The Jam songbook I had bought along the way, it was basically two chords, A and G with the occasional D. And we took on 'White Riot' for much the same reason. We then went one better. Spurred on by our surroundings – the Clash had the Westway, but *we* had the Railton Road – we added 'Police and Thieves', despite my total inability to successfully copy Mick Jones' rudimentary guitar solo.

There was one more new wave song we covered. The Stranglers had just released their third album, *Black and White*, and the first 75,000 copies came with a free EP, in white vinyl no less, that included a song celebrating 'Tits'. It was a straightforward twelve-bar blues, recorded live with lots of sexual innuendo, and for obvious reasons, an immediate anthem with us third years. It was fun to play, as well. Jeff certainly enjoyed it. But the day he brought a tape recorder to the Advice Centre, so his parents could hear how we were getting along, he told us we'd have to change the words.

'Why?' Chris and I wanted to know.

'It's rude,' he responded.

'Rude? It's just "tits".'

'So? They could ban me from the band.'

'Ban you?'

'They could take away my bass. They bought it for me, remember?'

'Aren't you an anarchist? How can an anarchist let his parents stop him saying the word "tits"?'

But it was like arguing with a puppy. Jeff was as reluctant to get angry with us as he was to listen to reason, and so the words were changed. We sang about a woman with '36-24-36 hits'. Jeff subsequently reported that his parents were impressed.

We began playing our own songs, too. I'd been writing them since I was eight, at the rate of about one every two years, given that I was determined to get each of them perfect in the misguided belief that they would then be 'discovered'. I'd moved on now, from an early 1970s acoustic ballad called 'It's Winter', and then a mid-seventies hard rock number creatively entitled 'Rock 'n' Roll Singer', to a couple of songs that better reflected my newly rebellious nature. One was called 'I Don't Need You', which reflected the disdain with which I intended to treat my ex-girlfriends once I finally got around to having them. The other was called, and I meant it, 'Don't Wanna Be a Face in the Crowd'.

Both of them were based around natural chord progressions: D leads to G and A and maybe throws in an E. F leads to B-flat and C with maybe a G, and so on. It was the familiar I-(II)-IV-V pattern we were taught both in music lessons and rock history books, and therefore it had to be the right way to approach things. Jeff disagreed. He hadn't grown up in a musical family. He didn't take music classes. This bass guitar was his first instrument. If he played a D on the bass and liked the sound of an F as the next note, then that's what he'd play. And if he then went down to a C-sharp, because it sounded good to his ears, he'd do that, too. If I argued that he wasn't playing the 'right' way, then it was *his* turn to remind *me* about punk values. What was all this about proper chords and progressions, eh? Where was my freedom of thought, my individuality? Did I want to just be another face in the crowd?

Chris didn't write any songs, nor declare his intent to ever do so. He didn't get in the middle of me and Jeff, and our energetic debates about the right and the wrong way to do things either. He was too busy being a drummer, turning up late for practice (if at all), threatening to quit the band on a monthly basis, inventing potential approaches from other non-existent acts, protesting a lack of money even for drumsticks though he always had enough to take girls out and then, just when it seemed as if the whole thing was about to collapse under the weight of his excuses, proving able to switch from a driving rock style to pure reggae at the drop of a hi-hat. We couldn't help it: the Railton Road was getting to us.

I had come up with a name for the band already: Direction, written on the inside of an arrow that pointed forwards. Chris was fine with it, and if Jeff was bothered by such an obvious reference to The Jam and The Who, he kept quiet for now. He was more concerned with my singing. Throughout that third year at school, my form-mate's voices had been dropping at the rate of at least one a week, Chris and Jeff's among them. Kids who had been singing soprano in the choir in first year were dropped to alto, then tenor, and some even to bass, at which point, given that their new register gave them licence to chase girls, even get served in pubs, they dropped out of the choir entirely. And yet every day, I woke up to find myself emitting the same high-pitched shrill as ever. Not only was this opening me up to ridicule, especially among the tough kids, but it was preventing Direction from getting any further than the Brixton Advice Centre.

The situation was hardly helped by the fact that Jeff's newly broken voice was strong and distinct. Jeff and I were close friends and companions now, but at the heart of our friendship was a brutal rivalry. Direction was my band, I figured. I'd formed it, in the first year, with Chris. Just because Jeff had woken up to rock 'n' roll via Sid Vicious, and decided one day to get a bass so he could join my band, and just because he could play that bass instinctively, and just because his voice was strong and distinct, didn't mean that I was going to let him sing anything he didn't write. I knew the rock band dynamic well enough already to know that if I handed over the vocals, I was handing over everything.

Having someone else sing my songs, though, someone who was *not* Jeff, who was not playing any other instrument . . . that was an entirely different matter. And so, acting on my leadership position while I had it, I demanded we recruit a fourth member: a singer. I wasn't asking to play the Paul Weller role in the group; I was happy to be Pete Townshend. Let someone else twirl the microphone; let someone else get all the girls. I'd be the song-writer, the one they came to for all the interviews, the one that, deep down, everyone knew was the band leader.

We talked about it at the Advice Centre. Jeff and Chris were resistant to the idea. Their attitude was that we'd only just got going and we should see how things fell into place before we rushed to recruit someone else. I didn't feel like we had just got going: I felt like I'd been working towards this since I got up at the front of the assemblies at Langbourne with my glitter shirt, and that we needed to make the most of what we had going for ourselves while we were still enthusiastic about it.

Eventually, I won the battle, and I placed an advert in the back of the *Melody Maker*. It announced our South London location, our relative youth, and our influences, which included 'reggae'. We must have hit a nerve, or a need, because we got a lot of excited applicants. I could tell from their voices (the calls came to my house of course) that some of them were West Indian, just as I could tell that one of them was a girl. I hadn't thought to mention that we were only looking for a male singer any more than it had occurred to me that we were looking for a white one. So I wrote down everybody's details, told them I'd call them back with an audition date, and, at school, informed Chris and Jeff of the various candidates.

'I'm not playing with a black person in the band,' said Jeff.

'I'm not playing with a black person in the band,' said Chris. 'Especially not a girl.'

I hadn't expected this. We went to school in Kennington,

we rehearsed on the Railton Road. We played reggae, or we wouldn't have listed it in the ad. I'd just attended the Carnival Against the Nazis, a massive march from Trafalgar Square to Hackney, where the Clash and Steel Pulse and X-Ray Spex and someone called Patrick Fitzgerald (who had been bottled off for his efforts) had all opened up for the Tom Robinson Band. There'd been about 50,000 people on the march, and many more than that in the park. It was the biggest political-musical event most people had ever been involved in. It felt like a major moment in history, like the great British public was finally standing up and telling the National Front to fuck off. It made me, personally, feel involved. Relevant. Important, even. Plus, I'd got to see the Clash and they were brilliant – even though I had to watch from the very fringe of the crowd because the core of it, a mere 30,000 people or so, seemed to be moving to the music with the fury of a major battle on the terraces.

Chris and Jeff were fans of the Clash, too, and Steel Pulse, and I was sure they supported Rock Against Racism and the Anti-Nazi League. And if I put it to them like that, they wouldn't argue. In fact, after a fire at their home, Chris's family had recently moved from their mostly white street off Denmark Hill to a mainly West Indian street just off Brixton Road itself, almost directly opposite the tube station. Once in the new location, however, the Boyles took to leaving the radio on at full volume all day to give the impression that they were home, with the implication being that the house would otherwise be burgled in a drum beat. Jeff's street, as close to the Elephant and Castle tube as Chris's was to Brixton, had different concerns. It was still white, it was very working class, and you could tell that the locals wanted to keep it that way; it was never far off the neighbours' lips that the immigrants had it easy, getting their housing for free, claiming unemployment benefits, robbing people and stealing our women and so on. I had a go at Chris and Jeff for allowing these attitudes to fester, but the more I did so, the more I was reminded of my own situation. I lived in a nice little middle-class housing estate in the back streets of Dulwich, a long way removed from the front line, from the all-night music, the burglaries and the muggings and the drugs. I had been brought up feeling middle-class guilt for how the country treated its immigrants; now I was being force-fed middle-class guilt for how the country treated its white working class. I couldn't win.

I didn't return the phone calls. One or two of the potential singers called me back anyway, including the girl, who sounded really nice, like she understood what we were trying to do musically. I felt bad lying to her about why she couldn't audition for us. I wondered if she knew the real reason, and how often she came up against it in life. But if she did, then I guess she was used to it by now. She didn't put up a fuss and Direction continued to play reggae as only three white boys could.

Number 32:
WHO ARE YOU

Tom was proving to be a frustrating pen pal. I'd followed up on his offer of a future interview by writing to his manager at the given address, but didn't get a reply. At first I couldn't think why. Then it occurred to me. Shortly after Elvis Presley had died, the previous summer, I had read that *his* manager, Colonel Parker, had once offered Elvis up for interview – for $100,000. Apparently there weren't any takers – but maybe that was only because the price was too high. So I wrote back to Tom, and apologised for the fact that I didn't have any money to pay for an interview.

He replied almost immediately. 'I don't charge anything for interviews,' he assured me, this time in his own handwriting, on paper printed with the logo for his band's debut LP, *Power in the Darkness*, up top, and EMI's Harvest label logo at the bottom. 'Nor does anyone else I've heard of. The artist is usually grateful for the coverage.' Motivated into action perhaps by my offer of no money, Tom suggested I send him a cassette and a list of questions and then, 'I'll tape-record the answers and send it back to you, OK?' I wasn't sure that this was how it worked for the people at *Sounds* or *NME* – they always seemed to conduct *their* interviews backstage, on a tour bus or in a recording studio – but given Tom's status, I wasn't going to object.

So I sent Tom a cassette, with a list of questions, and I waited. And waited. And after I got a little impatient waiting – I'd told everyone at school that *Jamming* was about to get its first interview, and with Tom Robinson of all people – I wrote to him again. Eventually, a reply came in the post, this one half typed, half handwritten, on a torn sheet of regular typing paper. It turned out he'd lost my cassette. But he had a solution. 'If you could write a list of questions,' he suggested, 'I'll answer them onto a (new) cassette and send it back, OK?' He signed the letter in his own writing, 'Sorry mate, love Tom.'

The sheepish apology meant that I couldn't be too mad at him. But I was eager to take *Jamming* to another level, and I was no longer sure I could rely on Tom to help. That spring and summer we had put together another couple of issues, run them through the Roneo machine at school, and one of them had turned out pretty good. I'd written a long, enthusiastic account of my day at the Carnival Against the Nazis, and also a double-page history of The Who. Jeff and I wrote up our impressions of an American powerpop band called the Rubinoos we'd gone to see at the Marquee. (Jeff was desperate to get to the Marquee and the Rubinoos were harmless enough that his parents didn't object. I was thrilled to have someone to finally attend gigs with.) Jeff also got free tickets to see Eddie and the Hot Rods and Generation X record a Radio 1 In Concert at a theatre just off Piccadilly Circus, and he wrote that one up as well. And he started his own column called 'Rattus', which was one long monologue, poorly spelled, full of stupid asides and bad puns, and which wound up a lot of people at school. (This, I knew, was his intent.) We even ran a couple of photos through the school Roneo machine, and the way they came out – in harsh black and white, with no grey areas – made us look a little more like a fanzine than a school magazine. Lawrence Weaver, still officially my co-editor, wrote about Rush and Rainbow, and for the fourth issue, he took the cover with a piece on the Electric Light Orchestra, to which I countered with a review of the New Hearts at the Marquee (again) – and The Jam at the Lyceum, the famous theatre off the Strand. That show had raised The Jam even higher in my estimation. They had played for longer, included some unreleased material, and wore flash grey mohair suits rather than the traditional black office wear, and being that this was a largish venue, without seats downstairs, I was able to get close to the stage without being crushed. As far as I was concerned, even if The Jam weren't getting bigger, they were definitely getting better.

I had been waiting until I had a magazine that I thought was good enough. I wasn't sure it was there yet, but I couldn't wait around on Tom forever, so after we got that fourth issue of *Jamming* out, at the end of the school year, I wrote to Paul Weller, at The Jam's fan club address in Woking, to see if *he* would give me an interview. It wasn't just that, though. Given how much stick they were getting in the music press, I wanted to let him know how popular The Jam were among us third-formers, and to emphasise the point, I told him how impressed we all were about something we had read in the music papers. Apparently, at the Speakeasy – a rock 'n' roll hangout in Soho – a drunken Sid Vicious had aggressively cornered Paul Weller, egged him on about something or other, and when the dust settled . . . Sid was in need of hospital treatment. The incident made Paul Weller that much more of a hero: not the kind to push other people around, but someone who would stand up and defend himself when it mattered. All us Jam fans figured Sid had it coming to him. Not Jeff Carrigan. He sided with Sid.

The Jam may have been out of fashion with the critics, but they couldn't have been *that* unpopular with the public, because they were announced as the headlining act for the first night of the annual hippie/hard rock Reading Festival at the end of August – and given that the New Hearts and a great band from Newcastle called Penetration were also on the bill, suggesting a determination by the promoters to draw in some of us new wavers, I planned on ending my summer holiday there. And I figured on starting it in equally music fan fashion, at the Institute of Contemporary Arts on Pall Mall, next to Buckingham Palace, for an exhibition launched by Who fans, entitled 'Who's Who'. I had a sneaking suspicion that members of The Who themselves might show up for the opening day. They were just the kind of rock stars that would do such a thing.

I was right. I went with Christopher and Adrian – both now firm Who fans, thanks largely to my encouragement – and when we got there, we found ourselves immediately drawn to a crowd surrounding Pete Townshend himself, being interviewed for radio. The Who had a new LP coming out soon, *Who Are You*, and it included songs like 'Music Must Change' that reflected Townshend's support for the new wave. All the press I'd read suggested that he wanted to retire The Who but couldn't bring himself to do so. A compromise had apparently been reached: The Who would not be touring to support the new album. I was just glad I'd seen them at Charlton, before it was too late.

We hung around at the back of the crowd, more or less the youngest kids in the ICA. And it was probably for that very reason that, when they finished interviewing Pete Townshend, the hosts from Capital Radio's Sunday magazine show *Hullabaloo* turned towards us, thrust their microphones in our faces, and asked us what *we* were doing there. What possible appeal could The Who have for the younger generation?

Christopher went first: they smashed up their instruments, and that was 'brilliant', he said. I went next. I said that they were from the sixties but their music was still relevant today, and that that was 'brilliant', too. The DJs told us to listen out on Sunday, that they'd probably use us, and with the confidence that came from being potential radio celebrities, we set off about the ICA with a spring in our step.

The exhibition included all The Who's single sleeves (except for the now mythically rare *Ready Steady Who*), Roger Daltrey's jacket from Woodstock or something equally important, a stage set up with their equipment, a film of the group in their early days, smashing up their equipment, and one of Townshend's broken Rickenbackers nailed to the wall in pieces, with a frame around it like the work of art that it was. And, upstairs, there was a hologram of Keith Moon at the drums.

Holograms were the new thing: three-dimensional projections, like how Princess Leia looked when beamed onto other planets for an intergalactic phone call in the *Star Wars* film we'd all gone to see the previous summer. The Who, already famous for their use of lasers, were apparently among the pioneers of the form and it had to be said, it was an impressively lifelike optical illusion. I got to see just *how* lifelike when I felt someone sidle up next to me and turned round to find myself looking right at Moon himself.

I knew that Keith was in the building; the buzz had been going around all morning. And I had hoped I might find him at some point and get his autograph, even if it meant his pouring a bottle of brandy over me or doing something similarly in keeping with his reputation for lunacy. But I had never anticipated that I would find myself standing next to him – with no bodyguards, no radio or TV interviewers, nobody at all around us other than a kid much my own age who seemed to be in his company.

I was nervous, but I wasn't going to waste the opportunity. I turned to him – he was only about my height – and made a shy comment about how weird this must feel for him, looking at a three-dimensional image of himself. He agreed – quietly, calmly, nothing like his public persona. Emboldened, though still dead nervous, I dropped my hand into my sports bag and removed the issue of *Jamming* I'd brought with me – the one in which I'd written up the two-page history of The Who – and asked him, ever so politely, if he would mind signing it for me.

Keith took the magazine, checked the cover, had a quick look at the story – two pages of regular type, no photos – and said, 'I don't think I've seen this one.'

You wouldn't have, I said to myself, given that we'd only printed 150 copies and, apart from those I got placed in the local newsagent and, impressively, the Virgin store at Marble Arch, most had been sold at school. 'It's my own magazine,' I said out loud, instead.

'I'd like to read this article some time,' Keith said.

'You can keep it if you want,' I replied. And I meant it. Of course he could.

'No, you want it autographed,' said the drummer, and he signed his name across the top corner of the page with a flourish. 'Tell you what, though,' he continued, and he produced a slip of paper from an inside pocket and scribbled down an address. 'Here's where I live,' he said as he handed it to me. 'Come and see me. Bring a copy of your magazine. Any time's fine by me.'

And then he moved along.

As he departed, I studied the scrap of paper. The address said Curzon Place, W1. When I got home, I found out it was in Mayfair. The most expensive piece of property in Monopoly.

A few days later, I was back on the number 3 bus into central London. I had in my bag all the issues of *Jamming*, and a couple of Who records to get signed, and in my stomach I carried enough butterflies to launch an exhibit of my own. I knew Soho well enough now, but I had never had any reason to venture the *other* side of Regent Street. All I knew about Mayfair was what my mother told me – that it was full of wealthy Arabs, and, apparently, the wealthy prostitutes who serviced them.

Curzon Place was tucked in just behind Park Lane – the second most expensive property in Monopoly. I expected to find a security guard blocking my way at number 9, but there was no one there. The whole building was eerily quiet. I felt a little like an intruder – I knew I didn't *belong* – but then I reminded myself: I had been invited. I had permission. I took the lift upstairs, and then walked down the carpeted corridor to flat number 12. When I got there, I could hear music. I just couldn't tell which flat it was coming from. Keith's? Or the one next door? I hesitated before knocking. Suppose that he was living like a rock star, making love to a beautiful blonde or something equally fantastic, and I interrupted him? Suppose that he opened the door and didn't remember me? Suppose that he was drunk and obnoxious, like the papers said that he always was?

. . . And suppose that I walked away without making the most of his invitation? I would never forgive myself. And think how nice he'd been at the ICA. Not drunk, not loud, not rude, not even funny. Just . . . nice. I took a deep breath and knocked on the door. And waited. Nothing happened. I could still hear the music. It sounded like a radio. I still couldn't tell which flat it was coming from. I knocked again. And waited. And again, nothing happened.

I'd prepared for this eventuality. I pulled the letter from my bag, and slipped it into a large envelope alongside a copy of *Jamming*, the one with the story of The Who. I had to work on sliding the package underneath the door: these were posh flats after all, where everything fitted together properly, with no draughts, no peeling paint and certainly no outdoor toilets. The letter had my name, and my address, and my phone number, and it offered the suggestion that perhaps Keith Moon might like to be interviewed for *Jamming*. I was hopeful, but nothing more than that. I honestly didn't expect to hear back from him.

Number 31:
IF THE KIDS ARE UNITED

The letter was postmarked central London, it arrived in late August, and I thought I recognised the handwriting on the front. I opened it up eagerly, and it was everything I'd dreamed of, and more.

'Dear Tony,' it began – which was funny, because nobody called me Tony, which meant that either I'd signed my own letter that way to appear cool, or he'd taken it upon himself to call me Tony because Anthony was way too posh. 'Thanks for your letter and the fanzines, I'd be glad to do an interview if you can make it this week sometime,' and then he listed the address of a recording studio in North-West London. 'If you can't make it get in touch,' he continued, as if worried that I might have too busy a schedule, and he provided a phone number for me to call. He concluded, 'Try and make the studios so you can hear the new LP (EXCLUSIVE!)'

And he signed it, Paul Weller.

Up until now, I'd been somewhat OK about Tom Robinson's disorganisation. It was obvious the man meant well, and he was *trying* to give me an interview (of sorts), and he was a busy rock star after all, but still . . . he was no Paul Weller. And yet Paul had written back immediately, with no deliberations, no vague promises about the future, no requests for a cassette in the post. Instead, in his own writing, without any middle man, he'd invited me to meet him face to face for an interview. This week. In the studio. EXCLUSIVE!

Then I saw the P.S. on the bottom left corner of the letter and an arrow pointing downwards. I turned the letter over.

'P.S. As regards the 'SID' episode tell your friends *that THERE AIN'T NOTHING TOUGH OR ADMIRABLE ABOUT VIOLENCE*. Cheers.'

Wow. I had been thanked, befriended and then admonished by my idol, all in the space of one short handwritten letter. No wonder he was The Jam's leader. His authority was written all over him.

When I got over the shock of it all, I worked up the courage to call the phone number he'd given me. (I knew it was a Woking number; I was enough of a Jam fan to recognise the area code.) And when I did, a lady answered and I asked if Paul was there and she said no, he didn't live there any more – but she said it like she was used to this and asked why I was calling. I told her about my fanzine and about Paul's letter. I said Paul had invited me 'this week' but it was Wednesday already and The Jam were playing Reading on Friday. Monday was a bank holiday. I needed clarification. I wasn't just meant to show up, was I? (Or was I?)

She laughed. She obviously didn't know anything about any of this and yet was completely used to it. She told me she was Paul's mother, Ann, and that she'd check into it all and get back to me later that day. And she did. Next week, after the Reading Festival, after the bank holiday, and just before school started again, I could go up to the RAK Studios in St John's Wood, around lunchtime. Paul Weller would be expecting me.

I may have been just another face in a crowd of about 20,000 at Reading that Friday night, but I had something the others did not: the knowledge that, just a few days later, I'd be sitting face to face with the group, or at least with Paul Weller, interviewing him, in the recording studio, like a proper music journalist.

We would have plenty to talk about. The Jam had just released their new single, and they'd declared it a double A-side. One of those A-sides was 'David Watts', a cover of a song by The Who's sixties contemporaries the Kinks (not that I had heard the original), and Bruce Foxton was singing lead vocals, again. 'David Watts' was all about some sort of pure and noble Victorian schoolboy ideal: the head boy, captain of the team, gay and fancy free. The other A-side, '"A" Bomb in Wardour Street', was its total opposite. Sung – shouted, rather – by Weller, it recounted the singer's journey into the dark heart of modern-day Soho, where he found himself at the Vortex, the punk club at the top of Wardour Street, his head having been 'kicked in' and 'fifteen geezers' having pinned his girlfriend to the door.

It was tempting to imagine this as Weller's way of recounting his fight with Sid Vicious, but there it had been the Pistols' bass player left bleeding on the floor, not The Jam's singer. No, the song seemed to be portending a violence more tribal and – as the lyrics moved that violence, verse by verse, from the Vortex floor to the West End to the city to the country – something far more universal. And in its reference to a size-ten boot and ultimately, to 'Doctor Marten's apocalypse', that final word of the song spelled out letter by letter (and just as well, as most of us had never heard it used before), Rick Buckler's snare drum rolling furiously to announce the trio's unified power-chord climax, there seemed little doubt as to what – or rather who – Weller was talking about.

Skinheads.

They were everywhere that day at Reading, a marauding army of cropped heads and turned-up Levi's jeans, suspenders worn over either Fred Perry tennis shirts or Ben Sherman button-downs, and, to a last man and boy, those regulation Doc Martens boots. They were all over the train I took from Paddington that morning with my new gig-going partner Ray. They were in the field already when we got there, throwing beer cans indiscriminately before the first band even came on, purposefully parting the crowd as if this was a football ruck. (I took a photo of them doing so, catching a skinhead in gormless grin as he threw one can with his right hand and prepared to launch another with his left.) They were especially aggressive during the New Hearts' set, scoring a direct hit on the temple of the group's new second guitarist, whose cream-coloured Gibson was soon splattered red. And when *their* band came on – because they hadn't come along *just* to cause indiscriminate trouble – they invaded the stage. For most of Sham 69's set, you couldn't see the band for the skins.

Sham 69 had not started out as a skinhead band. They had declared themselves true punk rockers. They saw the Sex Pistols manager Malcolm McLaren and his King's Road clothing shops as rip-offs; the Clash's willingness to embrace musical forms other than three-chord punk as a sell-out; the gathering 'new wave' as a bunch of artsy poseurs. They had one song that denounced 'rich boys', another that celebrated a 'Borstal Breakout', and yet another with a chorus that went 'What have we got?' to which the audience could shout back in unison, 'Fuck all!' Along with the likes of Menace, Skrewdriver, Chelsea and Bethnal, they had made the Vortex their home base, turning it into either the last refuge of authentic punk, or a mockery of the whole movement, depending on who you talked to.

Sham 69 were a four-piece, but really, they were all about their front man. Jimmy Pursey spoke in flattened vowels, the same way Tom Robinson sang that song 'Martin'. He made a big deal of the fact that he'd worked at a greyhound racetrack and been a barrow boy in the East End. But Pursey was not a cockney. His group came from Hersham, a distant suburb of London that was no more 'in the city' than The Jam's Woking. They had taken their name from faded graffiti on a local wall, and because most people knew that 1969 was the year the original skinheads had taken hold, so they figured Sham to stand for 'SkinHeads Are Mad' – as opposed to the truth, that it was the name of their home town absent its first syllable. Sham 69, Pursey in particular, were so desperate for fame that they allowed the myth to spread, and as a skinhead revival took root, Pursey readily set himself up as their leader. He said as much, that he saw himself as a spokesman. He thought that if the skinheads listened to his band, they would listen to what he had to say, that they would trust in him, and that he could trust them in return. He couldn't admit what most people already knew, that the skinhead revival was being sponsored and manipulated by right-wing fascist groups who were far smarter than he could ever hope to be.

Earlier in 1978, Sham 69 had signed to Polydor – The Jam's label – and released the single 'Angels with Dirty Faces', the run-on line of which was an almost comically exaggerated 'Kids, like you . . . and me!' It was the kind of record that appealed to the first and second years at our school, those who had missed out on punk but wanted to buy into what they thought was genuine working-class revolt in sing-along fashion. It also appealed to older kids who thought that buying Sham 69 singles made them tough by association – the same prats at Tenison's who'd waved the sleeve to 'Clash City Rockers' in my face.

The Clash had made up for their self-caricature with their next single '(White Man) in Hammersmith Palais', which took the reggae concept of 'Police and Thieves' and then turned up the volume and energy for four full minutes, the likes of which nobody had ever heard before. Lyrically too, it strode new ground, Joe Strummer name-checking all manner of reggae stars while simultaneously berating punk groups in Burton suits (The Jam, we presumed) and suggesting that Britain was moving so far to the right that 'if Adolf Hitler flew in today, they'd send a limousine anyway'. '(White Man)' wasn't a hit, of course; it was far too original, too confrontational, too musically and lyrically threatening to get Radio 1 airplay . . . Unlike Sham 69's follow-up to 'Angels', the even more ridiculous terrace chant 'If the Kids Are United' (. . . 'they will never be divided'), which Radio 1 played so bloody often that it soon went Top Ten. By the time Sham 69 played Reading, they could lay claim to being the biggest band on the bill.

Their army of skinhead followers certainly acted like it. Having terrorised the crowd all day, they started a nasty fight at the front just before Sham 69 were due to start, and there were public threats about the gig being cancelled. The band took to the stage anyway. When they did so, we expected Pursey to rein the skinheads in, or to warn them off, to at least do *something* to distance himself from their behaviour. 'Thank you to the best fans in the world,' he roared in gratitude instead, and within seconds, they were all over the stage.

It turned out Pursey was only getting warmed up. 'This is going to be a Rock Against Politics gig,' he shouted at one point; 'This is what happens when there's too much politics,' at another. Sham even covered the Clash's 'White Riot', perhaps not the wisest choice for an audience of skinheads whose culture had long been associated with Paki-bashing and the far right. It was possible that Pursey felt entitled to play 'White Riot' because, despite his thinly veiled attacks on Rock Against Racism and the Anti-Nazi League, he had sung it with the Clash at the Carnival Against the Nazis. (The Clash, so word had it, were not happy about his insistence on doing so.) But it didn't stop him insulting *them* at Reading as well. 'The Clash haven't accepted the invitation to come here . . .' he shouted, as if he was the festival promoter or that the Clash were duty-bound to be his backing band every time he wanted to co-opt their first single. The skinheads lapped it up, chanting 'White riot, I wanna riot . . .' Were those Hitler salutes we saw? It sure looked like it. Eventually Sham's set ended, and the skinheads, once convinced to leave the stage, promptly stormed off *en masse* to overrun the press tent.

A couple of hours later, darkness having fallen, Ultravox and the Pirates having played in between, The Jam came on stage. Weller thundered immediately, 'I don't care how long your hair is, or how short it is. I don't care whether you're wearing boots or plimsolls – rock 'n' roll is for everybody,' and that was it: into the music. There were no stage invasions, and no skinheads Sieg Heiling, though the barriers at the front collapsed and several people were pulled out from the crush looking as if they'd fainted, and Weller's amp kept cutting out until eventually, during the final song 'Here Comes the Weekend', he smashed his Rickenbacker against it and then threw the guitar across the stage, at which it promptly split in two. It didn't look half as exciting, or artistic, as when I'd seen Pete Townshend do it on film. In fact, as the conclusion to a nasty day out, it was only slightly less appropriate than Jimmy Pursey rushing back on stage after The Jam's encores to lead a chorus of 'You'll Never Walk Alone' – and being met by silence.

Number 30:
TO BE SOMEONE

I was wearing my brand-new black school jacket when I went to RAK Studios in St John's Wood to interview Paul Weller. Now that we were heading into our fourth year at Tenison's, starting on our O levels, we could finally leave behind the blue blazers that had denoted us as 'posh' grammar-school boys. (We had, actually, been a comprehensive school for a year already, the Labour government having decided to abolish the grammar-school system in pursuit of social equality. The option for rich people to send their children to so-called 'public' schools remained.) I had yet to sew the Tenison's school crest onto the front of the blazer and had no immediate plans to do so. That way, I was hoping I could pass as a 'new wave mod', like an everyday member of The Jam. Wearing it to the studio for the interview was something of a test.

'All right, you come straight from school, then?'

Paul Weller's opening words put me right in my place. There was fashion. And there was school uniform. And Weller, decked out in perfectly creased Sta-Prest trousers and a light-coloured, long-sleeved shirt unbuttoned at the top – clothing so similar to my own and yet so many miles apart – was clearly on the first side of that divide.

I'd never been inside a recording studio before, but RAK looked almost exactly as I'd expected. The place was modern, it was bright – daylight pouring in on the control room from the quiet street outside – and the atmosphere was casual, quietly humming along with what was, to those involved, the everyday business of making a record. The mood was clearly confident, too. 'David Watts' – the A-side much preferred by the radio stations – had just entered the charts and there was a feeling it was going to keep rising this time. Everyone around The Jam was taking bets on its position for the next week's chart, at £5 a go, the kind of money I couldn't imagine having in my pocket without immediately spending it on an LP, a concert ticket or, preferably, both.

The betting team revolved around three people, all of them considerably older than the group. There was John Weller, imposing with his boxer's nose, his silver hair and his rough voice; an even more daunting man called Kenny Wheeler, whose position in the camp I didn't quite understand but was not about to question; and an affable, bearded chap called Dave Liddle, who I recognised from Jam gigs as Paul's guitar roadie, though when I used that term he quickly corrected me. He was a guitar *tech*, he said.

And then there was Paul: handsome, tall, immaculately dressed, rake thin, and yet visibly tough. He was the reason that anybody was in the studio to begin with, and yet he seemed to shirk that responsibility, as if deliberately trying to vacate the centre of activity and leave a void there. He near enough chain-smoked, though he wasn't the only one, and he drank tea at a furious pace, though he wasn't alone in that activity either. And he was a constant bundle of nerves. When we conducted our interview, in the studio itself, sat on a couple of folding chairs pulled in and facing each other, my family's portable tape-radio propped up on a Vox AC30 amplifier, I noticed that his Sta-Prest trouser leg twitched constantly. In song he sounded so self-assured, so absolutely certain: I don't give two *fucks* about your review. But now that he was talking to a fourteen-year-old fanzine editor, he didn't seem quite so sure of himself. In fact, he was oddly inarticulate.

Was it me? I had no interview experience to base this on. I was sitting opposite someone who had become near enough a god to me over the last twelve months, and we were one on one, just inches apart, with nobody in the room to overhear and pass judgement on us, but also no one to assure me I was asking the right questions. I wanted to know everything, but I didn't want to pry. I wanted to be friendly, but I also wanted to make sure I got something out of him that was worth printing. I wanted to start at the beginning, but I didn't want to run out of time at the end. So I just kept asking questions. Paul's response to them, typically, was to study his fingers, and the cigarette ash burning slowly between them, and then to respond in choppy sentences that started, paused, rewound, started again, paused again, and often abruptly stopped . . . only to start back up again just as I set about asking a new question.

And yet, although his responses weren't exactly the height of literacy, there was nothing he didn't answer, nothing he avoided – although he did have an interesting habit of throwing my questions right back at me. When I asked, for example, if he'd gone to see the 'Who's Who' exhibition, he said that he had, and then he asked if *I'd* gone, and what had *I* thought of it? And when I told him that Townshend and Moon were there he wanted to know, 'Did they talk to you?' Not, 'Did you talk to *them*?' But 'Did they talk to *you*?' (Actually, he used the word 'yer', as in 'Did they talk to *yer*?' He wasn't one for the Queen's English.) When I quizzed him on his reputation for 'arrogance', he quickly projected it right back on me. 'It's like someone saying to you, "What do you think of your fanzine?" . . . If you say, "I think it's fucking great," it doesn't mean you're arrogant, it means you've got confidence and you believe in it and you believe in what you do.'

And then, when we talked about a recent *Sounds* cover story that had painted The Jam as being in the throes of crisis, Weller wasted no time explaining why he had refused to sit down for an interview with the writer. 'He was a cunt,' said Paul, using a word we rarely uttered even on the terraces. 'I only talk to people I think it's worth talking to. Like, you've come here for a purpose. But all he'd come for was to give us a slating, so that's not very positive. At least you're doing something.'

I was? I hadn't really thought of it that way. I just figured I was indulging in a hobby while my band got going, trying to have some fun outside of school hours (and, especially, during them). To the extent that Paul Weller or Keith Moon were giving me the time of day, I figured it was only out of kindness, sympathy, perhaps a memory of how they had been similarly eager at my age. The magazines I had sent Paul were nothing: just a bunch of third-formers' poorly edited music reviews, a couple of fawning biographies, and some hastily written gossip items, all run through a school copier. And yet here was Paul Weller sitting in front of me, giving up part of his valuable studio time, telling me I had every right to believe in it, to say 'It's fucking great' and mean it. He was *validating* it for me.

Halfway through the interview, Dave Liddle walked in, asking what we wanted for lunch. I looked at Paul. What *did* rock stars have for lunch?

'Fried egg,' said Paul to Dave. 'Lots of ketchup.'

Liddle looked at me. 'Fried-egg sandwich all right?'

I nodded. I'd never had a fried-egg sandwich before but I wasn't about to admit as much. It was bad enough that I'd given away my 'mod' credibility with my school blazer.

A few minutes later Liddle came back into the studio with two plates. Each contained a fried egg, laden with ketchup, wedged between two slices of white bread, with a cup of heavily milked tea to accompany. I tucked into mine. It tasted wonderful. Better than that, it *looked* wonderful. The studio was state of the art, and there was pristine equipment everywhere, and Weller looked sharp as a shop-window dummy, but still, The Jam ate like Jimmy out of *Quadrophenia*, like that picture in the album book that showed a café table full of chips and eggs, and fag ends and tea cups. I loved it.

Paul had promised me an exclusive and he was good to his word. Early on in the day, he disappeared into the studio with a Rickenbacker, which I now knew to be the most beautiful guitar in the world (even as I still suspected that the Gibson Les Paul made a better sound) and recorded overdubs for the final part of a song called 'In the Crowd'. ('Hey! That's my song title!' I wanted to say but of course didn't.) He allowed me to come into the recording room and take pictures of him; he had a faraway look in his eyes by the time I did so, fully focused on the psychedelic little guitar lines he was creating. It was like I wasn't there.

And then, later in the afternoon, I was allowed to hear the rest of the album. They'd decided to call it *All Mod Cons*, a pun on the mod movement per the shorthand of real estate advertising (for 'all modern conveniences', my mum told me), and it was immediately obvious that the critics who had it in for The Jam were going to be rudely disappointed. *All Mod Cons* was not so punk as its predecessors; it was deeper, more polished, better produced, more expressive. (Paul used the word 'subtle' during our interview.) By any musical or lyrical standards you could apply, it was obviously their 'best' album – and yet it still had plenty of anger. And swearing. There was a song called 'To Be Someone', about rock stars who 'shit out to become one of the bastard sons', and another in which Weller promised a character called 'Mr Clean' that 'If I get the chance I'll fuck up your life.'

But there was also this song called 'English Rose' and it threw me for a loop. The other members of The Jam weren't present on this recording (just as they weren't at the studio that day); it was only Paul and an acoustic guitar. It was a ballad, unlike anything The Jam had done before. The closest I could compare it to was 'Tonight At Noon', but without the band accompaniment. I was happy that Paul was in love (every Jam fan knew her name was Gill), and that he could write songs about it; I hoped to get there myself one day. But I loved The Jam because they were a *band*; I wasn't looking for Weller to be a solo artist. And I liked them loud: even 'Tonight At Noon' had power chords on top of the acoustic strumming. So when Paul asked me what I thought of it, like he wasn't quite sure of it himself, I said something about it being 'different' and left it there.

Fortunately, 'English Rose' was the odd one out. Everything

else was The Jam as I knew them and loved them while taking that vital step forward. I was especially moved by the tracks at the end of each side. 'In the Crowd' was well over five minutes long, suggesting that the group had finally broken free of their reputation as either a 'punk' or a 'mod' or even a 'punk-mod' band. (Even better, in the lengthy fade-out, Paul threw a vocal reference back to 'Away from the Numbers'. He knew, as well as anyone, that there had been something special about that one.) As for the finale, 'Down in the Tube Station at Midnight', everything about it – the rhythm, the lyrics, the rush of words at the end which told of an encounter every bit as violent as '"A" Bomb in Wardour Street' – suggested that it was the best thing they'd ever done. During our interview, Paul said they'd probably break with tradition, with the unwritten punk rule-book, and take more than one single off this new album.

'It's too good not to,' he insisted.

And that wasn't arrogance. It was the truth.

I heard the news from Nicky Horne, at the start of his show, at 9 p.m. on a Thursday night. Keith Moon had died at home, in Curzon Place, earlier that day. Whether it was a heart attack or something else – a drug overdose, perhaps – was yet to be determined. But the circumstances didn't change the reality. Keith Moon was dead.

My grandfather had died when I was four or five years old. (For reasons I had never figured out, my brother and I had not been told about it until after his funeral.) Other than that, I'd never known anyone who had died. Death was always something that happened to other people.

But this death happened to *me*. It hit me in the gut, like a bully had punched me there, and I felt myself go weak inside, the stuffing knocked out of me. Barely a month ago, I had introduced myself to one of my favourite people in the world – one of the most famous people in the world – and he had been nice to me. He had been sweet, gentle and kind. He had written down his home address and invited me to come round and see him. In the process, he had shown that I needed not be scared of, or awed by, rock stars, that they were human, like the rest of us. He hadn't responded to the letter I'd slid under his door in Mayfair, and whether he had ever intended to (indeed, whether he'd ever read it), I would now never know. But I felt like I knew him all the same, and I reacted to his death like it was a member of my own family. I bawled my eyes out.

Keith was all over the newspapers the next day. He dominated the front pages of the tabloids the same way the Sex Pistols had done after they swore at Bill Grundy. The *Daily Mirror* ran the headline 'Drugs Death Drama of Pop Wild Man Moon' and the other papers offered their own speculative accounts of his demise. He had been Moon the Loon, infamous for drinking and drugging his way across the world, leaving a trail of damaged hotels and ravaged women behind him, and now, they seemed to be suggesting, he had got his just reward.

They had no idea. Thousands of us looked up to Keith Moon, felt kinship with him for the way he had lived his life, free of convention, of expectations. For the example he had set to those of us who derided the nine-to-five life, who shivered at the prospect of ending up in a suburban semi-detached with 2.4 children and a dog, who decried that businessmen in Britain all wore pinstripe suits, that secondary-age schoolchildren were forced to wear uniforms, that the teachers had long stopped caring, that bullies ran rampant, that the streets were full of violence, that the buses never ran on time, that the country shut down at 11 p.m. – with the national anthem as a reminder of our pervasive monarchy – and that the sky was perpetually overcast and the air permanently damp, that the older generation clung to an Empire that no longer existed and had been built on violent conquest to begin with, that they genuinely believed that the return of National Service and beating with the birch would solve all the problems of us youth, that fascism was gaining ground, that skinheads were increasing in numbers, and that, by their very design, with their endless rows of terraced streets and parades of small-time shops, our towns and cities promoted anonymity and servitude. Keith Moon, a working-class boy from Wembley, had emerged from all of this and shown that you could rise above it, that you didn't have to sacrifice your dreams for the security of normality, that you could, by your talents and your determination – and yes, your lunacy – take control of your own destiny to live your life in the stratosphere, far above the miserable majority of the human race, like a comet streaking through the night sky. In his case that flame had burned out already, and I didn't know enough to fully understand why or how. I just knew, at this moment in time, while he was being slandered and libelled and pilloried in death, that I would do anything to set the record straight.

Number 29:
YOUNG PARISIANS

R ay was two years older than me. But he was small for his age, about my size, and he was scruffy, like me. He was in the bottom stream at Tenison's, but he didn't hang out with the hard nuts, the ones we occasionally saw pummelling less fortunate kids in the toilets. Ray lived along Croxted Road, a few bus stops closer to Tenison's than me, but we'd never spoken in almost three years of shared bus journeys. I didn't think we had anything in common.

Then, shortly after the first issue of *Jamming* came out, I got a letter in the post addressed to Ann-phony. (I'd printed my home address in hope of correspondence.) It wasn't signed anything other than 'Me', which was silly given that the writer was offering to supply a front-row review and photographs from the Carnival Against the Nazis, and I would have been interested, in the pictures at least, if I'd known how to contact him. Then again, the letter had a few snide comments, like the writer couldn't decide if he liked the magazine or not. Given that I felt much the same way about it, I printed the letter anyway. Ray soon came up to me at school and introduced himself, and after a couple more encounters in the hallways, admitted he was the author, and asked to get involved with *Jamming*. As an incentive, he sent in another letter, signed by several other fifth years; it felt like an official endorsement, and was recognised as such around the school.

I printed Ray's pictures from the Carnival in the last issue we put out before the school holidays. And then, over the summer, Ray started calling me every evening, as if we were friends already.

Mainly we talked about music. Ray was into bands like Ultravox and Wire, who went beyond the regular I-IV-V chord patterns of The Jam, the Clash and the Buzzcocks, or at least found new ways to arrange them. Wire's first album had an astonishing twenty-one (short) songs, with titles like '1.2.X.U.'. Ultravox used synthesisers, had a lead singer who sang in a style closer to David Bowie or Bryan Ferry than Paul Weller or Joe Strummer, and thought nothing of combining two foreign languages into one title, as on 'Hiroshima Mon Amour'.

I wasn't unfamiliar with this type of art rock: I'd bought the Be-Bop Deluxe LP *Sunburst Finish* after seeing them at the Great British Music Festival way back in early 1976, and still loved it. (On their most recent album, *Drastic Plastic*, however, they tried to jump the new wave bandwagon, and lost all sense of place and purpose in the process; Bill Nelson appeared to admit as much by announcing their break-up soon after.) I loved Wire's new single 'I Am the Fly', and I liked what I heard of Ultravox, too: they sounded confident in their originality, and seemed comfortable being grouped in with the new wave even though they would have been much the same group without it, and so I agreed to go and see them with Ray at the Marquee only two days before we were to see them at Reading. It was worth it: watching singer John Foxx's staccato stage movements and Billy Currie's frenetic violin playing under the strobe lights was that much more captivating in a club than in a field. Ultravox were hardly a secret – their run of five sold-out shows at the Marquee equalled the venue's long-standing record, and they were the favourite group of the real *In the City* fanzine, the one from Neasden that I was now buying regularly from Virgin Marble Arch and which I had come to admire (and envy) for its sharp graphics and quality photocopying – but they weren't on the lips of the other third years, that was for sure.

Ray was not much of a fan of The Jam or The Who, thought Nicky Horne was a boring old fart, and couldn't understand why football fans spoke about their clubs as if they were part of them. We argued as much as we agreed. Still, I liked that I had someone living local to develop my music tastes with and agreed that Ray could contribute to *Jamming*. I was barely back at school – Ray had left for good, like so many did at the end of their fifth year – when he called me to say he'd got an interview with John Peel. I was thrilled.

'Great,' I replied. 'When can we do it?'

'You're too late,' he said. Ray had gone to BBC radio's head-quarters on Great Portland Street, waited around for John Peel to show up to do his radio show, handed him a couple of copies of *Jamming*, asked for an interview, and was told to come back a couple of days later, around the same time. He did just that. The interview was already in the bag.

If I was put off by Ray's tactic, I wasn't going to turn down the interview. And though Ray's questions were largely rudimentary, Peel demonstrated why people respected him so much when asked about Jimmy Pursey's behaviour at the Reading Festival, where he'd had a stage-side view as the event DJ: 'It seems to me that he can only control his fans if he does what they want him to do – so really, the fans are controlling him.'

Then Christopher Modica called to say he could score us an interview with someone he had recently started following under his own steam. If we wanted to, we could sit down and talk with Adam Ant.

I knew the name. Adam Ant had hung out with the King's Road crowd that gave us the Sex Pistols, and his group's original front woman had been Jordan, the distinctive-looking punkette who had starred in this incredibly strange film called *Jubilee* that almost nobody had actually seen. But his band Adam and the Ants had, even after all this time, yet to release a record. More people had read about them than actually heard them. And according to what was reported, Adam Ant was a sexually decadent Nazi sympathiser given to dressing up in rubber and whipping people.

Christopher Modica was becoming, like myself, quite the fourteen-year-old gig-goer, but he was no more sexually experienced than I was, let alone decadent, and although his sister had once walked down the street wearing a dustbin bag, I'd yet to see him sport anything more outrageous than a torn shirt. Plus, he was well into Steel Pulse and Rock Against Racism: the chances of his following any kind of Nazi sympathiser seemed unlikely in the extreme – although, it had to be said, the page Adam Ant had just designed for top punk fanzine *Ripped & Torn* was full of swastikas. Any which way, Adam Ant was a name, of sorts, and so I agreed to the interview.

And yet I didn't ask Christopher to conduct it. Or even to share in it. I was the editor. And to prevent him getting the same idea as Ray, I announced that from now on, I would do the interviews. Christopher could be the *Jamming* photographer. The pictures he had taken at a recent Marquee gig were by far the best any of us had managed yet; from a vantage point he'd wrangled on stage, he had caught Adam Ant, in trench coat and eye make-up, staring straight into his camera lens. Another, taken backstage, perfectly portrayed the claustrophobia of the Marquee dressing room – Adam standing with his back against the wall, a spray-painted 999 logo hovering right above his head as if taunting him that they were the more important band.

If Christopher was offended by my cutting him out of the interview process, he didn't make a big deal of it. After school one day I took a couple of buses over to Notting Hill Gate where I found myself welcomed, to my surprise, into a vast management office, with large desks and white walls, complete with a sofa on which to conduct the interview. Adam and the Ants had finally signed a record deal with Decca, home to The Who back in the sixties, but generally considered the least fashionable of all major labels. Adam defended the partnership as evidence of his punk ideals: 'The way to kill something is to get inside and cause an awful lot of havoc,' he said. This sounded suspiciously close to the philosophy of his fellow punk pioneers Siouxsie and the Banshees, who had been similarly left on the shelf during 1977, perhaps also due to accusations of Nazi sympathies. (There were plenty of pictures to prove that the gorgeously outrageous Siouxsie, who'd been the object of Bill Grundy's affections on the famous *Filth and the Fury* interview, had most certainly worn swastikas in the early punk days.) The Banshees had just signed their own major label deal, and Adam was eager to make distinctions. 'I don't think they'll manipulate Polydor as well as we'll manipulate Decca,' he said, even though Siouxsie and the Banshees' debut single 'Hong Kong Garden' was already creating great excitement. He played me his own song that he hoped would have equal success: it was called 'Young Parisians'. It was a ballad with an accordion as its lead instrument, and it was about as far removed from the new wave as it was possible to get while still mentioning Patti Smith.

Throughout our interview, Adam Ant was the very model of politeness, even when I was forced to reveal that I hadn't ever heard the band before today, let alone seen them in concert. Or when I cited that page he'd designed for *Ripped & Torn* as evidence of his fascination with swastikas, at which he patiently explained that he'd done it 'to give them what they want, to show how ridiculous it is'. Like Paul Weller, he was eager to impress on me my generation's self-worth. 'There's no good band in London over the age of sixteen,' he told me early on, which gave me great faith in the possibilities for Direction.

Despite his businesslike approach to his new record deal, I believed Adam when he said, 'We are, and always will be, an underground group.' Nor did I doubt his sincerity when he closed our interview by saying, 'We like doing the small clubs, because we know the kids can see. You're my bread and butter, all your mates, and the kids in your class.'

I liked the idea that some underground musician, someone who had been shunned by the music press, falsely accused of Nazi sympathies, who was single-handedly setting out to make the Decca label hip again, believed in us kids like that, that he thought of us as his 'bread and butter'. But when I went back to school and told one of those kids in my class – Lawrence Weaver, my *Jamming* co-editor – he exploded.

'Adam and the Ants? What kind of a fucking name is that for a group? I quit.'

Number 28:
POWER IN THE DARKNESS

Jeff's house in Hastings was surprisingly modern and spacious, given the age and condition of his terraced home back at the Elephant. It was inland, on a hill, a couple of miles' walk through town from the sea. Not that Jeff and I saw much of the beachfront the weekend I spent there. Instead, we stayed up laying out the first 'proper' issue of *Jamming*. Gaining interviews with Paul Weller, John Peel and Adam Ant had confirmed that it was time to take the magazine in a new direction – mainly, one that would enable us to include photographs. But 'offset litho' printing, as the most common process appeared to be called, wasn't cheap. There was the cost of 'scanning' original photographs into 'half-tones'. Further costs originating 'plates' for each page. Time (which equalled money) spent ensuring each page was printing correctly before commencing the actual 'run'. The price per magazine only became reasonable once you got up to a run of 5,000 or so, a number beyond my comprehension – although *Sniffin' Glue* had supposedly shot up to 15,000 in the summer of 1977 before its founder, Mark Perry, gave it up to focus on his band, Alternative TV. Their brilliant single 'Action Time Vision' suggested that he had made the right move.

I'd have been just as happy to have *Jamming* photocopied – it was the preferred 'medium' of the punk ethic – but though it was cheaper in the short run, the cost didn't come down much as you increased your numbers. Faced with exorbitant estimates either way, I couldn't figure out how other fanzines managed it. Then Jeff's dad came to the rescue. He knew a printer in Hastings who would be willing to run off our fanzine, at cost. I was invited down for a weekend to oversee it.

Moving to offset litho meant not just that we could print photographs, but that we could 'lay out' the fanzine. We could use cuttings from other magazines, run the type sideways if we wanted. Rather than ending a story at the bottom of a Roneo stencil while typing it, we could glue the piece onto the page, cutting individual sentences out along the way and pasting the result back together. Not surprisingly, given so much creative freedom, by the time we made it to Hastings the Friday evening of the printing weekend, we still only had about half the issue laid out. And so, with multiple sheets of Letraset, a single can of Cow Gum, my mum's Smith Corona typewriter, and, of course, a pair of scissors at our side, we set to work finishing it off.

In the process, we almost pulled our first all-nighter. But at about two or three in the morning, after several cups of tea and coffee and after our tiredness had turned us into giggling wrecks (though it could as easily have been the Cow Gum), his parents forced us off to bed.

The rest of the weekend was spent shuffling back and forth between the work bench in his parents' basement and the printers itself. It was a race against time, and time won. By the end of the weekend we'd barely finished the layout, let alone got the thing printed. But what we did see coming off the presses looked surprisingly professional. We'd laid most of it out neatly, orderly, more like a regular magazine than a punk fanzine. There was a big picture of Paul Weller on the cover (stolen from a music paper; I didn't trust the quality of my own photos) below the Letrasetted words 'Exclusive interview with THE JAM', and the promise of 'More exclusive interviews' below that. Here and there, though, we'd experimented, especially at the back of the magazine, where Jeff designed a collage of all the artists featured inside, and I worked hard on a 'pop art' design for a page of 'overspills' that included a rave about a Scottish powerpop-punk band called the Rezillos and their hit single 'Top of the Pops', along with a farewell tribute to Be-Bop Deluxe – and a heartfelt but very short obituary of Keith Moon.

A full week later, we got the finished magazines delivered to London, courtesy of the Carrigans and their weekend jaunt to Hastings. Now all we had to do was put them together. The printer, run ragged by our disorganisation and my personal lack of gratitude, had drawn the limit at collating and stapling the magazine for us, meaning that approximately 18,000 sheets of freshly printed paper were deposited in my bedroom for me to figure out that part for myself. There was also the matter of finishing the front cover. When EMI had included a 12-inch stencil of the Tom Robinson Band's clenched fist logo with the *Power in the Darkness* LP, in the hope of encouraging a spray-painting campaign by fans, it had given me an idea: we'd design a stencil logo for *Jamming* and spray-paint every cover ourselves. It would serve to make each copy unique, for one thing. And it would come across as an act of punkish rebellion while indicating our understanding of the 'pop art' concept, for another. Plus, it offered a nod to The Jam, whose own logo was spray-painted. Finally, it enabled us to introduce colour on the cover of what was otherwise a distinctly black and white magazine. It was, perhaps, my first true act of inspiration.

It was also an act of insanity. If it wasn't time-consuming enough collating and stapling the magazines – even with the occasional help of Jeff, Ray and Christopher – the additional process of spray-painting each copy meant that there was barely any time left for sleep, let alone homework. Then there was the matter of the spray paint's toxic fumes left hanging in the air of my bedroom which, like any good fourteen-year-old, I rarely bothered to 'air' by opening the windows. But it didn't seem to matter. I was just amazed that we'd pulled it off. For there was no doubt about it: in one giant leap, we'd gone from producing a crappy school fanzine to printing a semi-profes-sional magazine.

Adam Ant certainly thought so. I sent him a copy, along with a spare page of my interview with him which I asked him to sign, and he wrote back quickly, on his own fanzine-like stationery, saying that he thought *Jamming* was 'excellantly presented and has its own very individual style, which I feel will help secure its long (I hope) and rosy future'. He was equally complimentary about The Jam interview, which was nice of him considering the bands didn't seem to have much in common. And he took my hint that I wanted to go and see the Ants live, but that their next London show was at an over-eighteens-only venue in Camden Town: 'I have put you on the guest list for the Music Machine, which should help some of your problems.'

The guest list! All of a sudden, I was on the inside.

Paul Weller also wrote back quickly, using the blank, reverse side of a front cover that I'd asked him to sign where the spray-painted logo would otherwise have gone. I'd dared mention in sending him the magazine that The Jam's next London headline, at a revived Great British Music Festival, this time to be held at Wembley Empire Pool, seemed at odds with the group's reputation for club gigs and that, coming so soon after the Reading Festival, I hoped it wasn't part of an ongoing pattern. As an act of provocation, it worked. 'There's two ways of looking at it,' he hand-wrote before even commenting on the magazine. '1. We're shitting out. 2. We owe it to all the kids that have supported us, bought our records, put us where we are, perhaps expect us to get bigger, they want THIER band to get somewhere.' He had a point: as a fan, one of 'the kids', I was ecstatic that The Jam were getting good reviews again, were selling singles, could headline something called the Great British Music Festival, and much sooner them these days than Bad Company. And I'd already bought my ticket; it was inconceivable that The Jam would play in London – even at Wembley Empire Pool – without my being there. But still, I thought there could be a happy medium somewhere, and so, it turned out, did Weller: The Jam had already booked an end-of-year show . . . also at the Music Machine. 'All *our* money will going to a charity,' wrote Weller, 'anyway it's no fucking lie and this IS AN EXCLUSIVE.' He signed off with best wishes, and then a P.S.: 'The feature was very good and I enjoyed the criticisms as well.'

The criticisms? Shit: The Jam were my favourite band in the world. (Though I proclaimed to love *Who Are You*, it was evident that The Who were not the musical force they had once been. Punk had left them high and dry, confused and not a little alienated. Besides, Keith Moon was dead.) What had I possibly written that could have been perceived as a criticism? Reading back over the five-page story, the answer was: quite a lot. In my determination to pen a properly mature 'music paper'-style piece, I'd been surprisingly distant and restrained in my enthusiasm. I'd talked about the bad sound at Reading. I'd quizzed Paul about his perceived arrogance. I'd taken him to task for denying his infatuation with The Who. (But rightly so on that score: The Jam had just offered their own tribute to Keith Moon by covering The Who's 'So Sad About Us' on the B-side of 'Tube Station', splashing a picture of a gorgeously handsome teenage mod Moon across the back cover.) And in reviewing *All Mod Cons* on the one listen in the studio, I'd commented that 'English Rose' was a 'disappointment', suggesting it was the sort of thing Weller could write 'later on, but not when you're twenty'. How was I to know that they'd add sound effects after I'd left that day to flesh it out? How was I to predict that just about everyone else on the planet was set to call it his finest moment, an act of great maturity, a sign that he was destined to join Ray Davies and John Lennon (and perhaps even Pete Townshend) in the pantheon of great British songwriters?

Still, he'd signed both the cover and a page of The Jam story I'd sent him, and he'd got Bruce and Rick to join him in doing so. And only a day or so later, I came home from school to find a postman's note: there was a package being held for me at the post office. This was a rarity, the kind of thing that only happened around Christmas. When I went to retrieve it, I was handed a 12-inch cardboard envelope: inside was a copy of *All Mod Cons*, signed by all three members of The Jam, with Weller adding the words up top: 'To Tony.'

Number 27:
TEENAGE KICKS

John Peel was old enough to be my dad. In fact, he already had several children, all borne by a long-suffering wife he referred to on air as 'the Pig', apparently as a term of endearment. Almost forty years old already, he had been on Radio 1 since it had started, back in 1967, and along the way had booked sessions from every hippie act you'd heard of and most of those you hadn't. He still had a beard. He looked like a boring old fart. By rights, the punk movement should have pushed him aside before it even considered taking on the likes of Pink Floyd and The Who.

But Peel was the exception, not the rule, and, like Pete Townshend but much more coherently, he had seen punk coming and thrown open the doors of his late-night radio show to welcome it. He had excitedly aired the first British punk single, 'New Rose' by the Damned, upon its release in late 1976, and for his efforts had received shit in the mail. (Literally, he had received shit in the mail.) Undeterred, he'd attempted to steer his show towards a fresh audience, one that would be more receptive to the new music that was soon arriving in crates. Gradually, he'd succeeded. As older listeners dropped off in disgust, younger ones came on board by the class-load. I was just one of tens of thousands of teenagers now listening, almost religiously, to his show every night that I was at home, tape deck at hand to capture the best of the new releases and, especially, his exclusive sessions. For, more so than any other DJ on Radio 1, or any radio station for that matter, Peel had licence to invite bands into a BBC studio for the day. The eight-hour union shift barely allowed time for overdubs, let alone proper mixing, but this worked in the sessions' favour; stripped of the production gloss that often came with a major label release, a listener – even a fourteen-year-old like myself – could quickly tell whether a song was any good. And if it wasn't a conventional 'song' (Peel's tastes were notoriously all over the place), it was still perfectly possible to listen between the notes and around the riffs, to ascertain whether a group had *it*, whether there was some emotion involved in their collective music-making, and better yet, some magic.

John Peel never talked down to his listeners, never presumed either to overestimate or underestimate our intelligence. He just figured that all of us, the fourteen- and forty-year-olds alike, were equal, which meant that he thought nothing of playing the Buzzcocks' latest single ('I Don't Mind' and 'Love You More' rapidly followed 'What Do I Get?' in their series of blisteringly perfect love songs) alongside a lengthy piece of instrumental music by an experimental synthesiser band from Germany. Part of the joy of listening to John Peel was turning to the radio in astonishment every few songs and exclaiming, 'What is this rubbish?'

Then there was his habit of playing either the wrong side of a record, or playing it at the wrong speed – or, occasionally, both. Given how much music on his show was weird to begin with, it would sometimes take a minute for him to realise his mistake. This fallibility was further part of his appeal – as was his contrarian nature. Earlier in 1978, when the Stranglers were being labelled as sexist pub rockers who, having successfully jumped on the punk rock bandwagon, now ought to be dropped off as soon as it passed the old people's home, Peel played the new album *Black and White*, the one that came with that 75,000-run 'limited edition' EP, in its entirety, one uninterrupted side at a time, simply because he thought the Stranglers were getting an unfair rap.

Similarly, he thought nothing of playing 'God Save the Queen' and 'Anarchy in the UK' every few weeks, partly to prove his belief that the BBC had never dared officially 'ban' them, but also, I suspected, to see if perhaps they *had* and whether anybody in the higher echelons of the BBC was listening in and would take him to task for doing so. (They never did.) And though his love of reggae was sometimes almost embarrassing – it wasn't like there were any Rastafarians where he lived, out in the flatlands of East Anglia – it had the desired effect of tempering the acutely angled, sharp-edged, sometimes abrasive or purposefully amateur music that increasingly dominated his show as wave after wave of self-pressed, or at least independently distributed, 7-inch 45s landed on his desk and, just as rapidly, found their way onto the airwaves.

Ultimately, though, John Peel loved a good pop song as much as anyone else, and right around the time that Ray interviewed him for *Jamming*, he started championing what he was soon referring to as the greatest pop song of all time. And you couldn't much argue with him: 'Teenage Kicks' by the Undertones, a five-piece band from Derry in Northern Ireland, was everything a 7-inch single was meant to be: short, sweet and sharp; full of life, lust and love; easy to sing along to; and completely unforgettable. This was the same format the Buzzcocks had been working on all year, to the point that with 'Ever Fallen in Love (With Someone You Shouldn't've)', they finally wore down Radio 1's resistance, got daytime airplay and had a genuine hit. But the Buzzcocks, as had been evident from their meticulously designed packaging, had been crafting the perfect pop single much like scientists in a laboratory – and they had the support of a major label to finance their experiments, to ensure that they sounded and looked appropriately professional. By contrast, the Undertones were on an independent label called Good Vibrations, run out of a Belfast record store of that name, and 'Teenage Kicks' came in a paper fold-out sleeve and sounded like it had been recorded in a cheap studio, in one take – which was not far off the truth. As a result, its greatest asset was the thing you couldn't quantify – the thing that you heard between the grooves, around the riffs, the unmistakable *it*. 'Teenage Kicks' had magic.

Shortly after the publication of that first properly printed *Jamming*, Ray invited me and Christopher Modica up to BBC Radio to hang out with Peel. We could, so Ray told us because he'd done as much himself the night he conducted the interview, sit in the studio while the great man presented his show. We took the number 3 bus to Great Portland Street and, sure enough, Peel invited us upstairs, into the inner sanctuary of Radio 1 – eerily silent that late at night, the offices all hushed, the corridors deserted – and let us sit behind him while he broadcast to the nation. He even mentioned our presence there, plugging *Jamming* in the process, and he may have said something about how we ought to have been indoors, doing our homework. Christopher and I were keeping a careful eye on the clock anyway: we knew from going to the Marquee that the last number 3 was due to leave Piccadilly Circus at ten minutes past eleven, but that the last bus was also the only bus that you could guarantee running *ahead* of schedule. (The driver and conductor wanted to get home, you see, and what did it bother *them* if someone was daft enough to trust the timetable on the bus stop? Should have just got there earlier, shouldn't they?) So we sat there quietly for the first forty-five minutes of Peel's show, and then we scarpered off home before we had to walk.

A week or two later, Ray invited us back, and Peel again let us sit in behind him. It was like he didn't know how to say no. All the same, I could tell that he found our presence off-putting. I knew he didn't want us making a habit of it, but I suspected it wasn't just *us*: I wondered if he didn't just prefer broadcasting alone. Peel lived an odd existence. Although he was hired to DJ big festivals like Reading and for weekend university concerts, the timing of his nightly radio show meant that he couldn't attend gigs during the week; he was on air while the vast majority of bands were on stage. He didn't hang out at London nightclubs either; no drunken Speakeasy incidents for him. He just drove in from East Anglia every night with his records, recorded his show, took a whole bunch of new records (and cassette demo tapes) home with him, and repeated the process the following night. He didn't even witness the sessions he commissioned, which took place at the BBC's studios in Maida Vale, a hefty car journey across London, during the daytime. So I wondered if he wasn't just self-conscious about our presence, as if we might think there was something wrong with a man on the verge of forty proclaiming a song called 'Teenage Kicks' the greatest single ever made – whereas, left alone with just his records, a couple of turntables and a microphone, he could perhaps persuade himself that nobody else was listening, that no one would question his motives.

But people *were* listening – and we didn't question his motives at all. We trusted him implicitly, even more so after the night that he played 'Teenage Kicks', said something about how wonderful it was, put the needle back to the start of the record – and played it again! This was how *we* listened to music – us, the kids, the teenagers, frequently leaving the arm up on the record player so our favourite new 45 would repeat for eternity. But nobody had ever heard a radio DJ do this before, and to do it on Radio 1, where the daytime hours were given over to obnoxious, self-obsessed, so-called Romeos who were slaves to the official Radio 1 playlist, seemed like an act of insurrection.

'Teenage Kicks' was soon picked up by Sire Records, the American label behind both the Ramones *and* Talking Heads, which now, as if the steam had run out of the New York new wave scene, seemed to be focusing more on British bands. Before taking on the Undertones, Sire signed the Rezillos, whose album *Can't Stand the Rezillos* came in the loudest record sleeve I had ever seen, a gorgeous riot of bubblegum cards that screamed, 'Buy me, I'm fun' – and so I bought it, and it was. The Rezillos had two lead singers – one male, who wore lime-green jumpsuits, the other Fay Fife, a short-haired girl who wore miniskirts and dangly earrings, suggesting her own fascination with the modette style of the sixties, but in modern fluorescent colours. Fay Fife sang in a broad Scottish accent and she danced like a lunatic. She wasn't Debbie Harry, but she was sexy all right.

That autumn, Sire did what every record company would do under the circumstances: it put the Rezillos and the Undertones on tour together. And in the middle of November, by which point both groups had been on *Top of the Pops* – although 'Teenage Kicks' cruelly missed out on the all-important Top Thirty by just one position – that tour came to the Marquee for two nights.

I went on the second night, a Monday, in the company of some sixteen-year-olds who had braved Tenison's' rapidly declining reputation to stay on into the sixth form. They were the same ones who had co-signed Ray's letter of support to *Jamming* earlier in the year. So when one of them found me at school, told me that they had cornered the Rezillos at the Marquee the previous night and had scored an interview, I responded enthusiastically: of course I'd include it in the next *Jamming*.

That Monday evening, those sixth-formers walked me backstage and introduced me to the Undertones. There was nothing to it: we just rounded the Marquee bar, went through the door behind it, and then through another door off to the right, one that led directly behind the stage and into the dressing room. It was a path I'd followed before, introducing myself to the New Hearts after seeing them the second time at the Marquee. (But I'd had to wait fifteen minutes outside the inner door as they screamed and shouted at each other. I later found out that they broke up that night; the new line-up at Reading had only been put together to honour the booking, meaning that the guitarist had got a gash in his head from a beer can for nothing.) It was a path Christopher Modica had taken to get his pictures of Adam Ant. Still, those bands had not been on *Top of the Pops*. They were not the Undertones.

The dressing room was a hive of activity, the Undertones

getting ready to take the stage. The singer, who went by the exotic name of Feargal Sharkey and sang not only in a strong Northern Irish accent, but also with a constant trill to his voice, was nowhere to be seen. But the other members of the band – the guitarist brothers John and Damian O'Neill, the drummer Billy Doherty and the bassist Mickey Bradley – were all there. They welcomed us, invited us to have a seat, asked how we were doing. It was as if we were one of them.

And we were. Or rather, they were *one of us*. I'd never imagined that a band could behave so naturally, or look so bloody young: Mickey and Billy were indistinguishable from our sixth-formers – except for looking less fashionable. Some people reckoned that the Undertones' clothing – lots of V-neck jumpers and turned-up jeans and laced-up boots – was a gimmick, a little like Jilted John, whose hit single earlier that summer had been, in some ways, a celebration of the fashion reject. But it wasn't like that, I could tell now that I met them. The Undertones dressed that way because they dressed that way. Maybe there weren't any decent clothing shops in Derry. Maybe there wasn't any money for clothes. Maybe fashion just didn't mean anything in Northern Ireland, what with the IRA bombs and the UDA revenge attacks and the RUC for a police force and the British Army on the streets, and the kneecappings and everything else that went with 'the Troubles'. What the Undertones had in place of sharp clothing, though, was charm. When they appeared on *Top of the Pops*, their joy shone through; they had clearly loved every second of it in a way that the English bands, brought up on punk rock cynicism for the system, could never risk showing. That same enthusiasm at being able to make something of their lives was equally evident backstage at the Marquee.

So we chatted a bit. I told them how much I loved 'Teenage Kicks' and I may have asked about getting an interview some time. And when one of the O'Neill brothers picked up his guitar to check its tuning before taking to the stage, I decided to push my luck. I asked if he'd show me how to play the song.

'Sure,' he replied, and he invited me to sit down next to

him, there on a bench in that graffiti-scrawled closet of a dressing room.

It was all barre chords, starting with a D major up the top of the neck, working down a semi-tone at a time to C major, then back up again, after which it was straight down to G major, up a semi-tone and again to A major, and finally back up to D. It was the basic I-II-IV-V, and playing it all as barre chords meant that you didn't have to even change the position of your left hand's fingers, you only had to move them up and down the frets in time to the bass and drums. Not that we talked about it in terms of semi-tones and stuff. Either John or Damian just played it and I watched and said, 'Great, I can play that.'

And so he said, 'Why don't you?' And he handed me the guitar.

I would have felt nervous next to an expert – no way would I have dared ask Paul Weller to show me anything on a guitar – but the Undertones were so unassuming, so affable and down to earth (the teenage equivalent of John Peel, essentially) that it felt like one of my mates was showing me the chords instead. I played the riff a couple of times and O'Neill helped correct me a couple of times and that was it. I had it. Then he took the guitar back and a few minutes later, he was on stage and I was in the front row watching him play 'Teenage Kicks' to a sold-out crowd. And I felt no divide between us whatsoever.

Number 26:
SKANK BLOC BOLOGNA

Rough Trade was the name of a record store located at the top of Kensington Park Road, sandwiched in between the more famous Ladbroke Grove and Portobello Road. By the autumn of 1978, Rough Trade was known as the headquarters for all things musically independent, and so, on an October Monday afternoon, my sports bag laden with copies of *Jamming* that had been freshly collated, stapled and spray-painted as soon as they'd been delivered from Hastings over the weekend, I made it my first port of call. It was symbolic to me that Rough Trade should have the new issue ahead of anyone else. They took ten copies and paid me up front, 20p on the 25p cover price. This, I was about to learn, was as good a deal as it got.

Rough Trade was small, barely half the size of Counterpoint in Crystal Palace. But it was packed wall to wall with records, almost all of them on independent labels. The BBC's recent expansion of its chart from a Top Fifty to a Top Seventy-five may have been intended to reflect on the flood of new music being released in the wake of punk (and, to be fair, in the wake of disco-mania too) but walking into Rough Trade was like stepping into a parallel universe: most of the records here had been pressed with little concern for the charts, and if they had been, with no idea how one got on them. They were the product of a new, alternative music industry that had already fashioned its own basic formula: up and down the country, the staff at stores like Rough Trade were receiving demo tapes across the counter from aspiring local bands, enthusing about some of what they heard, and pressing those more interesting recordings up as 7-inch singles and EPs on their own labels, distributing them in turn to the other stores doing exactly the same thing: Good Vibrations in Belfast, Beggars Banquet in Ealing, Small Wonder in Walthamstow and dozens more besides.

The Rough Trade label refused to confine itself either to geography or genre. From offices behind and above the store, it put out records by Cabaret Voltaire from Sheffield, Stiff Little Fingers from Belfast, Subway Sect from London, Kleenex from Switzerland and Metal Urbain from France. None of these groups sounded remotely like the others: they ranged from almost unlistenable synthesiser dirges to immediately accessible punk anthems. What united them, other than the Rough Trade logo (laid out in Letraset, so it seemed, by a drunk, in a travelling car, at high speed), was a sense of artistic freedom, the notion that in this new, post-punk environment, anything went.

As I frequented more of these stores, distributing copies of *Jamming* across all four corners of London in the space of four consecutive after-school journeys, it became increasingly obvious that for all punk rock's attitude, it was the hippies who were running the show. At Rough Trade they did so as a 'co-operative', which meant that everyone took turns to sweep the floors, clean out the toilets, make the tea, work the counter and, I could only presume, given how they'd come up with such an all-encompassing roster in such a short space of time, choose which records to release, too. Still, it was quickly apparent that the business – or rather, the ideals behind it – revolved around its founder Geoff Travis, who was older than most punks, and better spoken too; he had the air of the worldly wise ex-public schoolboy, as topped by an Afro. Rather than look down on me and my comparatively conservative tastes in music, he set about quietly trying to influence them, and I immediately appreciated him for it.

Over at Small Wonder, the long-haired Pete Stennett ran his record store and label more or less single-handed. Small

Wonder was located at the far, *far* end of the Victoria line, all the way out in Walthamstow, a hell of a journey to undertake for the sake of just ten magazine sales, but it was part of the circuit and I wanted to get *Jamming* in every one of those stores that would take it. Like Rough Trade, Small Wonder seemed little bothered by the concept of label identity: it put out records by punk folk reggae singer Patrick Fitzgerald – he who had been bottled off at the first Carnival Against the Nazis for daring to come on stage without a band, and sing about a 'Safety Pin Stuck In My Heart' in a whiny cockney voice – but also by Menace, whose ode to London's governing body, the 'G.L.C.' (chorus line: 'You're full of shit, shit, shit shit shit shit') sold to the same aggressive skinheads and punks who had bottled Fitzgerald in the first place.

Hippies ran the Compendium book store on Camden High Street too. A clearing house for right-minded leftist thinking, the walls were lined not just with music fanzines, but with political publications: feminist texts, socialist propaganda and books upon books about every subject in the world that they didn't teach at school. (Along with alternative views on every subject that they did.) Compendium made no apologies for its politics. When I brought *Jamming* in, a woman working the counter examined it closely before agreeing to take ten copies on the always troubling 'sale or return'. (Troubling because no money changed hands, and if the magazines failed to sell, no money would ever change hands, though it would still require a return journey to pick them back up.)

'If there's anything racist or sexist in here, we'll pull it off the shelves,' she warned me, and I promised her that there wasn't. I couldn't guarantee, however, that Adam Ant's love of bondage wouldn't fall into a slippery crack somewhere in between.

There were occasional exceptions to the hippies' domination of punk distribution – Shane MacGowan from the Nipple Erectors, the singer who had famously had his ear bitten half-off by some girl at the 100 Club Punk Festival in 1976, worked the Rock On stall in Soho and took a few copies from me – but they were few and far between. If anything, the punks themselves were turning into hippies, and none more visibly than Mark Perry, who, when we went to interview him at the Step Forward label offices in Notting Hill, looked nothing like the short-haired yob who had stared menacingly from the cover of *Sniffin' Glue* just a year earlier. Now he had straight hair falling down to his shoulders and was wearing a grey V-neck jumper like the least fashionable of Undertones. His group, Alternative TV, who we were interviewing based on their brilliant first LP *The Image Has Cracked*, had just completed a joint tour with the Here and Now, a hippie band who had spent the summer of 1977 not on the front lines of the King's Road or Lewisham but in the fields of Wiltshire at the annual Stonehenge free festival, the central date on the calendar for every unwashed hippie in the country. Perry was particularly excited that their recent shared jaunt had, itself, played out 'in a field' somewhere; in fact, he said that he would no longer play clubs because 'they're all run by bullshit promoters'. Besides, he didn't want to play live again at all until he found somewhere that would let him play a two-hour show. Two hours? The Jam had barely made it to one!

Alternative TV's new album, *Vibing Up the Senile Man*, Perry warned us that day, featured 'a lot of poetry, with atmospheric music', which was understating the case; it turned out to lack anything approximating a song. (Still, I was grateful that Step Forward took out a full-page ad for it in *Jamming*; I desperately needed help paying the bills.) It perhaps followed on, then, that Perry didn't seem much bothered about the future, especially as Alternative TV. 'It may go completely,' he said, suggesting he'd just perform under his own name and that of anyone else in the group on a given night (or day). 'After all, jazz musicians do.'

I copped a similar attitude from Step Forward's day-to-day boss, Nick Jones. (I had no idea that, back when he was a teenage mod, he had been the first person to review The Who, on the opening night of their residency at the Marquee in 1965, and for *Melody Maker* no less. He looked like just another hippie to me.) When he called me Tony, despite the fact that Paul Weller was doing the same thing and it was time I took the hint, I stressed that no, my name was, in fact, Anthony.

'Ah, but what does it matter?' he said. 'It's only a name.'

And it was only a simple comment, tossed off casually, but I sensed it as something quite profound, and it stuck with me. Society was collapsing all around us, and the punk generation – backed by its hippie financiers – was doing its part, dismantling the foundations of the music business brick by brick. Now everyone was standing back, examining the mess they had created, clearly fascinated by the possibilities of rebuilding. What about if we put this brick here – but that one over there? What about we put more bricks on one side than the other, so that everything's out of balance? What about we use mud, or sand, or paper instead? What about we leave out building materials altogether? What does a band name matter? What does an individual's name matter? What does *any* of it matter?

During one of my periodic visits to Rough Trade, mainly to see how *Jamming* was selling amidst the dozens of other fanzines (against which it stood out like a sore thumb for its neat and tidy approach, spray-painted logo notwithstanding), Geoff Travis told me about an upcoming concert at the nearby Acklam Hall. All the groups were involved some way or another with the store or the label, something I might have guessed by the fact that three of them (Cabaret Voltaire, pragVEC and Scritti Politti) appeared to have taken their names from foreign languages though they were all in fact English, and the fourth, the Red Crayola, the only ones whose name appeared to make the slightest bit of sense, were foreign, being Americans with something of a history dating back, surprise surprise, to the hippie era.

I went to the Acklam Hall with Ray and Christopher that Saturday night, just five days after seeing the Undertones and the Rezillos at the Marquee. The Acklam Hall sat underneath the Westway, where the riots took place every year, like clock-work, at the end of the Notting Hill Carnival. You could see why: it was dark down there, even in daylight, and easy to either hide or get lost in the shadows, for screams to go unheard above the constant noise of the traffic. Still, I found the Ladbroke Grove area perpetually exciting, what with its steady pulse of reggae and punk, and the street markets and the record stores and the vast Georgian houses and the clothes shops and so on. It felt like Brixton, London's other major Rasta quarter, might feel if it had more space to stretch out in.

Armed with a tape recorder and a sense of purpose, we made straight to the Acklam Hall dressing room, where we found pragVEC and Scritti Politti hanging out together and, just like the Undertones, perfectly happy to welcome our intrusion. Ray immediately asked Scritti Politti for an interview. They immediately said yes. And so we all sat down to conduct it.

As an exercise in dismantling the typical interview process and building it back up again, with most of the bricks missing – after all, none of us knew anything about each other – it was as entertaining as it was enlightening. We were informed, primarily by a shaggy-haired punk-hippie called 'Green', that just two months ago, the group had not existed. In the eight weeks since, they had brought an old friend from Leeds down to London, to live with them in their Camden Town squat and learn bass from scratch, then they had booked a studio, recorded three songs, taken the tape to Rough Trade, been encouraged to press up 2,500 copies on the assurance that Rough Trade would buy and distribute them all, and had the record taken up by John Peel, who had booked them in for a session as well. Just as importantly, they had used their fold-out paper record sleeve as a propaganda sheet of sorts, listing all the costs of making the EP, and printing the phone numbers and addresses of the various pressing plants and mastering facilities they had used, so that everyone could see how easy – and inexpensive – the whole process had been.

It was a pretty impressive start to any band's career, but

Scritti Politti were not interested in a career. They were only playing the Acklam Hall, said Green, because someone had put their name on the poster without asking them first. They were still working out the live line-up, he said, and it included a chap called Simon who was going to play 'tapes'. Their bass player Nial had only just got his own guitar and amp. They had barely rehearsed.

'I think it's important that when you get a group together you shouldn't wait until you've got an hour and a half's worth of material before you go on stage,' said Green, as explanation for this rather daring approach.

I replied, instinctively, 'Yeah, but you've got to have a certain amount of professionalism . . . before you go on.'

It wasn't intended as a question and Green didn't take it as one. 'Well, don't tell us that,' he said, 'because we haven't got it.'

Green was right. Following on from Cabaret Voltaire, whose music got lost in shrouds of cinematic fog, synthesisers, taped drum beats, and impossibly long fringes, Scritti Politti were anything but professional. They played just three songs, featuring Green's delicate but largely unintelligible vocals (as in, I couldn't understand what he was trying to say even when I could hear the words), scratchy guitars and dub bass lines, with the drummer Tom, appropriately given his dreadlocks, leaning towards a reggae rhythm, and the 'tape player' throwing in radio transmissions, and lots of reverb whenever it sounded like it was going nowhere. The experience – I could hardly call it a show – was like nothing I'd ever seen or heard before in my life. It wasn't necessarily very good, but then what did any of *that* matter?

Number 25:
WHERE IS JAH

Scritti Politti's squat was on a side-road bordered by Camden Street to its east, Camden High Street to its west and Camden High Road to its north. It was dirty and dishevelled, furniture was at a premium, the sink was forever full of dishes and tea cups, people came and went every five minutes, and there was a persistent aroma of hand-rolled cigarettes (and stronger substances, too). But at the same time, the place was alive! Books and magazines crowded every surface, instruments lay in every corner – though never for long, as someone was always picking one up to play it – and the kettle was constantly on the boil. Conversation flowed as freely as did the tea and coffee (and stronger substances, too), and music filled the air constantly.

The band had invited us to stop around any time we liked, and we took them at their word. We arrived, Ray and myself, to find an *NME* journalist, Ian Penman – a recent hiring who confused me in print with long words and even longer sentences – sitting in a corner of the living room, opening his post. It appeared to consist of nothing other than free records. We watched, transfixed, as he tore into yet another brown 12-inch cardboard mailer and withdrew an album cover featuring three peroxide heads staring down a camera lens. The band was called the Police.

Penman sighed in disgust. 'I'm not even listening to this one.'

Ray quickly pounced. 'I'll have it, then.'

And Penman was equally quick to respond. 'How much you

got?' Turned out that he sold all his unwanted review records at Honest Jon's, on Camden High Street. Everybody did it, he said. It was part of a freelancer's income.

Ray wasn't letting go. 'You're not even going to listen to it? What's wrong with the Police?'

'You want a list?' Penman asked. Ray said he did. So Penman set off on it. All this stuff about faded old has-been prog-rockers from the sixties trying to get hip with the new wave, riding the bandwagon, pandering to the lowest common denominator, selling out to capitalist institutions like Wrigley's Chewing Gum at the first possible moment. (The Police had dyed their hair blond to score a TV commercial as a 'punk' band.) And the greatest sin of all? Playing bad reggae.

Scritti Politti took their reggae seriously. They listened to the stuff recorded in Kingston, Jamaica, and released either on Virgin or Island or Greensleeves, or the 7-inch singles and 'dub plates' imported from the West Indies and sold at Rough Trade. I took my reggae seriously, too. I'd seen both Aswad and Misty in Roots at the second Carnival Against the Nazis, this one held closer to my house than any other concert I'd attended, in Brockwell Park at the Herne Hill end of the Railton Road. (The show also featured Rough Trade's own Stiff Little Fingers and the great Elvis Costello.) I was so enamoured of a single by a British group called Reggae Regular, 'Where is Jah', with its middle eight that would have made Townshend or Weller envious, that I wrote to them via the Greensleeves label asking for an interview. (There was no reply.) And there was a record out by a Jamaican Rasta called Dr Alimantado, the title of which I couldn't remember but which had a chorus line about 'life' and which seemed to me about as pure and perfect as reggae could get. (Without owning a copy, or bothering to find out that it was called 'Born for a Purpose', I reviewed it for the next *Jamming* in almost as many words.) All in all, I might have agreed with Penman's view of the Police if I thought that they merited the discussion. But they didn't. Nobody had bought their singles and no one was likely to buy their album, either.

The new issue of *Jamming*, the one with Paul Weller on the cover, had served as a breakthrough, but its meticulous layout had generated plenty of flak from the more established punk fanzines: Tony D, whose *Ripped & Torn* sold a whopping 2,000 copies, even wrote to us personally to accuse us of 'giving fanzines a bad name'. Ray leapt to our defence with a war of words fought out not just via the Royal Mail but in the letters pages of various other fanzines, even though it was obvious he largely agreed with the criticisms. For as we started designing a new issue, Ray put together his own pages of ripped and torn cut-and-paste: a review of *Give 'Em Enough Rope*, the *long* overdue (and bitterly disappointing, or at least bitterly American-sounding) second LP by the Clash, and a collage that attacked the people behind the Radio 1 playlist. At the same time, he figured we should advertise *Jamming* in the classified sections of *Sounds* and *NME*. He headed these ads with the words 'Free Sex' in bold letters to distinguish them from all the others that read 'For Sale'. We didn't sell enough copies to cover the cost of the ads.

At school the previous year, I'd managed to keep *Jamming* to more or less a bi-monthly schedule, which wasn't too hard when dealing with just a few typed pages and a print bill of about £10. But we had overprinted this first 'proper' issue, in part to keep the cost per copy down, and now, with 500 uncollated copies of *Jamming* on my bedroom floor and a printer in Hastings sending polite requests via Jeff Carrigan for the £100 I still owed him, I wasn't so sure we needed to rush ahead with a new issue. Yet there was one solid reason for pushing on regardless: we were gathering interviews faster than we could transcribe them. We already had Mark Perry's Alternative TV, Scritti Politti and the Rezillos (who had broken up almost immediately after playing the Marquee, disillusioned by their brief encounter with the money-churning side of the music business). And Tom Robinson's cassette had finally arrived in the post; the questions now appeared desperately dated, but his replies were appropriately frank and hopefully, despite his recent absence from the Top Thirty, people would still be interested.

And then Ray scored an interview with Pete Townshend.

Ray hated The Who. But he knew how much I loved them, and how much an interview would mean to me (and to Ray, in terms of his authority), so he'd travelled out to Townshend's book shop, Magic Bus, in Twickenham, and dropped off a copy of the current issue and a letter, and although he was told not to hold out any hopes, he got a phone call barely three days later from Pete's assistant, setting up an interview date. Why Townshend agreed to the request, we weren't sure. Perhaps he was spurred to call us by the sight of Paul Weller on the front cover. Or maybe he was rarely approached by fanzines and figured it was about time one of us gave him the time of day. It was always possible he really liked the magazine. But it didn't really matter. It was Pete Townshend and he had said yes.

I stared at the pictures on my wall. That photo of him in mid-air, Gibson above his head, at Woodstock. The poster from the Marquee residency of '65 (also given away with *Live At Leeds*) with his arm raised high above his Rickenbacker. And the full-colour poster I'd had on my wall since Charlton, of The Who in their mid-seventies glory, with Daltrey twirling his microphone and Townshend, alongside him, in mid-glide, his upper body located directly above his legs, but with his hips somewhere else entirely, like an optical illusion created by standing in front of a hall of mirrors. No matter how he held it, where he wore it, the guitar always looked good on Pete. And now I would be going to meet him, to talk with him one on one.

Well, not quite. Four of us set off for his office in Richmond that October half-term morning: Ray, myself, Christopher Modica and Jeff Carrigan. And because there were four of us, we were inevitably late getting together and getting going. And because we were late getting going, and it was a long journey via public transport, we arrived for our 11 a.m. interview at lunchtime.

Townshend's assistant, thoroughly unimpressed, told us to wait, though at least she didn't tell us to go home and come back when we were more professional. Eventually, we were shown through to a kitchenette, where we found Pete, in customary short beard and moustache, wearing a nondescript black jumper with a white shirt collar folded over the top, looking more like a schoolteacher than a rock star whose new LP was currently number two in the American charts. He made an opening remark about the surprising size of our 'posse', which didn't exactly put us at ease. Then he sat down in a wicker rocking chair that almost swallowed him up, at which point I – because I wasn't going to let anyone else steal this moment, regardless of who had actually secured the interview – started asking questions.

I didn't do a very good job. As with Paul Weller, I really wanted to start at the beginning and work my way to the end, but unlike that day at RAK, our time was clearly limited (arriving so late hardly helped our cause), besides which, it would take much longer to get through fifteen years of The Who's history than it would just three years of The Jam's. And then there was the fact that, unlike Weller, Townshend didn't get nervous at the sight of a tape recorder. Quite the opposite: I'd ask him a question and he would quickly answer it – and then he'd keep on talking, answering it several more times in several different ways, some of which appeared to contradict his earlier summations, before veering off-subject for a few minutes. It was fascinating – as in, I clung to every single word – but I could feel our precious time slipping away, especially when I asked an open-ended question about his spiritual guru, Meher Baba, and had to wait ten minutes before getting the opportunity to speak again. Not being *that* interested in mysticism, I steered the conversation back to the group that smashed up hotel rooms.

At this, he suddenly got nostalgic. 'We used to make an art

of it,' he recalled, leaning forward in the chair, which served to make it rock gently. 'Keith, in particular, was an artist. He used to go through so that there was no fragment in the room left longer than an inch.' There was reverence for the dead drummer in his voice. 'He once burrowed through a wall with his bare hands,' he said, recounting the incident I'd read about in the *Bellboy* programme, before concluding, 'I'll probably never smash another hotel room in my life now, because half of it was the fact that Keith and I used to do it for one another.'

This opened a massive window of opportunity: to ask Pete what he *really* thought had happened to Keith, how badly he missed him, and why he had felt it necessary to announce, the day after Keith's death, that 'we feel more determined than ever to carry on' . . . But I failed to seize it. I didn't want to upset my rock god. I wanted to enjoy the occasion in case it turned out to be the high point of my life. I worried that asking about Keith might open up a deep wound; given that *I* was still dealing with his death myself and I'd only met Keith the once, how could I imagine what it felt like for Pete? He seemed remarkably cheerful for a man who had just lost a lifelong musical partner, but that may have meant he was merely hiding his real feelings, that he was ready to crumble and cry at a moment's provocation. Better then, to talk around the issue, to celebrate Moon's destructive tendencies than to discuss what caused them.

We moved on to The Jam, instead. I told Townshend that Weller had played down The Who's influence when I interviewed him, saying that they were 'just one' of his favourite bands. Townshend digested that and agreed. 'I think that Paul Weller's got more of a thing about me than about the Who,' he said. 'I really like what they do, but I don't think they're one of the great bands. I think that maybe they're still a bit too young.'

Weller had turned twenty that May. Would he prove capable of composing something like *Tommy* at the age of twenty-three, as had Townshend? Who knew? I couldn't envision being twenty, let alone Townshend's age, an ancient thirty-three. I was barely able to plan beyond the following week. One thing I *was* sure of with regards to The Jam, though, was that Paul Weller had put me on the guest list for the Great British Music Festival. I hadn't even had to ask. It was a truly noble gesture, a mark of, if not necessarily friendship, then something similar that I didn't dare examine for fear that it might prove an illusion. The only problem? The 'Great British Music Festival' was taking place the same evening as what Archbishop Tenison's liked to call its 'Speech Night', otherwise known as its annual awards ceremony. Despite both forming a band and starting a fanzine in my third year, despite my chemistry teacher's recent comment in my report book that 'He would need to concentrate far more on his work and less on his own (un)importance,' I'd still managed to excel in enough subjects to be slated for a number of prizes. An invitation came in the post, to my mother. She was thrilled that, in a single-parent family with a minimum of oversight, I seemed to be doing so well. She rarely made it to parent evenings, but she announced her intent to attend this Speech Night. I had to explain that if she did, she'd be going without me.

There followed, inevitably, a verbal tug of war. Hadn't I seen The Jam often enough? (No, there was no such thing as seeing The Jam 'enough'.) Wasn't school more important than a rock band? (No, not this rock band. Probably not any rock band.) Didn't I owe it to my teachers to accept the prizes they'd graciously awarded me? (No, I didn't owe anyone anything, least of all the establishment.) How was I going to get home from Wembley, all the way on the other side of London? (We'd figure that one out when I got there.) And, when would this ever end? (Probably, never.)

Naturally, I won. I was used to winning any kind of emotional or intellectual argument. I was relentless. I always had a retort and I would never back down. Like Pete Townshend, I was a Taurus.

* * *

The 1978 Great British Music Festival was almost a carbon copy of the 1978 Reading Festival. The Jam headlined. A respectable but not yet populist new wave act was second on the bill. (Ultravox at Reading, Generation X at Wembley.) The Pirates – the 1950s rock 'n' rollers whose 'Shakin' All Over', immortalised by The Who on *Live At Leeds*, had been released when Paul Weller was still in nappies – were third on the bill. And a skinhead band was booked to ensure plenty of audience aggro.

In their defence, Slade had been skinheads a decade back, when the image was brand new. They'd released a couple of albums dressed up as boot boys on the cover – and nobody had paid the slightest bit of attention. It wasn't until they grew their hair out, donned sequins and glitter and top hats as part of the glam rock movement – and got into the habit of misspelling their song titles – that they enjoyed that remarkable run of number one singles. The hits had dried up now, and so their appearance at Wembley as a 'Great' band as well as a 'British' one provided them with a welcome opportunity to prove they could still cut it. And if the new generation of skinheads wanted to take them up as a cult cause, well, Slade could certainly do with the fans.

The skinheads were quite well behaved during Slade's set; there were none of the ugly scenes witnessed at Reading. They waited until Generation X for all that. The Bromley band were, nominally, punks, but their near-hit single 'Ready Steady Go', with its tribute to the mid-sixties mod-friendly TV show, had expanded their following to include Jam fans who, in their own recognisable uniforms of black jackets and ties, made their enthusiasm known in the front rows. And as soon as they did so, the skins attacked. Bodies went headfirst over seats, fists and boots flying with them; it was like the occasional ruck you'd see in the seated section at football matches, except that here there didn't seem to be any police on hand to deal with it.

I watched it all from my seat above the floor. I'd got to

Wembley nice and early, and found that there was indeed a ticket waiting for me at the box office. I'd also found a back-stage pass in my name – another first – and had nervously used it early in the afternoon, at which I'd been shown to The Jam's dressing room. (There was nobody there.) After Generation X played, I went backstage again, and this time I found Paul Weller, in The Jam's dressing room, looking thoroughly pissed off. Word was that someone had been stabbed, and Paul was trying to get information, figuring whether he should go to the hospital after the show or what else he could do. Why he had expected things to be different after the events at Reading, I couldn't say, and I certainly wasn't about to ask him, not after having already posed a similar question in writing and received such a defiant response. He was clearly preoccupied, and almost as an apology, he asked if I was going to be able to hang around after 'the gig', so that we could have a chat then. I said that no, I had to get home. I didn't want to remind him that I had school the next day.

But I went backstage at the end anyway. I knew, thanks to seeing the set list in advance, what was going to be the last song of the night and before The Jam were halfway through it, I'd shown my pass at the backstage curtain and made my way to the foot of the steps that led up to the back of the stage. Out front, there were at least 5,000 people, most of them cheering and jumping in front of their seats. But back here, there was almost no one, and yet the area was cavernous, the size of several Marquee clubs, and that before you even headed off down the corridors to find a dressing room. Out front, though Wembley was hardly celebrated for its acoustics, you could at least hear the music, identify the songs; from behind the stage, it was all a mess of echo, reverb and all-round white noise. When I'd interviewed him, Weller explained that on stage at Reading, 'we couldn't hear each other,' that it was 'like trying to guess what the other two are playing'. Now I had a sense of what he had been going through. But then The Jam hammered out their final power chords of the night, propped their guitars against the amps – with volume up full, judging by the wail of feedback – and, to a thunderous roar of approval, left the stage. Moments later, they came charging down the scaffolding steps, drenched in sweat, draped in towels, John Weller and Kenny Wheeler flanking them. Paul's girlfriend, Gill, appeared from out of nowhere and gave Paul a big kiss. He put his arm around her and the two of them walked towards the dressing room, passing me by without even noticing my presence. But that was OK, I had no desire to interrupt the moment. To be someone must be a wonderful thing.

Number 24:
DON'T TAKE NO FOR AN ANSWER

We were all discovering girls. Or rather, *they* were all discovering girls. I didn't stand a chance. My voice still showed no signs of breaking, and early in the fourth year, I was horrified to find, on taking a shower at school after PE, that everyone else had grown hair on their balls over the summer holidays and I hadn't. Unfortunately, I wasn't the only one to notice this and a new phrase made its way around the school, chanted in the hallways and occasionally scrawled in physical graffiti on notebooks and desks: Fletcher is bald. I denied it, of course, having no other idea how to handle such an accusation, not knowing that it would only make the rumour spread faster and louder. The bigger lads made a frequent habit of checking on my status by trying to pull my pants down in the playground. Or the classroom. And especially the gym.

Then I came out with that first properly printed issue of *Jamming*, and it only made things worse. I was daring to do something with my life, and I was being highly public about it, and a lot of kids didn't care for it. Lawrence Weaver, now that he'd quit the magazine over the inclusion of Adam and the Ants, no longer had to pretend to like me. He was a tough kid, and because he hit me occasionally, I had a habit of flinching in his presence, and it became highly obvious to everyone that I was easily scared and so they were all constantly making me flinch – and occasionally punching me for real, as when I did something to annoy John Gregory, captain of the cricket and football teams, in the gym changing room, and he walloped me in the nose, drawing blood. Plus, Adrian and I had fallen out, towards the end of the previous school year, in a minor playground incident that was escalated by others into an organised Friday-afternoon fight in the churchyard after school. I bunked off the last lesson rather than show up – not so much because I didn't want to fight my friend (though I didn't), or because I was scared he'd win (though I was), but because I knew that all the hard cases were going to jump in on his behalf and beat me up. I got caned for missing that lesson, but it served its purpose; the proposed fight was forgotten over the weekend, the cane didn't hurt half as much as a beating would have done, and I learned from the experience how to play truant without getting caught. Adrian and I, though, stopped talking to each other. Three years as best friends ended, just like that.

In my own class, which was meant to be the top stream, I had to contend with the resident Scotsman, Munro, who had tormented me for three years already, and who only seemed to be getting bigger and more physical, and though I surprised even myself one morning in school assembly, before the teachers showed up, by responding to his bullying by throwing a chair at him, it only made matters worse in the long run – and for a while I brought a knife to school just in case. (My brother found it and took it away from me.) Even Jeff Carrigan, growing rapidly in size and stature and finding himself increasingly accepted by the mainstream, temporarily joined in the relentless teasing – though when he recognised that it was turning to outright bullying, he backed off and resumed his outsider status, and our friendship grew closer.

As for Chris Boyle, he had been latched on to by Raymond and Glover, our school year's confirmed troublemakers, and now they did their best to latch on to me, as well. They started showing up at my house on a Saturday night, when my mum was typically out, making up for lost time raising me and my brother on her own. I tried telling Chris that I didn't want to be their friend, but he seemed either unwilling or unable to shake them off. It was like if I wanted Chris in my life – and

I did – I had to have Raymond and Glover as part of the package. When they came round, I always wanted to say to them, if you're so tough and handsome, why aren't you out with the girls tonight? But I already knew the answer. And anyway, I wouldn't dare.

Raymond and Glover never beat me up on my home turf. They teased me, instead. They'd go through my records, roughly, as if hoping to damage them, playing some, insulting others; they'd pass judgement on the musicians I put in *Jamming*, and step on the uncollated pages on the bedroom floor; they'd light up, knowing perfectly well I wouldn't be able to get rid of the cigarette smell and I'd have to explain it once my mother got home; they'd ask if I'd grown pubes yet and when I insisted I had, ask why I was so afraid of showing them at school; and sometimes they'd steal something petty just to prove they could. They knew I wasn't strong enough, mentally or physically, to fight back, so they preyed on me.

I understood all that with perfect clarity. And yet I wasn't smart enough to know how to repel them and I didn't seem to have any other Saturday-night options to get out of the house. Adrian and I had separated. Christopher Modica had just got a girlfriend, and besides, he was increasingly put out that I wouldn't let him write anything for the magazine. Jeff was often in Hastings, and otherwise didn't have permission to take to the streets on weekend evenings. Jeffries had girlfriends, or was out at the pub, or was busy getting arrested at football matches; we didn't spend so much time together when we weren't following Palace. And I wasn't sure that I liked Ray enough to hang out with him when we weren't working on the fanzine.

So one Saturday night when I was home alone and I heard the doorbell ring, I tried turning off the lights. Raymond and Glover just laughed through the letterbox. 'We know you're home. We saw the lights go off. You're not fooling us. Come on, open up, we won't harm you. Don't you wanna be our friend? We'll get you on Monday morning if you don't . . .'

I held out as long as I could that night. But after fifteen relentless minutes, it was obvious they weren't going to go away. In a war of nerves, mine wore down first. I went to the door, rubbed my eyes, and told them I'd been asleep.

'What, at eight o'clock on a Saturday night? What are you, some kind of girl?' They were halfway up the stairs before I'd closed the door. Chris just smiled and shrugged as he stepped through, like it was all part of the Saturday-night routine and I was game for it.

Raymond told me to get them some Coke. (My mum always made sure to leave me a full bottle when she went out Saturday evenings. And she was always surprised that I got through so much of it and could still sleep through the night.) I didn't have to get them a drink – but only to the extent that I didn't have to let them in to begin with. So I went downstairs to the kitchen.

When I came back my bedroom curtains were on fire.

'It was an accident,' said Raymond, laughing as he did.

'We were only trying to light your poxy candle,' said Glover, matches in his hand. The candle, a decorative gift that was rarely used, was, indeed, burning.

Chris quickly put out the flames – by throwing the cold drinks over them. They flared up a little, like the sugar or the acid was acting as an incendiary, and then they fizzled. I ran to the bathroom and grabbed a towel and wrapped it around the foot of the curtains and held it tight until it felt like the fire had stopped completely. The room was full of smoke. The curtains were smouldering. And Raymond and Glover were giggling.

'It was an accident,' Raymond kept saying.

'It was the candle,' repeated Glover.

'You fucking idiots,' said Chris. But he was laughing too.

I didn't say anything. I was trying to think what I'd tell my mother.

'You won't tell your mum, will you?' asked Raymond, a little nervously.

'You won't tell your mum, will you,' said Glover. Coming from him, it didn't sound so much like a question.

'I'll have to tell her something,' I said. And sure enough, the moment she opened the front door later that night, the smell of the smoke hit her, and she found it thicker still in my bedroom despite the fact that the windows had been wide open for an hour or two already, and she saw the blackened curtain tips, and, of course, she wanted to know what the hell had happened. And like a good boy, I didn't tell her.

'I was playing with matches,' I said. 'I was just fooling around, I lit the candle and it set fire to the curtains. I wasn't paying attention at the time. I'm sorry.'

'Why on earth would you want to light the candle?' she asked me. 'We've got electricity.'

I couldn't answer that one.

'Who else was here this evening?'

'No one,' I insisted. I had no real reason *not* to tell her I was getting bullied at school, except that I knew that it wouldn't protect me in the long run. Mum seemed really good about handling the tough kids at Stockwell Manor – and hers were genuinely tough kids. But at Stockwell, she had the authority to do so. At Tenison's, she had none. Even if I'd told her what had happened, she couldn't go to my school about it; this incident was off hours, off premises, nothing to do with them. And if she tried calling anyone's parents, the only guaranteed result was that I would be in for yet more hell in the playground, the hallway, the midweek playing fields and at the bus stop. Until I figured out my own means of revenge, I would have to deny everything. All she could do was quiz me some more, make me promise I was telling the truth, and then add to my layers of guilt and self-pity by staying home the next Saturday night.

I told Raymond and Glover as much, that I hadn't grassed, but that my mum was staying home on Saturday nights from now on. And it worked. They never came round again. They claimed to be going out with girls instead.

* * *

On the terraces I was doing just fine. I knew it didn't make sense, but that's just the way it was. The Dulwich crew, having encouraged my musical tastes all along, had no reason to be jealous of me for *Jamming*. If anything, they were proud of their small contribution to my pastime. So when Gary, an apprentice at a printing firm in Streatham, asked how I was getting the fanzine printed, I told him: with difficulty. I still owed the printer in Hastings a lot of money, and I didn't know anyone else willing to print at cost, and I was back at square one. Gary said he'd have a word with his boss, see if he could cut me a deal, and he called me up at home soon after to say that he could. We would need to print 1,500 copies to get it down to a decent price per copy, but we figured that with Pete Townshend on the cover – and all the other stars, too – there was a possibility of selling that many. We were even going to get it printed on A3 paper – meaning that the pages would fold out like a 'proper' magazine. I had to borrow almost £200 to pay the printer up front, but Ray, who had a day job now, was so keen to see his work in print that he came up with over half the money.

As with the previous issue, there was the small matter of getting it finished on time. And I didn't have Jeff's help; it wasn't just that he spent most weekends in Hastings, it was that I seemed to be on my own right now with regard to schoolfriends. So I stayed in my room for the last weekend, for forty-eight hours solid, typing furiously, scissors and Cow Gum and Letraset and ruler at my side, The Who and The Jam and the Rezillos and the Undertones and maybe even Scritti Politti on the record player. Come Sunday evening, it felt like there was still half a magazine to go. I stayed up as late as I could, hoping somehow to meet the Monday-morning deadline, but the typing kept my mum awake, and eventually I was told to pack it in. At about midnight, I did so, resigned to the fact I would be late to the printers. Again.

Monday afternoon, I rushed home from school, went straight to my room, and carried on with the job at hand like I never did with my homework. And yet the final page just wouldn't come into sight; there were too many other pages to finish first. So when my mum insisted I turn my lights out at 11 p.m., I had to find a way to keep going. I couldn't afford to be another day late, not if I was going to get the magazine out by Christmas. I turned out my light, waited thirty minutes, turned it back on, resumed the layout, and then, when I couldn't wait any more, started typing again, in the middle of the night. It worked: my mother and my brother slept through the noise.

I'd pulled my first all-nighter. Finally. I'd been looking forward to it all my life, but I couldn't admit to it now I'd achieved it. Instead, here I was, at 7.30 in the morning, in my pyjamas, pretending that I had been asleep all along, though the circles under my eyes told a very different story. And I *still* had to catch two buses to get to the printers.

I managed it, despite dozing off on the journey several times. I dropped off the layout. I explained everything to the printer to the best of my ability. I caught a bus from Streatham to Kennington . . . and fell asleep immediately. When I woke back up, I realised there was no point going to school only to fall asleep in class. I'd just have to play truant. Again. I got off the bus at Brixton tube station, crossed over the street and waited (and waited) for a number 3 to take me in the opposite direction, home to bed. I was careful to set the alarm, to be back in my school uniform before Mum got home. The next day at Tenison's I made up some excuse or other. It was getting to the point that the teachers barely thought to ask for one.

Friday afternoon, we got the magazines back as scheduled. Fortunately, the printer had managed to make up for the lost day. Unfortunately, to do so he had skimped on the quality. Big time. We hadn't exactly made his job easy: several pages, including the cover, featured pictures taken from music papers alongside our own photographs that still needed to go through the 'scanning' process to become half-tones. A few other pages, including the Scritti Politti interview as laid out by Ray, featured the photos we needed scanning *underneath* the text.

But rather than call me about it, the printer had scanned some pictures, and then left others to look as they had done back when the magazine was printed at school: either black, or white, with no grey areas in between. Worst of all was the front cover. Without Jeff's assistance, it was atrocious to begin with, a jumble of Letrasetted band names and cut-out headshots. But the printer had made it worse still by scanning the *entire* page, ensuring an ugly grey coating across it. He hadn't even bothered to clean up the cut-and-paste marks and glue lines before making the plate. We'd wanted the new issue to look more like a fanzine, but not like *this*.

Ray and I talked about it. We decided to photocopy the front cover and one other page in the hope that they might prove legible. On blue and yellow paper, for the hell of it. And so, instead of spending the Saturday before Christmas loading up London's independent record stores with our hot-off-the-presses fanzine, we spent the weekend dealing with photocopiers, then stapling the additional pages into the existing magazine. The first A3 fold-out edition now had ten staples per copy.

Come Monday, deflated and defeated, I started on my rounds of the major stores anyway. Naturally, I took the day off school to do so. I had to come back home from the West End in the middle of it, all the way back to West Dulwich to stock up on more copies, but that was OK; a 'wholesaler' called Phoenix, just down the road from Rough Trade, had agreed to take fifty copies to send around the country, the biggest single sale I'd ever had. And Small Wonder bought twenty-five up front, making the journey back from Walthamstow that much lighter. Perhaps we were still in business after all.

But I couldn't get over the feeling that the printers had done us wrong. And so, the next day, after school, I went to my mum's bedroom, where there was a phone with some privacy, and I called the head of the printing firm, and when he came on the line, I took a deep breath – and told him how disappointed we were, that we'd worked so hard for this to look great, and that we knew what we were doing (most of the time) and that we had, to be honest, expected a better printing job. I'd never had a conversation like this before. I was the kid that always ran from a fight.

The printer listened to me, and he argued his own case, about how the job had come in late, and he had done his best because he was doing it in a rush, and he was doing it cheap to help out one of his apprentices, and I had to say, in response, I know all that *but*: doing it cheap doesn't mean doing it badly. We need money back.

I'd said it. And once I did, I felt my heart racing from the shock of doing so. The printer went silent. Then he asked how much. I took another deep breath, said we needed to be refunded at least the cost of the photocopies . . . and another £50. After another long pause, he agreed. It didn't make it OK. But I had learned something crucial about business. The customer has the right to be right.

Number 23:
STRANGE TOWN

Mark was still a teenager when he answered my latest *Melody Maker* ad for a fourth member. (Jeff and Chris had finally accepted that we were going nowhere without one.) But he may as well have hailed from another planet. Nineteen years old, he listened to dub, funk, avant-garde, electronic music and everything else experimental, lived with his girlfriend in a squat on the other side of London, had been in bands since he was fifteen and, to cap it all, had written for an original punk fanzine, *Skum* – for which, in December 1976, he had interviewed Sid Vicious.

Back then, Sid had been in the Flowers of Romance, alongside Viv Albertine, Palmolive and Keith Levene. The first two had gone on to form punk's first original all-girl group, the Slits, and at the point that Mark joined our band, Palmolive had just left the Slits for a band called the Raincoats, while Keith Levene was suddenly famous as the guitarist in Johnny Rotten's new band, Public Image Ltd. As for Sid, he was dead, having overdosed on heroin in New York City, the day after he was released from Rikers Island on bail. (He was not in jail for allegedly murdering his girlfriend, Nancy Spungen, the previous October, as most people thought. He was in jail for beating up Patti Smith's brother with a broken bottle while on bail for killing Nancy.) The February morning that Sid's death hit the British tabloids, Jeff Carrigan wore a black armband to school. Our form teacher promptly made him remove it. We all laughed at his subservience to authority. Jeff vowed vengeance on Judgement Day.

Within a week of Sid's death, Virgin Records released a new Sex Pistols single: Sid Vicious singing Eddie Cochran's 'C'mon Everybody'. This was the same Virgin Records that had just had a Top Ten hit with the single 'Public Image', on which Johnny Rotten – preferring now to go by his birth name John Lydon – screamed at full tilt about his hatred and mistrust of the music industry. You could hardly blame him.

Then again, I had gone to see Public Image Ltd perform their second-ever show, at the Rainbow Theatre in Finsbury Park on Boxing Day (their first-ever show was on Christmas Day itself) and came away feeling cheated. I'd been excited about attending the Rainbow; it had a better reputation than the Hammersmith Odeon – even more so when the seats were taken out. But I wasn't one for dancing, and neither, that night, after opening sets by future reggae band the Basement 5, political reggae poet Linton Kwesi Johnson, and dub reggae DJ Don Letts (our own old Tenisonian), was anyone else. Public Image were aloof, distant, cold. Jah Wobble's thunderously deep bass lines and Keith Levene's blunt guitar riffs bounced off the vast walls and reverberated around the hall like they were ghosts, and Lydon whined about a God who spelled backwards was dog (like we couldn't figure that one out for ourselves), all while seemingly revelling in upsetting those who had expected him to show up Rotten. Those who didn't vacate the premises either hit the bar, sat down on the floor or began booing.

It was the last show I went to with Ray. He had nosed his way into a series of backstage relationships with bands I didn't much like: we'd spent a whole evening in the farthest reaches of North London, hanging out with a group called the Raped, who did little more than preen, and bitch about how Rough Trade refused to stock their records because of their name; I got home so late at night that I found my mum on the phone to the police, reporting me missing. Ray was now pathologically seeking John Lydon's approval and friendship; after the Rainbow, I wanted nothing of the sort. Ray wanted *Jamming* to change

its name to *Sniffin' Glue*; I figured he must be joking. He had
visions of an even bigger print run despite the fact that we'd
barely sold a third of the 'Pete Townshend' issue; I was terrified
of rising debt. Ray wanted to be the official co-editor of what
he considered a 'real fanzine', with more cut-and-paste artwork
and none of my conformist rock groups; I told him he could
start his own fanzine. He demanded his money back from the
last print bill; I didn't have it yet and told him he'd have to
wait. He wrote me a letter saying, 'My lawyer has told me I
have a good case.' I ignored him.

Soon after we split, my home phone started ringing at all
hours of the day and night. The calls were from men looking
for a woman called 'Ann', who had advertised her services, as
such women did, via business cards left in telephone boxes
across London. Ray's first letter to *Jamming* had called me
Ann-phony; it wasn't hard to connect the dots. Still, there was
only one woman in our house, and once the calls started my
mum assumed it was her job to answer them. Upon being
subjected to the sexual inquisitions of London's seemingly
endless supply of dirty old men, she would tell them to go fuck
themselves, and hang up, at which, evidently excited by the
prospect, they called straight back. She would pick up the
phone again and put it down again, this time without saying
anything at all, which wasn't really a good idea, because it
would immediately ring yet *again*, and then keep ringing while
we pretended to get on with our evening. Or morning. Or
afternoon. Or sleep. As for Ray, on the couple of occasions I
spoke to him, I didn't want to give him the satisfaction of
knowing that his ploy had been effective. So he resorted to
stronger tactics. I came out of the house one weekend morning,
walked up past our terrace – and saw graffiti all over the end
wall. Twenty feet of it at least. It called me names. Said I was
a mummy's boy and worse. I was embarrassed. Ashamed. I
wanted to cry, but I didn't. I knocked on the door of the end
house, people who didn't have kids and who I didn't really
know, and told them about it, said that I thought it was directed

at me and that I was sorry. They told me not to worry about it. When I came home that night, they'd painted over it. They never even asked for a contribution, never even told my mum. They were good neighbours.

I could have gone to Jeffries. He'd have sorted Ray out in a heartbeat. But I had the respect of all my tougher friends on the terraces, who always figured I was one of them; to admit that I was being harassed like this, just like to admit that I was being bullied at school, would mean to lose that respect. All I could do was keep singing 'Away from the Numbers' – especially that line about 'all those fools I thought were my friends' – and get on with my life.

Everything had turned upside down. The name of the Sex Pistols was now mud for anyone who cared about it thanks to the Sid Vicious sing-alongs, and Sid was dead now anyway, and yet Johnny Rotten's new group – or John Lydon's, whatever – was a joke. The Clash had lost much of their street credibility with *Give 'Em Enough Rope* but at least they had toured Britain with a vengeance to reclaim it, and people who went to see them at the Lyceum said they were brilliant. The Stranglers released a live album and we all yawned and moved on. The Buzzcocks, having finally taken their perfect pop song formula into the charts, decided to send the whole thing up with 'Everybody's Happy Nowadays' and promptly alienated their long-term fans. (On the other hand, 'Why Can't I Touch It?', the six-minute extended B-side, was possibly the most amazing song they'd recorded.) The punk baton, it seemed, had been handed down to the next generation: Stiff Little Fingers, X-Ray Spex, XTC, Siouxsie and the Banshees, and, sadly, Sham 69 . . . who had somehow taken their music yet *further* downmarket with 'Hurry Up Harry', a record I could have dismissed for its comical stupidity if not for the fact that it inspired a nation of sixteen-year-old skinheads to chant 'We're going down the pub' on the top deck of the buses every weekend night. Under the circumstances, it was understandable that Paul Weller announced that The Jam's new single, 'Strange Town', was about a London he could no longer recognise. 'Strange Town' was as strong as almost everything on *All Mod Cons* and though it did not perform especially well in the charts, the B-side, 'The Butterfly Collector', an electrified ballad about some kind of groupie, confirmed The Jam's ongoing musical superiority compared to their previous punk peers.

Still, our own new group member, Mark, encouraged us to abandon our debt to (and cover versions of) The Jam, the Sex Pistols, the Clash and the Stranglers. He was more excited by our way with reggae, and told us we had the talent to see it through. On cold winter Sunday mornings at the Brixton Advice Centre, he showed us how to play it properly, by getting inside the groove rather than focusing so strictly on the beat. He also encouraged us to stop writing songs in verses and choruses, and instead start jamming around extended riffs. Jeff responded enthusiastically, quickly mastering the reggae rhythm, on guitar as well as bass, and, for his first composition, 'Case of Non Conformity', followed Mark's advice by sticking to the same two chords throughout. He also turned up at school one morning raving about someone called Shrink that he'd just seen play at the London College of Printing. Shrink wore a gold lamé suit and red Doc Martens, his face painted half gold, his head half-shaven (the other half dyed red and spiked high), playing a Flying V guitar. 'He's the personification of electricity, the genesis and revelation of music,' he wrote in a review he handed in for the next issue of *Jamming*, with all the unreserved enthusiasm of a fourteen-year-old on his fifth gig.

A willing disciple to his appointed messiah, Jeff took to visiting Shrink at his flat in Kennington after school – without his parents' knowledge. This seemed a bit dodgy to those of us he shared the information with; we figured that, what with all the gold make-up and equally lurid clothing, Shrink had to be queer. This was confirmed the day Jeff came to school and told us he'd met a bloke at the flat who had a tattoo on his elbow:

it indicated how far he'd managed to stick his hand up another man's bum. *People stuck their arms up other men's bums?*

Then one of the sixth years told me I was wanted down at the record shop by the bus stop. I didn't go there often; they hadn't shown any enthusiasm for selling *Jamming*. But when I stopped in after school all the same, the person who'd asked for me told me he was also working with a band that rehearsed in the basement, and he wanted me to check them out. They were called the Homosexuals.

I had been raised never to accept invitations to go *anywhere* by people who called themselves Homosexuals – let alone into basements. But when I went downstairs anyway, I found an enthusiastic and relatively harmless trio of musicians. They all seemed to think that *Jamming* was 'honest', in a way that the regular music papers were not, and their 'manager' – the one who worked upstairs – asked if I would write about them. I said that I would – like John Peel, I didn't know how to say no – at which I was informed of the conditions. The Homosexuals wouldn't allow themselves to be interviewed. They wouldn't even tell me their names. On the other hand, they *would* take me to see them play live, once they got a show together, and in the meantime, they gave me a copy of a self-pressed single. The A-side was called 'Hearts in Exile' and was constructed like a dub version, with scattered lyrics about 'empty continents' and 'pink triangles'. The other side, 'Soft South Africans', was funky, almost like disco, but for a blazing guitar and harmonica solo in the middle that sounded like something dropped in from The Who's *Live At Leeds*. I found it curiously brilliant.

So Jeff had Shrink, I had the Homosexuals, and as we recognised that we were the school's resident musical outsiders as well as its only active band members, we resumed going to gigs together. We went to the Marquee to interview the Undertones, whose second single 'Get Over You' was almost as brilliant as 'Teenage Kicks'. But one of the band had taken sick and the show had been cancelled, their place taken by the Lurkers. We went backstage and interviewed them anyway.

The Lurkers were surprisingly honest about their status as a second-division, second-generation punk band in dire need of a proper hit single. (Their latest, all about a girl who was 'Just Thirteen', had barely scraped into the Top Seventy-five.) Later in the evening, Jeff disappeared with a girl he had met in the bar, who probably wasn't much more than thirteen herself. The bouncer, Big John, later found them in the coat room with their hands in each other's clothing and warned them never to try it on his turf again. But he said it in a friendly manner, like he cared.

Jeff had gone through puberty almost overnight, and now exuded sexual confidence in his closely shorn curls, leather jacket and tight jeans; me, I was still a pre-pubescent mess of floppy hair, turned-up denims and hand-me-down shirts. In part I looked so dishevelled because I was determined not to subscribe to any one fashion, which Jeff quite admired, but in part it was because I didn't know *how* to be fashionable, and that he had strived to correct. He successfully dissuaded me from sporting a series of saucer-sized band button badges – like the one with the massive Jam logo that took up half of my chest, or the mirrored Who badge that made me look like a refugee from 'Tommy's Holiday Camp' – and to opt for smaller badges, a couple at a time, casually displayed just below the collar. Even if it was only for the sake of the band, he cared how I looked, and I cared about him in return.

A few days after the Lurkers show I dragged Jeff along to see my new friends Scritti Politti play their second gig, in a room above the Chippenham pub in Maida Vale, where they were 'opening' for Rough Trade's new 'signing', the Raincoats. The room was poorly decorated, standard pub flock wallpaper highlighted by a few cheap chandeliers; there was shared equipment in a back corner and the most minimal of PAs. Jeff and I stood on chairs along the side to see Scritti Politti better and, leaning back against the wall, Jeff accidentally connected a couple of exposed wires. The room went black. Scritti Politti made up a song on the spot, called 'Please

Turn the Lights on'. It wasn't the kind of thing you could imagine The Jam doing, that was for sure.

The Raincoats featured not just a female drummer, guitarist and bass player, but a violinist, too, every bit as unusual as X-Ray Spex and their saxophone player. And like X-Ray Spex, they made not so much a racket as a piercing screech, the thin guitars and biscuit tin drums augmented, if that was the right term, by the scraping sound of the string instrument. The overall effect was surprisingly addictive. The crowd of about 100 people, most of whom either worked at Rough Trade or lived in the squats surrounding the pub (or both), loved them. So did I, up to a point. If the Slits – yet to release an album – didn't get there first, surely the Raincoats were going to be Britain's biggest all-girl new wave weirdo feminist group.

What with the fact that an independent label called Cherry Red had started sending me free records, it seemed like a good time to be running a fanzine. There was something extraordinarily healthy going on under the mainstream music business radar, and every chance of *Jamming* being a part of it. All the same, when Bill Nelson announced that his new band Red Noise would be releasing an LP and going on tour, I decided to go after him for an interview. I was still allowed my heroes.

Nelson didn't have a fan club, didn't run a book store, didn't send out newsletters. I had no choice but to approach him the official way. I called the EMI switchboard a few times and was eventually given the number of his 'publicist', Tony Brainsby. (And there was me thinking that publicity was part of the record company's job.) I called Brainsby's office and found myself on the phone with a girl called Magenta Devine. The conversation was productive, and a couple of days later I went to their office in central London and hand-delivered the last two issues of *Jamming*. There were gold and platinum discs lining the walls, and there were conference rooms and sofa chairs. I had been spending all my time recently in record store basements and rooms above pubs, hanging out amidst the backstage graffiti at the Marquee or rehearsing alongside the political slogans at the Brixton Advice Centre; I had almost stopped considering how much money there was in the music business for those who knew how to make it.

A few days later Magenta called to schedule me an interview during Nelson's tour rehearsals – which were conveniently taking place inside the old Astoria cinema opposite the Brixton police station. But more important than location was the matter of acceptance; this was the first time anybody working with the major record labels had recognised *Jamming* as some sort of proper publication.

And then, a few days before the interview, I got another late-afternoon call from Magenta. (All my weekday phone calls were late afternoon; I had no idea how often the phone rang when I was at school.) She told me, with brisk sincerity, that she was cancelling it. There were too many people wanting too much of Bill's time, and the band leader himself had asked her to postpone my interview. 'I'm sorry,' she said when I protested, 'but Bill's priority right now is to get his shit together.'

Get his shit together? That was the kind of thing an American rock star might have said – before punk came along. It certainly wasn't the kind of thing I imagined Bill Nelson saying to anyone.

So I turned up for the interview anyway. That following Saturday, earlier than originally planned, I went to the old Brixton Astoria and I waited for Nelson outside the stage door. When he arrived, in a chauffeur-driven car, I approached him and explained my situation, and just as I thought, he knew nothing about any of it. He thanked me for my enthusiasm and persistence, invited me to come in with him and told me I was welcome to stick around all day. It was only when we were an hour into the interview itself that he suggested he really ought to get on with rehearsing his new band for his big tour. He never once uttered the term 'getting my shit together'.

He was, though, highly critical of the newly political punk bands – like Stiff Little Fingers, whose *Inflammable Material* LP was riding high in the charts, turning the Rough Trade label into a major player. Among its many songs about sectarian

Belfast was one with the line, 'Killing isn't my idea of fun,' which had recently been used in a music paper to caption a picture of the band.

'Everyone knows killing ain't an idea of fun,' Nelson insisted. 'But they take the most obvious statement like that as a revelation. People don't need to be told the obvious, they need to know how to get out of the mess they're in.' Not surprisingly, he was no more enamoured with his label-mate at Harvest, Tom Robinson. 'I think he would make a better politician or campaigner than a musician, because I don't really think he's a great musician. If I were him and that sincere, I wouldn't pick up my guitar, I'd get out and do something.'

Nelson's own idea of 'doing something' no longer entailed being a rock star. 'I've got a lot more to do than being on the road all the time,' he said. 'I'd like to get a few bands to record, and maybe get involved with films, and maybe a few one-off projects under my own name.' In the meantime, however, he had a high-profile tour to rehearse. I watched from the sidelines, highly impressed; Red Noise seemed to have adopted some of the more quirky aspects of the new wave – the synthesiser riffs and odd rhythms of Swindon's XTC, for example – without sacrificing Be-Bop Deluxe's artsy integrity or guitar solos. Songs like 'For Young Moderns' and 'Revolt into Style' seemed to be discussing the changes in culture from a reassuring distance but were commercial enough that I figured them for potential hit singles. During a break, the group's hired drummer, a Canadian called Steve Peer, took me under his wing. He had a band back home called TV Toy, and he promised to send me their self-pressed single and other new music from his side of the Atlantic. Peer also promised to get me tickets for Red Noise's show at the Drury Lane Theatre, and he kept to his word. (I didn't dare ask for them through Tony Brainsby's office.) The show was OK. The audience, in reverence of the surroundings, stayed seated throughout, which upset Nelson, who had somehow failed to anticipate this likely result of playing a major theatre – but by the encores everyone was up on their feet, and it looked like Nelson was still a rock star, assuming he could maintain the enthusiasm for it.

At last, then, I had a new issue of *Jamming* to take to the printers. It had interviews with Bill Nelson, the Lurkers – and pragVEC, who we'd met back at the Acklam Hall. When we went to their flat in North London for an interview, they explained their song 'Wolf' by using the term 'metaphorical cannibalism', which was about as helpful as naming their EP 'Existential' to begin with. And then, shortly before he quit our band because, ultimately, he had better things to do with his Sunday mornings than try to tutor a trio of fourteen- and fifteen-year-olds, Mark let me reprint his interview with Sid Vicious from 1976. I could have announced it as a 'Sid Vicious Exclusive', like I had with Paul Weller, but I was getting more into the idea of running a proper fanzine, and proper fanzines didn't sell themselves on the back of murderous dead junkies. I advertised it as the Flowers of Romance and trusted that people would know who I was talking about, that this was the band whose members had gone on to the Sex Pistols, the Slits, the Raincoats and Public Image Ltd.

With his quotes edited, cut up and pasted onto a single page, the then nineteen-year-old former John Beverley came across as he always had and, now that he was dead and unable to change his ways, always would. 'If I feel like killing a hippie, I will,' he had told Mark at one point. And later, he'd said, 'As long as I don't have to compromise for any cunt, I'll be totally happy . . .'

And there was this: 'I don't think anyone can get above their own station in life. If I ever got the urge to do something like that, I'd consider myself a total cunt, and I'd blow my brains out.'

Sid hadn't blown his brains out with a gun. He'd done it with drugs. But he was gone, all the same, and it was time to move on.

Number 22:
IS SHE REALLY GOING
OUT WITH HIM?

Kate was at my bus stop most mornings. She was about my height, with medium-length reddish-brown hair, a thin face, straight nose and a sharp chin. Not beautiful, perhaps, but pretty for sure. From her uniform I knew that she went to Charles Edward Brooke, and now that I was occasionally starting to mix with CEB girls in the classrooms, I knew she wasn't in my year. She had to be a fifth-former. No way was she younger than me.

In the year since I had first noticed her, we had sometimes smiled at each other at the bus stop in the morning, and once or twice we even said hello, but that was as far as it went: the idea of chatting up someone older than me never crossed my mind. I'd 'copped off' at various parties since the weird incident with Cindy, but they were all of a similar sort, with parents never far from barging in and demanding an end to the slow music and the kissing and canoodling in the corners. There'd been nothing any further. I'd resigned myself to the absence of a girlfriend.

And then, one evening in the middle of winter, Kate called me at home.

'We know each other,' she said, as she told me her name. 'I'm the girl who smiles at you at the bus stop.'

I blushed. Fortunately, she couldn't see me. 'Right,' I said, and stopped there. Damn it. My voice still hadn't broken. What did she want from me? She told me that copies of my fanzine were doing the rounds of her school. It was pretty neat, she said, me doing that at my age.

197

'Thanks,' I said in return, all the while thinking, this is very nice but can't she just come out and say why she called – or who gave her my number in the first place – so we can get it over with and I don't have to keep stammering?

She did. 'Do you want to come to a film with me one night?' she asked.

Did I? I fancied that and a whole lot more. And I wanted to say as much immediately, except that, knowing some of the boys at school, and not knowing this girl at all, I wasn't sure she hadn't been put up to it.

'Are you serious?' I asked.

'Why?' she said. 'You're not interested?' I almost thought I heard some disappointment in her voice.

'No, no, it's not that. It's just . . .'

'I won't bite,' she said, half giggling. 'I promise. What are you doing Saturday evening?'

What *was* I doing Saturday evening? Nothing – other than staying home and worrying that Raymond and Glover might come round with Chris Boyle and set fire to my curtains. I told her I didn't really have any plans. Kate sensed my nervousness and she eased me through it.

'So let's go to a film,' she said. 'Do you want to meet me at the Palace Parade? Seven o'clock OK? Great. See you then.'

And she did. We met at the Parade, we went to a film in Streatham, me staring blankly at the screen throughout for fear of what else I was meant to do, and after catching the bus back, we walked down from Crystal Palace Parade together and all of a sudden we were holding hands. Just like that. When we got to her flat, on a terraced street just off Gipsy Hill, she let me walk her to the door, which was already more than I'd done with anyone else . . . and there she gave me a proper kiss. Not a long one, but a proper one. She knew what she was doing, too. Then she let herself in the door and promised to call me the next day. When she kept to her word, I found it much easier to talk. I knew she wasn't having me on. And with that, I officially had a girlfriend.

By Monday afternoon, everyone at school knew about us. Not from me. But there was no way you could keep anything like that a secret. Either someone had seen us at the cinema or on the bus or she'd got talking at her school and the news had just wafted up Camberwell New Road on the wind.

All of a sudden I was seen in a new light. The last few months at school, I'd been Fletcher the Bald, hiding through lunch hour to avoid being de-trousered in public, bunking off last lessons to avoid getting beaten up in the churchyard, teased in the classroom and even in my own bedroom. But there they all were, going out with girls in the third year or lower, assuming they were going out with girls at all. And here was I, going out with a fifth year. I may have still had a high-pitched voice. I may have still been bald for all they knew. But I had Kate waiting for me at the bus stop after school, and that trumped everything. They had no choice but to stop picking on me. The whole reasoning behind it – that I was a weak little mummy's boy, prone to crying fits at the slightest provocation and with an annoying habit of extracurricular overachieving – no longer held up if I was going out with a good-looking sixteen-year-old.

Kate and I made a nice pair. We didn't hang out with any of the cliques from either school, didn't feel like we had anything to prove to them. We didn't go to any gigs together either. To be honest, she wasn't into the same music anyway; she was more of a soul girl. We did go to the occasional film, but even that wasn't really our style. We seemed happy just to hang out in each other's rooms, chatting, playing records, helping with each other's homework and, of course, making out. Kissing. She had to show me how to get good at it – there was an art to rolling those tongues round each other's mouths, I soon discovered – but because she knew I was innocent to begin with, she didn't make a big deal of it. She made me feel comfortable. She did tell me that her friends had taken to calling her a 'cradle snatcher', but she stressed that she didn't care.

It seemed natural to expect that I'd soon start having sex with her. As far as I could tell, she was experienced in that department – more experienced than me, at any rate – and it was widely assumed I must be getting my share, given that was the main reason boys and girls went out with each other.

Unfortunately, I couldn't boast about my sex life because I didn't have one. Me and Kate were boyfriend and girlfriend, and when we got together, every few evenings, we kissed extensively, but that was as far as it went.

The main thing she wanted from a boyfriend at this point, she said, was good company. She wanted someone with at least half a brain who she could enjoy hanging out with. Someone like me.

Compliments aside, that left me in a tight spot. I had been brought up to respect women's wishes. But I had also read all this stuff in the papers about women saying 'no' when maybe they meant 'yes'. So the next time we were in her bedroom, snogging, I tried brushing my hands across the front of her blouse. She gently moved them away. And the next time, the same thing. The time after that, as well. Every time I tried moving my hands across her breasts, she'd gently move them around to her back.

So, I decided to seize the opportunity I was presented with. At our next kissing session, I worked my way under her blouse and up her back, and she didn't object. Finally, I was getting somewhere. I had some flesh to play with. What I wanted to do was reach up to her bra, and unclip it in one swift move, leaving her suitably impressed (and undressed). But of course, I had no prior practice with a bra, and after I fumbled with the metal clips, she reached up behind her and pulled my hands back down.

'No,' she said, softly.

'Why?' I asked.

'Because,' she said. 'I told you. I like you. But you'll have to be patient.'

I walked home that night without the usual warm farewell kiss to keep me company; she was upset that I was trying so hard to get somewhere with her, and I was upset that she wouldn't let me. I liked Kate like she said she liked me. But I knew it wasn't love. What was the point, then, of having a good-looking, older girlfriend if she wouldn't even let me inside her bra?

I stopped seeing her. I went back to my fanzine instead.

Number 21:
REVOLT INTO STYLE

Joly was a hippie. Of indeterminate age – as was anyone beyond their early twenties, in my eyes – he was rail-thin, wore black sweaters, and kept his hair in a pony-tail that ran all the way down his back to the very top of his black jeans, which were, at least, tight at the ankles, not flared. He smoked hand-rolled cigarettes, favoured dub reggae, and spoke with great intensity and enthusiasm. Joly lived and worked on the Portobello Road, just a few doors north of the Westway, in between the Acklam Hall and Honest Jon's, in a couple of floors above a store front, floors that reeked of cat piss and cannabis. And it was from that building that he ran his unlikely empire: Better Badges.

The 1-inch button badge had become *the* fashion statement of the new wave. And Joly's company had become *the* place to get them made. He had figured out that badges were ordered primarily for publicity purposes, and that most bands and labels were happy to give them away – but at the same time, that if the badges were trendy, witty or well designed, the public was happy to pay for them. Joly offered to print badges at a better price than his competitors, on the understanding that he had the right to sell some for himself – which he could be seen doing on a nightly basis at various concerts across London. Joly didn't limit his badges to those that he was paid to print, though; if a new image, or catch-phrase, or band came along, he'd design a relevant badge – and if someone then came knocking on his door going on about 'copyright', he'd give them a pep talk on street credibility along with 1,000-odd badges or £50 as compensation. Each week, he ran ads in the back of the weekly music papers that listed the latest badges and their prices (20–25p, depending on colour) alongside a chart of the best-sellers and a simple order sheet for getting your own badges made. Step by step, he had cornered the market.

I didn't know all these details when I first rang Joly's door bell. I was after an advert for the new *Jamming*. Printing costs were so exorbitant for a small-run fanzine like mine that the only way to even think about breaking even on the venture was to secure as many ads as possible. And yet having ads in a fanzine seemed like a sell-out, which was why it was so important to get them from companies like Better Badges. But even as I first rang that doorbell, I was feeling defeated: the latest printer I thought I had struck a deal with had just raised the price on me by a full £100 – or about 50 per cent. I was starting to wonder if I'd ever get another issue out.

Joly wasn't necessarily keen on paying for an ad. But he *was* interested in bartering for the space, and upon hearing my plight, he made me an offer. After years of using outside printers for his badges, he was finally buying his own A4 offset litho machine. To get the ball rolling – to test out the equipment – he offered to take on *Jamming* as his guinea pig. In other words, he could print *Jamming* for cost, on the understanding that it might not be printed perfectly. Oh, and he'd get his ad for free, as well. My previous issue had been printed *far* from perfectly – and the company had tried to charge me full price. I accepted his deal on the spot.

So began a routine. After school, I'd make my way by bus to the Ladbroke Grove area, walk over to Better Badges in that shadowy area by the Westway, Joly would buzz me in, make us both cups of tea, put on the latest dub reggae at a thunderously loud volume, and then lock us into a dark room where we'd work on scanning the pictures and making the plates for the next issue of *Jamming*.

Of course, being new to the printing process, we ran into our fair share of problems. The litho machine was no less temperamental than a piano, a guitar or, indeed, the rock star who played them, and I began to understand why printers charged for an initial 'pre-press' run. However much Joly adjusted the amount of ink on his brand-new A4 printing press, the pages came out with streaks all over them. Some of the streaks looked kind of cool, the way a fanzine should; others just looked bad, like the printer didn't know what he was doing. And the whole process took time. A lot of time. Joly had thought he could print my 1,000 copies – a realistic reduction on the previous issue, which, like the one before it, remained largely unsold and, indeed, uncollated on my bedroom floor – over a weekend, and at first I decided to hang out with him to watch it 'come off the presses'. But it proved such a slow process that he eventually sent me home and told me he'd call when it was done. Monday came and went, Tuesday too, and Joly was no closer to completion. And when, on Wednesday, I went up to the Portobello Road after school anyway to find out what was going on, I found him with his head inside the machine, his fingers covered in ink, his hair tied in a rubber band and tucked down the back of a black pullover lest it get caught in the printing press. He looked tired, as if he knew he'd taken on more than he could easily handle. And yet he was no less committed to seeing it through than I was.

For me, every day without the new issue of *Jamming* on the street represented not only lost sales but the threat of that issue's obsolescence, and I wasn't used to the casual confidence of the hippie entrepreneur, with his calm assurances that everything would surely turn out all right if I only stopped worrying about it. But at the end of the week, we had achieved what we had set out to do. Joly had mastered – well, just about tamed – his printing press. And I had roughly 1,000 copies of a new *Jamming*, printed at cost.

I also had something of a friend. Johnny Rotten had told us all to 'Never Trust A Hippie' (a phrase that Joly had duly printed up, placed on a 1-inch badge, and sold by the case), but he was the first person to ever cut me a real deal. Sure,

I had had plenty of support already, from Paul Weller to Adam Ant, Step Forward to Rough Trade, but Joly had seen something in me that he felt was worth an actual investment. In return, I felt that, whereas I could no longer trust Johnny Rotten (or John Lydon), I *could* trust Joly. The new issue of *Jamming* was not the strongest, in content, layout or quality of print, but it was the first to be printed by someone on the scene. It was the first that looked and felt like a proper fanzine. It had attitude, whether it was the stark premonitions of the teenage Sid Vicious, my rant about the lack of gigs for under-eighteens ('But *are* the kids all right?'), or Jeff's clinically drawn mock-investigative report into the music papers' profit motive ('Proper-Gander'). And it didn't harm our credibility that it also had a full-page Better Badges ad.

Number 20:
THE PUNK AND THE GODFATHER

I was still in the habit of listening to Nicky Horne on Capital from 9 to 10 p.m. before switching over to John Peel on Radio 1. Four days after my fifteenth birthday, Horne made an announcement almost as surprising as when he had told us of Keith Moon's death. The Who were playing live in London again. At the Rainbow Theatre. *Tomorrow night*. Tickets would go on sale at the box office at ten o'clock in the morning.

Any question as to whether The Who – especially without Moon – meant as much to me as The Jam these days was suddenly irrelevant. The opportunity to see the greatest group in the history of the world at a small theatre like the Rainbow was one I simply could not pass up.

My mind kicked into overdrive. Buying a ticket – assuming I could get to Finsbury Park early enough to secure one – would mean bunking off school for the morning, possibly the whole day. I could manage that; I'd already got it down to a science. The bigger problem was the ticket price: £5.

I didn't have £5. Nobody I knew had £5. Not in my age group, anyway. Singles were less than a quid; the Raincoats and Scritti Politti at the Chippenham had cost all of thirty pence – though admittedly, that hadn't included functioning lights. Had The Who announced their show the previous week, I might have had cash from my birthday sitting around. Had they announced it a couple of weeks before that, I'd have had change sitting about from taking the new *Jamming* round town (money that otherwise was going straight to the printers – all of them). But this particular Tuesday night, I simply didn't have the money.

I waited until breakfast. I made sure I was up early, dressed properly, ready – apparently – for school.

'Mum, can I borrow £2?'

'Why?'

'The Who are playing tonight, at the Rainbow. I want to go.'

'Then we'll talk about it after school.'

'We can't. The tickets go on sale at ten o'clock. It'll sell out in minutes. I have to get to Finsbury Park this morning.'

It was a dumb thing to say. Especially to a teacher.

'No! Absolutely not! No way! Impossible!' I caught a flash of the manner in which she controlled the kids at Stockwell. 'You're going to school and that's that.'

I wanted to say, 'Make me,' but I didn't need to. She had to be at her school the same time I had to be at mine. Short of forcing me into her car, setting off for work early, driving past Stockwell to Kennington, depositing me in my classroom and literally locking me in until my form teacher arrived, there was no way she could control my movements. I scraped up every last penny I could find, which brought me to barely £4, and then I caught the number 3 bus to school, earlier than usual for someone who was chronically late, which meant that I was more or less on time. At each stop, I looked to see if a Tenison's kid was getting on board, especially someone in my year, someone I had a relationship with. There weren't any. (Adrian, sadly, didn't count any more.) I had to wait for the two-mile straight line from Brixton to Kennington, where the route was shared by a dozen or more different buses, and you never knew who might get on.

. . . Like Khalil. Khalil was smart. He worked hard. And he was a Pakistani, the only one in our class. All these things stood against him, but he had compensated by only speaking when spoken to, never saying anything to aggravate anyone, and, above all, remaining polite in the face of all-round adversity. I never saw him get picked on by anyone.

So when I approached him and asked if he could lend me a pound or two, he knew I wasn't trying to steal from him.

And because I'd been bullied so much over the course of that school year, he may have even had some sympathy for me. Khalil, confirming my long-term suspicions that he came from a well-off family, handed over a pound. Better yet, he agreed not to tell our form teacher he had seen me.

I emerged from Finsbury Park tube station shortly before 10 a.m. to find a line snaking around the Rainbow. I had expected that; I was just praying it wasn't already more than 3,000 people deep. The thing I had not expected was to see so many other teenagers. Especially so many mods.

I knew I wasn't the only one who'd heard *Quadrophenia* several years back, studied the photo book that accompanied it, and thought, *I wish I could have been part of that.* Not alone in my excitement that The Who were now making a feature film out of it. Not the only one too young to have been a real punk rocker, but old enough now for a movement of his own. Not alone in having latched on to The Jam as the next best thing to The Who, to have bought into the younger band's own sense of style, fascinated that they would list their hairdresser on the back of a 7-inch single and that they would release two albums in a row with the word 'mod' in the title. Hardly the only person who swore by the singles on *Meaty Beaty Big and Bouncy*, or had The Who Marquee poster on their wall from the *Live At Leeds* souvenirs . . .

I just hadn't realised there were this many of us. I had been distracted recently, immersed in the do-it-yourself music scene over in Notting Hill and Camden Town (and the temporary duties of having a girlfriend). I wasn't aware that the *Quadrophenia* film was finished already. I had missed entirely the *NME*'s multi-part cover story on mods just three weeks back, a story which ensured that their talk of an imminent revival would become a self-fulfilling prophecy.

And now, here they were. The mods. There were dozens of scooters parked outside the Rainbow that morning – proper Vespas and Lambrettas, with all the extra side mirrors, the beautifully painted bodywork. And there were hundreds of teenagers wearing green army parkas over the top of carefully tailored suits, just like Jimmy in the *Quadrophenia* photographs. Some of the kids were wearing 'Jam shoes' too – the black and white, triangular-toed footwear I'd first seen on the cover of 'All Around the World'. There were plenty of hard-core Who 'lifers' out there, too, but the queue was notable for being that much younger than the band itself.

While we were waiting for the box office to open, a man in his thirties, wearing a long coat but with a recognisably large nose, came strolling casually down the road, examining us from a slight distance like he was trying to figure out this new generation of Who fans for himself. And the strange thing was, we all knew it was Pete Townshend, and yet we didn't mob him. As I'd seen back at the ICA only eight months ago, there was something about the relationship between The Who and their fans that forestalled that kind of hero worship. So Townshend didn't say anything to the kids, and we didn't say much to him. I certainly didn't ask, 'Do you remember me showing up for that interview a few months ago, with three of my mates? We were over an hour late?'

The queue remained orderly. And unlike at Charlton, it moved. Around noon, I reached the box office, handed over £5 in change, and got my concert ticket. Then, using my free school bus pass, I took the underground back across the river, and made it to my form room for afternoon registration. Nobody had grassed on me, even though many of them guessed where I'd been. After school, I went home, got changed, and told my mum I was off to the Rainbow. She didn't ask, and so I didn't tell, that I'd been there once that day already.

My seat was for the balcony, sadly. But at least it wasn't at the back. And so, the moment The Who came on and launched into 'Substitute' – which, on about five days out of seven, was my favourite single of all – I joined hundreds of other Who fans in a mad dash for the front row of the aisle.

The bouncers, naturally, pushed us all back. The exercise

was as much one of futility as of enthusiasm. But when it was my turn to be forcibly returned to my rightful seat, the bouncer stopped pushing me almost as suddenly as he'd started.

'You're Lawrence's friend.'

It was Alf Weaver. I'd met him the couple of times I'd gone over to Lawrence's house, maybe at school events once or twice as well. I knew what he did for a living, but I'd never seen him in action. He was intimidating; I could see where Lawrence got it from. Lawrence had shown no interest in writing for *Jamming* ever again, but Alf lifted his arms, and let me glide past him to the front of the balcony, even as he pushed other fans back up the stairs. I was left with a bird's-eye view of the show.

For the most part, it was phenomenal. There were moments when I wanted to jump over the balcony, I was so excited. Admittedly, it was hard to look at the stage and see someone other than Keith behind the kit, but presumably, if we cared for the group's continuity, we'd need to get used to it. And although Kenney Jones was a very different kind of drummer, much more restrained, much less flamboyant, still the power that emanated from Townshend's guitar and Entwistle's bass, let alone Daltrey's voice, more than made up for it.

But something didn't seem quite right. It may have been the haircuts. Townshend still had his beard and moustache, but Roger Daltrey had cut off his long mane to star as a hardened criminal in the film *McVicar*, and his newly tight curls came across as a deliberate attempt to seek respect from the new wave mods. And Entwistle had cropped his own hair closer to Townshend's length. There was something different about their clothing as well; it wasn't just that the flares had been brought in, it was that they seemed to be making a conscious effort to look street credible.

None of that mattered, until they embarked on 'My Generation' – and the lead guitar work that had emblazoned *Live At Leeds* and the Charlton show, Townshend's explosive and yet always rhythmic improvisation, was suddenly missing.

He disappeared off to a corner of the stage, and began engaging in a kind of soloing that was less the mark of his generation than of the one The Who had always stood apart from: the self-indulgent progressive hard rock bands of the mid-seventies.

Perhaps Townshend was out of it. It was hard to know from where I was standing. But even a fifteen-year-old couldn't help noticing how Daltrey stared over at the guitarist's side of the stage, confused and uncertain, looking for clues on how to bring Pete out of his trance. Previously, this would have been Keith Moon's job, the guitarist and the drummer having an almost telepathic understanding of each other. Kenney Jones, playing his first show with The Who, had no such instinct for Townshend's next move, let alone the authority to direct it. For a few minutes there, the show seemed in danger of collapsing entirely.

. . . But eventually Townshend snapped out of his reverie, the band recovered their poise, they found a way to wrap up 'My Generation', and they finished the set with a rousing 'Won't Get Fooled Again'. Then they encored – yes, encored – with 'The Real Me', the opening track from *Quadrophenia*. Everything was back on course. The Who had returned to the concert stage. They were triumphant once more. They remained the godfathers – and not just to punk, but to a whole other movement. The mod revival was on.

Number 19:
FRUSTRATION

The *Surrey Vomet* was the funniest thing around. Rather than write about new music, like other fanzines, the editor took existing cartoons and rewrote the speech bubbles with incredibly rude words. He developed his own characters like W*nker Watson. He insulted politicians, pop stars and TV celebrities. He wrote about how to do a runner from an Indian restaurant. He cut-and-pasted and rearranged newspaper cuttings, especially from his publication's namesake – suburban weekly the *Surrey Comet* – and he laid the whole thing out with incredible wit and precision. He then photocopied it perfectly, without a single blotch or smudge, and on larger pages than most other 'zines, too.

It was a work of art, and the music press knew it. The *Surrey Vomet* was hailed as the pinnacle of punk irreverence. But here was the catch: the editor, Roger, was not a punk. He was a mod. The clue came in his fourth issue, when he finally profiled a music group, and chose a sixties revival band from Southend called Speedball. It turned out that he had just become their manager, and because Roger and I had started a correspondence – receiving free fanzines in the post was one of the rewards for spending every penny I didn't have on print bills – he invited me to come and see them play live. We agreed on a Friday-night gig, at the Moonlight Club in West Hampstead, where they were opening for a band called the Purple Hearts.

It had been a busy week already. Wednesday I'd seen The Who at the Rainbow. Thursday, I had been driven to Kingston to see the Homosexuals at the Polytechnic. I liked the band's inherent weirdness – the fact that they played about seventeen songs that stopped and started abruptly and sped up and slowed down and appeared to borrow from every musical style – but the night was most memorable for the multiple televisions they arrayed across the stage. The general election had taken place that day, and everyone wanted to know, for certain, what they suspected for sure, that Labour was on the way out and Margaret Thatcher was set to be the country's new prime minister.

I'd been doing my best to follow some of this. I knew that the last few months had been dominated by strikes – there was talk of it as the 'winter of discontent' – and there were, certainly, millions who believed that the trade unions had far too much power. I knew also, from when I'd been to see him the previous summer – he'd moved back from Canada to a job in Leicester, a city fast becoming Asian – that my dad believed immigration from the former British Empire was out of control, that he was voting for Thatcher in the hope she'd put a halt to it. But then I knew from my mother, and other teachers and parents, that as a former education secretary, Thatcher had stopped our daily bottle of free milk at primary school. They knew her as 'the Milk Snatcher'.

Most of all, though, I knew that with unemployment having recently exceeded 1,000,000 people, Thatcher's Conservative Party (or their advertising agency) had come up with the election slogan 'Labour Isn't Working', accompanied by the image of an endless line of people snaking away from a dole office, and that the moment it hit the streets, in the shape of 1,000 billboards, the election was guaranteed.

May 4, then, was the dawning of a new era. At the Moonlight Club that evening, it certainly seemed that way. There were scooters parked up outside and young mods lined up at the bar inside, sweating it out in their green army parkas with Union Jack patches sewn into the sleeves and The Who and/or The Jam's logos carefully inscribed on the back. They were there, in theory, to see the Purple Hearts, who came from Romford in Essex and were named after a popular brand of sixties 'speed'.

The Purple Hearts had been profiled as one of the mod revival's two leading bands in the NME's cover special a few weeks earlier, where they admitted that they had previously been punks. They used to cover the Clash's 'London's Burning', just as my own band, Direction, once covered the Clash's 'White Riot'.

But the Clash had been seen to sell out to America with *Give 'Em Enough Rope* at the very moment The Jam had made their most emphatically British album, *All Mod Cons*, and a movement's worth of teenagers had switched allegiance accordingly. So now here were the Purple Hearts, wearing sharp suits, covering the Monkees' 'Stepping Stone', telling people to 'stop pogoing', with a large following up front, similarly rechristened as mods, loving them for it. They had a couple of their own songs, 'Frustration' ('I wear it like a suit') and 'Millions Like Us', that spoke to the same kind of teenage identity crises as had made Townshend and Weller such heroes. They were on to something, for sure.

So were Speedball. Front man Robin Buelo, dressed in a blue army tunic, opened their set with a sharp guitar riff loosely based on 'Substitute' – the song was called 'Don't You Know Love' – and the four-piece had me, instantly. Maybe it was their role as underdogs. Maybe it was their dress code; Speedball weren't so obviously mods as they were, simply, fashionable. Perhaps it was their cover version of the Boys' 'First Time', a new wave pop classic that should have charted but didn't. Or maybe it was the fact that Roger from the *Surrey Vomet* was busy sneaking me halves of lager. It was impossible to keep going round London pubs and clubs to see bands and not get a taste for beer. I loved the fizzy allure of lager, the way it gave me a pleasant high and made me silly if I drank too much of it, and I had a special fondness for anyone who had more money than me and was willing to spend it getting me drunk.

Attending the Moonlight Club might have put me further ahead of the other fourth years, but catching a mod revival band did not. As the *NME* had announced in its cover story, there was a large pub opposite Waterloo station, appropriately named the Wellington, promoting mod bands at weekends. A couple of schoolfriends and their mates who lived in the area had started going there these last few weeks: the Wellington was local (for them), it was free (for everyone), and it didn't turn away fourteen- and fifteen-year-olds. Leading the pack was John Matthews, of course. Shortly behind him was Richard Heard, the two of them undeterred by their love of the Clash, who they'd seen regain their punk crown at the Lyceum, from retailoring themselves as mods. And so, the night after seeing the Purple Hearts and Speedball, I agreed to meet them at the Wellington to see what was going on for myself.

What I witnessed, for the first time in my life, was a scene. Though the Wellington was basically just a large pub by a train station, and anyone could walk through its doors and order a pint, it seemed like everyone there that night was there for a reason – to hang out with other people of a similar mindset. At the Marquee, the Acklam Hall, the Moonlight Club, the audience would change every night according to the bands on the bill. At the Wellington, it seemed the other way round, like the bands might change but the audience would stay the same.

The Merton Parkas were headlining. They were named after their home suburb, a place we passed through on our train journeys to our school's athletics field in Motspur Park; the kind of place, like so many others on that train journey, populated by the white middle class, a place where nothing much ever happened and the elders seemed to like it that way. Accordingly, the Merton Parkas – who had no choice, given their name, but to dress in green army coats – were nice boys, led by two brothers: the younger and better-looking one, Danny Talbot, up front on guitar and vocals; the older and better musician, Mick Talbot, off to the side, on keyboards. Like the Purple Hearts, they covered 'Stepping Stone', and like me, they had written a song entitled 'Face in the Crowd' – but unlike me, remained undeterred by The Jam writing one with such a similar title. Their music owed more to traditional rhythm and blues and Merseybeat than rock. They were inoffensive, and they were fun, and they were almost inseparable from the audience, and that was another thing that made it a scene.

I went back the next night, Sunday – my fifth gig in five nights – to see the Chords. They, too, were South Londoners, but from the eastern part, Deptford down to Eltham with a bit of Lewisham thrown in. In football terms, that made them Charlton with the potential for some Millwall. Their tougher background came across in the music, full of big, blustering power chords and suspended fourths as favoured by Townshend and Weller, raucous choruses with instant sing-alongs: 'Now It's Gone', 'Something's Missing', the obligatory sixties covers (in their case, The Who's 'Circles') and the regulatory anthem for a youth movement, 'Maybe Tomorrow'. Like the Purple Hearts, with whom they'd shared the *NME*'s focus on 'new' mod bands, the Chords weren't far removed musically from Eddie and the Hot Rods or Generation X. But two of them played Rickenbackers, and at least one of them sported taped arrows on his shirt like The Jam on the cover of *This Is the Modern World*, and the drummer, Brett – known as Buddy – played just like Keith Moon. I loved them, instantly.

And yet, for all that the scene at the Wellington felt like it could have been the start of something wonderful, it was, already, the end. The following Tuesday, the Wellington hosted a free gig featuring both the Chords *and* the Purple Hearts, filmed by the *London Weekend Show*, a Sunday lunchtime programme hosted by Janet Street-Porter, whose entire career had been built around reporting new street trends before anyone else. Given that the *NME* had already put the mod revival on its cover, Street-Porter had no choice but to put it on the TV, too. The bands barely had any say in the matter – except to turn down the coverage, and what new, unsigned young band would ever turn down free TV exposure?

As the gig's sponsor, London Weekend Television called the shots. The bands played just a few numbers each; the crew jostled the audience throughout. Two nights earlier the

Wellington's landlord had caught me drinking beer and told me never to come back. Seeing me now in the front row during the Chords' set, he grabbed me and, rather than cause a scene in front of the cameras, pushed me behind the makeshift stage. Meanwhile, the crew from *Maximum Speed* were busy selling their all-mod fanzine to every new convert in the room, including a couple of parka-clad ex-skinheads (their hair had still not grown back), who were loudly considering whether to 'boot out' any non-mods. I went back to the Wellington ten days later, to see the Merton Parkas again, but the *London Weekend Show* had broadcast its mod 'exclusive' in the meantime and you could hardly get inside the Wellington's door – not least because the crowd had become three years younger in the process. The sight of a floppy-haired, chubby blond kid on TV, barely fifteen years old, happily jumping around behind the Chords may have had something to do with that.

Besides, the scene had already moved on to bigger venues. Right in between the two Merton Parkas gigs that May, I went with some other fourth years, our resident punk Jeff among them, to the Marquee, to see a mod band from Hastings called the Teenbeats open for a London mod band called Secret Affair. Jeff was no more likely to wear a parka than I was, but down in Hastings all the different youth cults hung out together, punks, mods and skins united by their mutual fondness for youth fashion and hatred of adult conformity, and he enjoyed the Teenbeats for what they were – a moderately competent bunch of likable sixties revivalists.

As for Secret Affair, it turned out I already knew them – in the singer and guitarist's previous guise as the New Hearts, whose devotion to sixties powerpop was largely why I liked them in the first place. But even more so than the Purple Hearts, Secret Affair seemed to be denying their past. The bright suits had been reined in for more conventionally muted mod attire, and singer Ian Pain had changed his name to Ian Page. (Unless that was his real name all along, of course.) The New Hearts had declared their cynicism for youth movements in songs like 'Revolution? What Revolution?' and 'Just Another Teenage Anthem'. But now that they were fully fledged leaders of the mod revival, they had a whole bunch of teenage anthems especially composed for the movement's moment in the spotlight: 'Glory Boys', 'My World' and 'Time for Action'. The last of these had a line that seemed to sum up their philosophy: 'Looking good's the answer, and living by night.' That message was about as far from 'Anarchy in the UK' or 'Complete Control' as it was possible to venture in just two short years.

I couldn't figure out what to make of all this. I was aware by my suspicious reaction to Secret Affair that I must have held on to some of the New Hearts' cynicism, whereas they appeared to have let go of their own. Maybe I was just jealous of the fact that I had been championing the sixties sound all along – and that a mod revival had somehow started without consulting me. But my reaction also came from alternating these mod gigs with shows by the Homosexuals, the Raincoats, Scritti Politti and Swell Maps, from receiving self-pressed 45s and self-published fanzines from around the country, and from knowing that, regardless of Johnny Rotten's detachment, Sid's demise, or, for that matter, Strummer and Jones' fascination with the USA, the fall-out from punk would continue to create excitement for years to come. That even if looking good *was* the answer, looking backwards most certainly was not.

Number 18:
SUMMER HOLIDAY

S hona was only fourteen, but she was already beautiful. She had long blonde hair that fell neatly to her shoulders, a perfectly rounded face refreshingly free of freckles, spots *and* make-up; startling bright blue eyes; and a ready smile crowned by perfect teeth. She spoke with a pronounced cockney accent, only one step removed from Barbara Windsor in the *Carry On* films. Shona was talkative and cheeky, cheerful yet modest – and the other girls didn't seem to be jealous of her any more than she set herself up as their leader.

Shona and her mate Samantha had located themselves strategically in the middle of the coach that pulled up outside Tenison's late one May morning, direct from Charles Edward Brooke Girls' School. We were all on our way to Nantes. Unlike the previous visit to France two years earlier, we had mostly passed through puberty. (I was even starting to show a few hairs, though my voice *still* hadn't dropped.) We knew a bit about girls now, how their bodies operated if not necessarily how their minds worked, and we fully intended to put that knowledge to use. The fact that my friends from school were going to France (Jeff, Chris, Richard, John and more) and my enemies were not (Raymond, Glover and Munro) allowed me to regain the confidence I'd been lacking in the classroom this last year.

So I was among the select group of fourth years who positioned ourselves, instinctively, in the rows directly surrounding Shona and Samantha. Within minutes, and long before we actually set off for Southampton, Shona was sharing the magazine she had been reading – *Jackie*, perhaps? – and I was in the aisle, reading the problem page aloud. There was a letter about bra sizes, and everyone laughed when I quoted it. But when I got to the next one, asking how to deal with exposed pubic hair on the beach, Chris Boyle motioned to me to shut up. It's embarrassing, he mouthed, though whether he meant for me, for them, or for all of us, he didn't let on. I shut up anyway. I didn't figure I had a chance with Shona, but that didn't mean I wanted to make a fool of myself in front of her.

We left that to Richard Heard. In the last few months, Richard had emerged from the shadows of relative anonymity – as a pupil who worked hard and bothered no one and who was strong enough to ensure that no one bothered him either – to become absolutely obsessed with music. He'd not only seen both the Buzzcocks and Blondie in concert, but the Clash and The Jam too, and in recent weeks had come down firmly on the side of the mod revival. On this he was influenced in no small part by his big brother and cousins, a clan of Heards that stretched up and down the A23 from Croydon to Streatham and all the way to the Elephant. The clan was large enough that several of the older ones had formed their own mod revival band (with a left-over punk name, Verge of Insanity), and it showed how quickly the movement was going that we saw them play at the prestigious tourist club the Rock Garden only a couple of weeks after I'd been exposed to the Chords, Purple Hearts, Merton Parkas and Secret Affair.

Richard threw himself into the mod lifestyle with impressive commitment, ordering up a made-to-measure, two-piece, navy blue suit from the Carnaby Cavern shop, which was advertising itself in the back of the music papers as The Jam's tailors of choice. (It may have been. Once.) It cost him £50, a hefty sum of money, and having obtained it only just before the French trip, he made sure to wear it on the bus to France – and pretty much every other day of the trip, too. It wasn't the flashiest suit in the world, especially for those of us who'd been in the same room as Paul Weller, but it was a damn sight sharper than a school uniform. When he added Jam shoes and a Fred Perry shirt, there was no doubt about it: Richard was the Ace Face of the fourth form.

More importantly Richard was my close friend. Earlier that school year, when merely showing up at Tenison's had put me in line for a beating, Richard, almost alone of the entire form, had stuck up for me. Several times, he'd stepped between myself and one of the bullies, told them to back off and, always confident of his own strength, had physically forced the point if need be. He also sat with me in class, subtly coached me in ways to avoid attracting their attention, to fit in better without sacrificing my individuality. And he did all this, knowing full well that we were, affinity for mod aside, cut from a different cloth. Richard was focused on his schoolwork; almost alone of our year, he was already thinking ahead to university and a career. He recognised that I was not. 'For you, mate,' he said one day, shaking his head at me as I was trying to plan my escape from Tenison's ahead of schedule so as to get into central London to sell some more issues of *Jamming*, 'school is just an occupational hazard of being young.'

For Shona, Richard was an occupational hazard of being gorgeous. On the bus to Southampton, spurred on by the Bacardi we had smuggled onto the bus inside bottles of Coke, he was all over her, and by the time our ferry set sail for France, he was literally chasing her up and down the decks. While there was a definite advantage to getting in this early with Shona, the rest of us fourth-year boys considered drinking to be of equal priority, and we headed straight to the bar where, thanks to the laxity (or was it complete lack?) of drinking restrictions on the high seas, we were soon throwing back pints with abandon. Jeff Carrigan, wearing his leather jacket with the same sense of ownership as Richard sported his suit, began channelling the spirit of Sid Vicious, and when he threw up over the side of the ship, it looked like he'd succeeded. Drunk as the rest of us all were, and not a little sea-sick ourselves, we didn't realise that when Shona came into the bar, she was not so much seeking to join us as she was looking for protection from Richard. The way he had his arm around her, we figured that they were a couple already.

Pretty much all of us got off with someone else over the next two weeks, French or English, and yet none of the snogging sessions seemed to affect our friendship with the Charles Edward Brooke girls as a unit. Among my instant new friends was Jeni, a smart, friendly and musically sussed dark-skinned girl who lived alone with her mother opposite the Rosendale pub that was popular with the Dulwich crew; Linda, whose dad was caretaker at Kingsdale, which meant that she lived in the bungalow on the school grounds, right opposite Langbourne; and Jean and Fran, both of whom lived round West Norwood way. None of us doubted that we'd all remain friends once we returned to London, but none of us were keen to look that far ahead. We had our time in Nantes to enjoy first.

Thanks to Chris Boyle quickly becoming drinking partners with the bus driver, we could usually guarantee finding a case of French beer, in conveniently miniature bottles, under the back row every day that we headed out for a day trip. (The CEB girls showed impressive restraint in declining to get drunk with us, though admittedly, some of them, like Shona, *were* only in the third year.) Evenings off, we'd gather in the centre of Nantes, sometimes with our host students, often without, and drink some more. And on the Wednesday afternoon of our second week, the school's half-day, most of us gathered in the garden of Jeni's host family, for a communal outdoor picnic.

Chris was among the few no-shows; he was off touring the bars of Nantes with the bus driver. But Jeff was there, and so was an acoustic guitar, and soon enough he and I were playing music. The fact that I knew the chords to key mod revival songs like 'I Can't Explain' and 'Substitute', 'All Around the World' and '"A" Bomb in Wardour Street', stood me in good stead. And as far as impressing girls went, being able to say that I'd learned the chords to 'Teenage Kicks' from the Undertones themselves was an instant pass to stardom.

But we didn't just play other people's music. We played Jeff's 'Case of Non Conformity', we played what I thought was my astute observation on the punk rock non-revolution, 'Poser's

Paradise', and we played 'Railway Station Love', an entirely juvenile, but enjoyably harmless, rhyming poem I'd put to music. And then we played our ace in the pack. During the couple of months that he had been in the band, Mark may have tried to turn us away from our punk cover versions, and encouraged us to experiment, to get funkier and dirtier and blacker, and he may even have left the group because he knew it would take years for us to do so. But at the same time, he brought with him the most insanely commercial song we had ever heard. It was called 'Summer Holiday', and though it wasn't the Cliff Richard song of the same name, it might as well have been given its unapologetically exuberant nature. Performed on acoustic guitars with a lightweight reggae beat, it relied on a rudimentary chord structure and yet didn't seem any less original because of it. The chorus was a simple refrain: 'It's a summer holiday, all you have to do is pay, and then fly fly fly away.' If there was any sarcasm behind the lyrics we never noticed – and nor did anyone else who heard it. They just reacted like we originally had, exclaiming 'It's a hit!', especially after being subjected to the middle eight, which deftly threw in a couple of minor chords and ended with the sweetest and most uplifting of vocal harmonies, something that Jeff and I were starting to instinctively figure out with each other. When Mark told us he was leaving the band, he said we could keep the song as long as we remembered to credit him as songwriter. We assured him we would do, even as we quickly forgot his last name and soon lost all trace of him.

We didn't forget the song, though. It was so easy to play, so instantly memorable, and we were so fond of it, that we came to regard it as our own. That afternoon in Nantes, we played it again and again and again, because more than anything else in our repertoire, more so than any cover version, including 'Teenage Kicks', it spoke to the moment. We were having the time of our lives.

The same was not true for Shona. She seemed to like Richard, who was, after all, the Ace Face of the fourth form, but it was obvious that she didn't want to spend her whole time in France with him. So she would sit next to him while hanging out with all of us, hoping that the presence of a larger group would prevent him from trying to kiss her. It did not, and by the end of our trip, on the coach home from Southampton, she was no longer talking to him. Some of us might have figured that gave us a chance of our own. Only when we got back to school did we learn that Shona was already seeing Chris.

Richard had asked for it. Literally. Recognising that his aggressive approach had backfired, Richard leaned on Chris, as a good friend and the most mature of the fourth years, to ask Shona out on his behalf. Chris had gracefully accepted his mission, and on the ferry home, taken Shona aside and popped the question: would she go out with Richard? When she responded that she would sooner eat mud (or words to that effect), Chris asked if she had a boyfriend back in London. When she answered negative to that one as well, Chris figured that he'd fulfilled all his obligations to his mate and asked if she fancied going out with him, instead. This time she answered in the affirmative, and the couple wandered off to a lower deck and started snogging. It was, Chris later told us that she had told him, Shona's first proper kiss.

The Monday afternoon back at school, they were at the bus stop together, holding hands, Shona looking genuinely happy in Chris's grip in a way she had never looked with Richard.

Richard, of course, was furious. As far as he was concerned, Shona was his. He had seen her first. He had 'gone out' with her first. He tore off his school jacket, threw down his sports bag, and pushed Chris in the chest.

'Come on then! We'll fight over her!'

Shona looked like she was going to cry. The euphoria of France, the team spirit that had bonded us through the last two ecstatic weeks, had evaporated the moment we found ourselves back on the Brixton Road.

But Chris just laughed, as a 159 bus came along and he and Shona boarded it together, hand in hand.

'I'm not going to fight you,' he said. 'You're my mate.'

Number 17:
FACE IN THE CROWD

Alaska Studios were located in the railway arches almost right behind the Wellington pub in Waterloo, which made them a perfect choice for aspiring mod revival bands, Speedball included. Roger, their manager, had called to tell me that both the band's second guitarist and bassist had left under awkward circumstances (specifically, they were looking at jail for stealing musical equipment on behalf of the group) but that Speedball had a new bass player already and he was so good, they were continuing as a trio. I should come and see them rehearse at Alaska, before conducting the interview for *Jamming* I'd promised him, back at the Moonlight club while Roger was plying me with lager.

I was barely inside the premises when I heard my name. It was Guy, the Who fan I'd met at the Boxing Day party a couple of years ago, the one who'd taught me the chords to 'Substitute' and 'Pinball Wizard'. He was wearing a target T-shirt and a snazzy black chequered jacket, looking every bit the mod. He was Speedball's new bass player.

I was thrilled. We could now resume the friendship that had briefly blossomed that day back in Sydenham. Guy and I had plenty in common: we were each of us South Londoner Who fanatics from musical families, each now convinced of our destiny as rock stars. I had working against me the fact that I couldn't sing. Guy had working against him his last name: Pratt. Curiously, given that most musicians adopted a different last name as a matter of course, he opted not to change it.

Roger had it right: Guy *was* an incredible bass player, an

excellent backing singer too, and he brought personality and looks to the band as well. It didn't occur to me for a moment that as a trio Speedball wouldn't become superstars, and overnight, I started 'following' them. In turn, like the Dulwich crew on the terraces, Speedball adopted me as a mascot. They seemed happy to have me tag along to rehearsals and gigs, despite the fact that I was under-age, would get pissed on a single pint of beer, couldn't afford the cigarettes we were all constantly poncing off each other, and had no idea how to roll a joint. And so, barely a month after our school trip to France, Speedball invited me to come with them to Southend for a Saturday night. They were playing in Bishop's Stortford the next day, at a mod festival with the Merton Parkas and a band called the Mods. (Yes. *The Mods.*) We could make a road trip of it. We would stay at Robin's house on Queen's Road, where he was one of three people paying rent on the place.

'There'll be a few more than that staying the night though,' he said as we set off in his car from a lunchtime rendezvous at the Wellington. 'There usually are.' The house had, he said, somehow become a halfway home for some of the city's most damaged teenagers. As with Jeff's friends in Hastings, they were mods, punks and skinheads alike – all aligned against the teddy boys who, said Robin, occasionally attacked the house at weekends. Just as long as I knew.

I expected to find a fortress. What I got, instead, was a run-down terraced house that could as easily have been buried in the depths of South London. There was nothing to it. No character, no charm, nothing but the barest essentials. Out back, though, in the garden, we found a tall, handsome mod in an impeccably tailored suit busy admiring the latest addition to his scooter. Whether it was yet another wing mirror (there were about ten of them), or the perfect painting of Southend Pier along the body, I couldn't tell, but it was a beautiful bike all the same. Robin introduced me.

'This is Charlie,' he said.

Charlie looked me over. I wasn't dressed like a mod; I had

no interest in following fashion like that. This made me something of an outsider, and he seemed suspicious of my intent. Eventually offering a nod of acceptance, Charlie then went back to examining his scooter, soaking up the admiration of the other mods. He would not be coming to the concert the next day; he had a scooter run in Margate to go on instead. He was the real deal, I concluded – before Robin let on, in private, that only a few months ago Charlie had been a skinhead.

Charlie would, however, be joining us at the party that night. A couple of teenage sisters with a fancy house on the posh side of town; parents away for whatever reason; invites extended round the pub the previous weekend. All that was needed to guarantee its success was some speed.

I'd never seen speed. But you couldn't be a fan of The Who, the Sex Pistols, or *Deep Purple in Rock* for that matter, and get into your teens without coming to understand its importance. The notion of it appealed to my mentality, which was to get up and go go go, much more so than the occasional puff of cannabis I'd taken, which had a habit of making me slow down and eventually just stop. So when a cheerful-looking salesman in full mod regalia showed up at the house with a sports bag that seemed to be practically full of little blue pills, five for a quid, I was instantly in for my pound.

The pills were about the size of aspirin, and like aspirin they could be broken in half if you felt the need. Nothing about them suggested that they would turn you into a junkie. I put mine in my jeans pocket and asked Guy and Robin to let me know when it would be time to pop them. About an hour before we planned to set off for the party, I was summoned to the kitchen and offered a swig from a can of weak beer. I took it and swallowed a couple of my pills. And then I waited for them to take effect.

Nothing happened at first. So I began tagging around Robin and Guy, more closely than usual, asking when I could expect the speed to take effect. After I asked the question for the tenth time in a row, Guy looked at me, with a broad smile matched by a gleam in his eye.

'Mate!' he said. 'I think it has!'

He was right. I felt a surge of energy, much more instant and powerful than a can of Coke. I felt more alert with it, too, like all my senses were becoming more finely attuned than usual. And I experienced a rush of urgency, as if it was incredibly important that we get to the party NOW! in case we miss anything. My impatience finally wore down my friends. Robin gave us a lift to the party house. On the way we stopped at an off-licence to pick up carry-outs of beer. Robin got some chewing gum as well, and threw me a packet when we returned to the car.

'I think you're going to need it,' he said. I noticed that I had, yes, started chewing, despite myself. I was speeding, all right.

So was almost everyone else at the party. Punks, mods, straights (of which there were several) and skins (of which there were mercifully few) – everyone had the same sense of urgency about them. And all of them seemed out of place in such luxurious surroundings. The fully detached house, located in a leafy suburb, smelled of upper-middle-class wealth. The furniture was expensive, the stereo tasteful, the bedrooms refined. It was like somewhere back in Dulwich Village. Or Sydenham, where I'd first met Guy.

In my urgency to do something, I decided to find the hosts. I went to the kitchen and asked one of the mods there, someone who seemed to know what was going on, to point them out to me.

'Oh, they're not here,' he said, chewing furiously.

'They went out?' I asked.

'We haven't seen them,' he replied. 'When we got here, there was no one home.'

'So who let you in?'

He looked at me like I was some kind of idiot. 'We let ourselves in,' he snorted.

'You mean you *broke* in?'

He opened the fridge, looking for a beer perhaps. There weren't any.

'The girls said they were having a party,' he explained, leaving it there. He closed the door again. 'You should see yourself in the mirror, mate,' he laughed as he headed on into the living room, where a dozen or so people were half-dancing to sixties music.

I followed his recommendation, went into the toilet. Sure enough, my pupils had all but disappeared. I went to take a pee. My willy had vanished too. I eventually found it, shrivelled to the size of a peanut, flattened against my balls. I shook it loose, tried to pee. It wasn't happening.

I headed out to the garden, got talking to a lovely-looking modette. Or was she a skin-girl? Both wore Fred Perry shirts, knee-length skirts and loafers. But skin-girls cut their hair short on top and let it grow long round the edges, often dyeing it blonde for dramatic effect; the look was instantly sexy and hard with it. Mod girls, even if they cut their hair short, didn't go for the shaved or dyed look, and you felt less endangered talking to them.

I didn't feel endangered talking to this girl. (I was speeding. I didn't feel endangered by *anything*!) Her name was Karen, she was sixteen, and she seemed intrigued by my rapid-fire talk about my fanzine and my band and my recent trip to France and my friendship with Speedball and my interviews with Paul Weller and Pete Townshend . . . We hung out in the garden together for what seemed like ages, talking about youth fashion and how silly it all was and The Jam and how great they were and what we were going to do in the years to come. At some point she told me she'd just chucked her boyfriend.

'He wasn't worth the effort,' she said.

'I know what you mean,' I enthused. 'Girls aren't worth the effort either.'

She wandered off soon after. I kicked myself. Robin came up to console me, talked about her reputation. He mentioned the word 'abortion'. It was intended to make me feel better, but I just kicked myself harder. That meant she'd had sex. Maybe I could have been in there if I hadn't said the wrong thing in my speed-ridden urgency to say *anything*. Then I remembered my peanut-sized willy and knew that even if she'd thrown herself at me, I'd have been incapable of getting it up.

I didn't notice who got to the party first: the short-cropped hard case – straight out of borstal as word rapidly went round the house – or the boy in mascara, lipstick, earrings and a blouse. I hadn't really seen someone like this boy before, not just openly homosexual but a transvestite, and I was fascinated by his confidence, despite his surroundings. When Borstal Boy started threatening him, he simply returned the insults, with additional bitchiness. But then the insults grew louder, the tension more apparent, until Borstal Boy threw a vicious punch to the gay boy's face . . .

And the gay boy promptly threw one right back, just as hard . . . at which the two of them were off, careening round the room like pinballs, smashing ornaments, breaking glasses. After letting them go at it for a minute or so, some of the mods stepped in, pulled the pair apart. The gay boy looked like he'd come off worst, but he was more concerned about the blood on his blouse than whose blood it may have been. Fearless or foolish – most likely, both – he held his ground and stayed at the party until the bitter end.

That came soon after closing time, signified by a scream of terror. I went to check it out, and found two girls crying near the front door, one in the other's arms. They were good-looking girls, but they weren't fashionable. Not mods, not punks, not skins. Just your average middle-class teenage girls.

'What the fucking hell?' one of them kept screaming. 'What the fuck is everyone doing here?'

'We're here for your party,' someone wisecracked. It was the mod I'd spoken to in the kitchen.

'What party? When did we ever say we were having a party?'

'Last weekend, at the Lion. You told everyone.' The mod

was smirking now. You couldn't help but wonder if there wasn't some history between them.

'Fuck off, Gary!' the girl swore. 'You and every one of your fucking stupid fucking friends can fuck off.' And then she started crying again. Her sister, the younger of the two, didn't say anything. Her expression, one of total and complete shock, told the entire story.

They did what they needed to. They called the police. Hearing as much, Robin and Guy suggested I follow them into the back garden. There we found Dave, Speedball's drummer, snogging a girl. It was Karen, the one I'd been chatting with earlier. It didn't bother me, though. Dave was nineteen, six foot tall, seriously good-looking. He was also the drummer in Southend's leading mod band. I'd been right all along: I'd never stood a chance.

Within ten minutes, a police car pulled up out front. Robin and Guy waited until they could hear the voice of authority from inside the house and then led us round the front to where Robin's car was parked. Despite the speeding, the drinking, the fighting and the arrival of the police, their work ethic had kicked in. There was a gig tomorrow and they wanted to make sure they'd be around to see it.

The night was not over though. Not by a long stretch. I'd popped my remaining pills over the course of the evening and now I was flying. No *way* was I ready for bed. Back at Queen's Road, we hung out in the kitchen instead, all of us talking furiously about everything in the world as we cursed the British licensing laws, made cups of instant coffee and talked some more.

Soon enough, others from the party arrived. Turned out that the two cops had been unable to establish control, and had called for back-up. Some of the partygoers had felt the need to act tough, and the whole thing had escalated. People were pushed, punches were thrown, and Borstal Boy was under arrest. Again. Nobody expected him to make bail. Nobody seemed that bothered, either.

With no alcohol to consume, and everyone out of speed – so they claimed – the night gradually ground to a halt. Robin headed off to a private bedroom, his reward for paying rent. Guy claimed another room, his own reward for suddenly pulling one of the mod girls who'd come back to the house. There didn't seem to have been any interaction; it was like they just attached themselves to each other out of late-night need. I headed upstairs to the 'spare' bedroom, and only just in time. One couple had already taken one single bed, and another couple quickly grabbed the other. Two more people laid down on the floor, and one settled into an armchair. I laid out on what had once passed for a sofa. Eight of us in the one room. No one seemed to find it the slightest bit unusual.

The one couple went straight to sleep. The other did not. They had sex, instead. They did so under the covers, so it wasn't like I could see everything. But it was unmistakable all the same. She was on her back, knees up and soles down, each of her legs forming a perfect triangle. He was wedged in between her, forcing the sheets up and down with his arse. They made a lot of noise, though her panting was much louder. I couldn't help paying attention. I'd never seen people at it before. I'd never heard a woman make these sounds before. Besides, I was still speeding, furiously. It wasn't like I could sleep.

The boy came, loudly, and the girl made all these wild sounds like she was going through something similar, something I had read about in the magazines but still couldn't quite imagine. Then they sat up, lit cigarettes and started talking, like none of us were there. I peered out of the corner of my eye: they were sat on the edge of the bed, and I could see the shape of her tits against the window. She was good-looking, with blue hair, something you didn't see too often. He was your regular teenage street type. They were only fifteen. I knew as much because they told each other. They talked, too, about where they came from – neither of them seemed to have a home as far as I could tell – and their hopes for a future that didn't seem to extend much further than the promise to spend it together. And when they were done talking, they got back under the covers – and had sex again. Same positions, same movements, same noises. The rest of the room stayed silent.

Then someone screamed. I sat up just in time to see a cockroach scurrying across the floor and under the sofa I was using for a bed. A couple of people swore, though whether in annoyance at being woken up or disgust at seeing a cockroach in the bedroom, I couldn't be sure. One by one, they went back to sleep. The young lovers resumed having sex. And after they'd come for the second time, they too called it a night. Me, I just carried on staring at the ceiling, jaws snapping open and shut as they had been for hours. Five pills for a quid. A night of euphoria for the price of a pint and a half of lager. This is the best feeling in the modern world, I kept saying to myself, until exhaustion finally took over and somehow, I surrendered to the night.

'Look at 'im! He's still speeding.'

I opened my eyes again. My jaw instantly clamped shut again. Then threw itself back open, involuntarily. It was true. I had succeeded in snatching some sleep out of sheer necessity, but the amphetamine hadn't yet worked its way through my bloodstream. That was fine, I figured. I'd just enjoyed a whole night's high for a pound and it looked like it would carry me through the day as well.

Around lunchtime, I rode with Robin and Guy to Bishop's Stortford, a full hour away. Guy had ditched his girl already, though he carried with him the glow of someone satisfied by his pulling prowess. Robin was focused on the gig. Dave followed along in a van that carried the equipment – and he gave the young lovers from my bedroom a lift in the back. I helped unload the gear, and the couple took advantage of the free space to lie down under a sleeping bag they'd found. They didn't seem so much in love any more.

'What's up with them?' I asked Dave, as I helped wheel an amp into the hall.

'Comedown,' he said. 'They've run out of speed.'

So? I had too. More than twelve hours ago. It didn't seem a big deal. Although the buzz I'd found upon wakening had gradually dissipated over the course of the day, and although I was starting to feel tired, it didn't seem anything to get down about.

. . . And then it hit me. Like a runaway train hitting a brick wall, I crashed, hard. I couldn't do anything about it. I couldn't do *anything*, full stop. I felt physically sick, but I couldn't throw up. I felt hungry but I knew that I couldn't eat. I felt thirsty but I didn't know what for. I walked into the dressing room and sat down. Tried smiling. My expression told the others all they needed to know.

'Mate!' exclaimed Guy. 'You're looking rough!'

How come *you're* not feeling it, I wanted to say, but I couldn't get the words out. It was suggested I go outside and get some fresh air.

I took the advice, but I couldn't walk far. I lay down, instead, on the grass verge surrounding the venue. The migraine had engulfed me now completely. I just lay there, inviting the evening to pass me by. I missed Speedball's set. I missed the Mods. At one point, I heard the Merton Parkas playing their single – 'You need a car, if you want to go far' – but otherwise, I didn't pay attention to the music seeping out of the hall. I slept, instead. Out there in the open air. Nobody bothered to wake me, to ask if I was all right, to figure out if I was alive or dead.

I was finally brought to by the sound of the crowd: 'We are the mods, we are the mods, we are we are we are the mods.' I dared open my eyes; sure enough, a small army of parka-clad sixteen-year-old mods were half-marching, half-skipping out of the venue, back to their suburban homes. The gig was over. And I was suddenly very cold.

I got back to my feet, and I noticed something missing. The migraine. It had passed. I'd somehow got through it. I'd battled my way through the comedown and I was still alive to tell the tale. In fact, I felt oddly exuberant, like I'd passed a test. Not the kind of test you sat at school. This was a life test, a journey, and, despite a few stumbles along the way, I'd made it to the finish line.

In the dressing room, the members of Speedball were relieved to see me – they weren't unaware that they'd brought a fifteen-year-old along for the weekend and carried some accountability for my well-being. The Merton Parkas were covered in post-gig sweat, looking pleased with themselves. The young lovers were laid out on the floor in front of us all – the van having become too cold for them – looking like I must have done a couple of hours earlier. Like they were dead.

But they weren't my concern. Or Speedball's. Or anyone's, come to that. I accepted the offer of a beer, and a cigarette, and a lift back to West Dulwich from Roger. It was a long drive, two or three hours around the ring roads of London, and we didn't get home until the middle of the night. Only when we were close did I realise that I hadn't called home the entire weekend. But then I hadn't time. Hadn't seen a phone. To be honest, it never occurred to me. I was too busy speeding through life.

Number 16:
BOYS KEEP SWINGING

Pete Townshend was not entirely against my suggestion of a joint interview with Paul Weller, when I successfully got him on the phone after a couple of calls to his office at Eel Pie. The idea had been raised before – in 1977, the *NME*'s Tony Parsons had set off with Weller, after a night on the piss, hoping to run into Townshend at the Speakeasy or somewhere – and given that I had just interviewed the two mod icons back to back, I thought I had a fighting chance of pulling it off. Paul, certainly, was up for it. We'd maintained regular contact in the months since the Great British Music Festival; Paul had even called me at home to tell me I was on the guest list for the Music Machine show at Christmas. He'd caught me the day I brought my report card home for the term, in the midst of a massive family argument concerning its noting of my multiple 'absences' that term, which my brother pointed out in no uncertain terms to my mother, who then picked up the phone when it rang and shouted into it as if it was part of the debate; I offered apologies to Paul, explained the situation as best I could and in his understanding laugh of a response felt my street credibility gain valuable points.

Townshend asked me to let him 'think about it', after which I couldn't get him on the phone again. In the absence of my ideal exclusive, I took the opposite path: I decided to make the next *Jamming* a 'New Group Special'. Along with Speedball, I interviewed the Chords – cornering, so I figured, the two best bands on the scene. Jeff sat down with the Teenbeats in Hastings, and I interviewed Verge of Insanity largely because they were mates of my mate, which, given that we were suddenly all socialising and going to gigs a lot and drinking too much for our age and occasionally popping little blue pills, meant they were fast becoming my own mates too. But I was not about to turn *Jamming* into a mod fanzine. I'd been to the Marquee to see the Human League, all synthesisers and drum machines and lop-sided haircuts, and had been impressed by the opening act. Spizz Energi were just a duo; they changed name every year (in 1978 it had been Spizz Oil); and Spizz was unapologetic about writing humorous songs like 'Where's Captain Kirk?' I contrasted his light-hearted outlook with my 'piece' on the Homosexuals, who I still couldn't figure out but who had just released an incredible 12-inch EP of six indefinable songs, in a pink paper sleeve intended to highlight their name, I supposed.

I invited Jeffries to write about his favourite band from Deptford, and some fanzine-exchanging friends up in Paisley, a particularly rough part of Glasgow that I was happy to keep at pen-pal distance, to write about their own scene. I asked another fanzine editor, Johnny Waller, who had just set up his own label, to pen a piece about 'D.I.Y. Records', which I accompanied with a full-page chart breaking down the costs of several recent self-pressed singles. I wrote a piece myself about getting gigs, based on my complete failure to do so as yet for my own band. I made sure the singles I reviewed were all by relatively unknown acts (i.e., the ones I was getting for free in the post), wrote up a bunch of other fanzines, dedicated some space to newer Rough Trade bands, and printed a couple of live reviews by a reader in Birmingham.

To cap it all, I wrote a two-page opinion piece about the mod revival. With what some would have called arrogance but Weller might have condoned as 'confidence', I called *Maximum Speed* 'the biggest and the bigotest' of fanzines, damned the Purple Hearts for telling people to 'stop pogoing', dismissed Squire and the Killimeters as 'not worth the space' and concluded by asking, 'What will be left in six months?' As if this apparent condemnation wasn't confusing enough given that the same issue included overnight mod revivalists like my mates in Verge of Insanity, I printed the piece over a hand-drawn red-and-blue target background – because, all of a sudden, we were printing *Jamming* in multiple colours.

I had Joly to thank for this. Having fine-tuned his printing press, he suggested that if I let him print a page or two of *Jamming* in whatever colour was on the press that day for his badges, he could save time and (as a result) we could both save money. We could then apply some of those savings to additional colours per page – a photo in blue, the type in red, that kind of thing. Joly then made another suggestion. He'd continue to print *Jamming* at cost if I would point other struggling fanzines his way. Almost every other fanzine was struggling. It was a no-lose scenario.

The result was not just the best written, most energetic, musically varied and yet thoroughly contemporary *Jamming* to date, but the most colourful – and easily the best value: thirty-six pages in all, only three of which were ads. For the first time, I had a fanzine I was truly proud of. And despite the absence of big names, I couldn't staple them fast enough; I was forced to hold regular 'collating' parties in my bedroom attended by my new friend Jeni and other girls from CEB, which in turn brought Tenisonian boys, suddenly eager to 'help collate' too. Rough Trade took 100 copies, money up front, sent them all round the country, and soon came back for more. (Eventually I got a handful returned to find that members of Swell Maps, working at Rough Trade, had written their own review of my review of their LP across the page. It wasn't favourable.) Virgin Marble Arch sold fifty copies almost immediately. The Purple Hearts slagged me off in the *NME* and made me look way more influential than I thought I was. The *Young Observer*, the 'youth' section at the back of the leading Sunday newspaper's magazine, finally ran an interview (and photo) that had been conducted with Jeff and myself in my bedroom several months earlier – in an issue with Pete Townshend on the cover. Other music papers now habitually referred to *Jamming* as 'one of the major fanzines', and I discovered how perception becomes reality. And so, as well as toting copies round the record stores, I started working up the courage to walk up to strangers at gigs and ask, 'Do you want to buy a fanzine?'

Sometimes it worked. I came home from a Teenbeats gig at the Fulham Greyhound with an empty sports bag and about £10 in loose change in my pockets. But that same week, I went to see Spizz Energi at the Nashville and was met with outright hostility. One punk took a copy from me, flicked through it and then threw it back in my face.

'It's all fuckin' niggers and mods,' he spat. Perhaps he had meant queers – as in, the Homosexuals – because to *Jamming*'s shame, there wasn't a single black face in the entire issue.

Quite why Spizz, who openly disdained politics, had attracted such a malevolent following remained a mystery. But it was sufficiently hardcore that a group of skinheads came to the Nashville that night to do battle with them. The police were called to ensure they didn't force their way in, and by the time we left the gig, the skinheads had moved on. The threat of violence, however, had not. After the gig, on the platform of the above-ground West Kensington tube station next door, a couple of punks started fighting. It was a terrace-style fight, with a blow to the stomach forcing the recipient's head down instinctively, allowing the attacker to follow up swiftly with a boot to the face, from which there was no recourse and it was just a matter of how badly the one wanted to maim the other. I didn't get to see the eventual extent of the beating. Like everyone else, I merely boarded the approaching train as if nothing was happening. We'd seen it before. We'd see it again.

Within the hour, it turned out, a couple of sixteen-year-old punks who had also been to the Spizz gig were stabbed by teddy boys or, depending on accounts, their approximate contemporaries, the newly revived 'rockabillies', down in the Elephant and Castle tube station, and more or less at midnight. John Matthews knew them like he knew everyone round that area; he was visibly upset about it at school the next day. All this violence was not exactly unrelated to the fact that *Quadrophenia* had finally opened in the West End that same night. Even before its release, the tabloids had used the upcoming film as an excuse to put teenage tribalism on the front pages. Now, you didn't need any more reason to attract trouble than to look like you were part of a youth cult. And if you were young, and into music or fashion, it was almost impossible *not* to look like you were part of a youth cult.

The arrival on the scene of the Specials only served to further confuse the matter. Their single 'Gangsters' – championed, but of course, by John Peel – sounded alien, the way all great records did when they (apparently) came out of nowhere, and it was vaguely menacing; there was a tension to the song that couldn't be put down to the choice of studio. 'Gangsters' was reggae at double-speed: ska, it was called, the sound of late-sixties Jamaica before the music got stoned and went global thanks to Bob Marley, and the Specials were intent on reviving it.

The Specials were five whites and a couple of blacks from Coventry, the British car-building capital rapidly going bust, and they put out 'Gangsters' on their own label, 2 Tone. The label's logo was a drawing of a sharp-dressed man in a black and white suit; he was, apparently, a 'rude boy' – a style named after the black Jamaican ska kids of the sixties, many of whom had emigrated with their families to England during the post-war wave of Caribbean immigration. In the film *Quadrophenia*, there was a prototype of these black rude boys among the lead characters. He was the drug dealer, of course.

That piece of stereotyping was only one of many in the film – none of which served to make it any the less enjoyable. *Quadrophenia* was a riot. It glorified teenage sex, it glorified teenage drug abuse, and, especially, it glorified teenage mob violence. Phil Daniels put in the greatest portrayal of a teenager we'd ever seen, taking the working-class mod Jimmy of Pete Townshend's imagination and turning him into a living, breathing, fighting, fucking fool, one who – because, not despite, all his evident faults – swiftly became every young male's icon. Leslie Ash, as the object of his affections, the beautiful super-market checkout girl Steph, similarly became every young male's wet dream. (Who didn't wish they could have been Phil Daniels as he groped his way through a shag with Ash in a Brighton back alley in the midst of a riot?) The Ace Face turned bellboy was played by Sting, the singer with that formerly forgotten group of part-time punks, the Police, and so effectively so that they received a new lease of life and began topping the singles charts. *Outlandos d'Amour*, the debut album that the *NME*'s Ian Penman wouldn't even listen to upon its release, took up permanent residency in the Top Ten. All the film's other key characters had equally identifiable personalities that seemed no less relevant to the present day. Similarly, the suburban party at the start of the film was almost a perfect portrayal of the night I'd just spent in Southend. The world had turned, these last fifteen years, but it hadn't much changed.

The violence in *Quadrophenia* was a fair re-enactment of what had taken place on the streets of London and the beaches of Brighton during the mod heyday of the early 1960s. But with the mod and skinhead revivals in full swing, and the rude boy suddenly thrown in the mix, it couldn't have been re-enacted at a worse time; it was like setting fire to a powder keg with a blowtorch. You couldn't necessarily blame The Who for this – they'd built their reputation on unapologetic violence – but then they weren't the ones who bore the brunt of the film's popularity. That fell to us, the kids on the streets.

All right, so I wasn't exactly a product of the streets. (Our Brummie teacher, the one who grew up with Steel Pulse in Handsworth, took the piss out of the piece in the *Young Observer*, noting that 'Anthony from Dulwich' did not have the same ring to it as 'Tony from Norwood'.) But many of my friends were working class, and as we travelled, increasingly in packs now, from tube to bus to gig to pub on an almost nightly basis, we seemed to be spending an increasing amount of time in the great outdoors.

Evidence came from the unlikeliest of sources: *Harpers &
Queen*, a fashion magazine that was so upscale, I'd never heard
of it. Neither had Jeff, who called me at home over the summer
to tell me that, nonetheless, there was a photo of me in it. His
mum, who worked a menial job at a fancy car showroom in
Mayfair, had been flicking through the new issue there, only
to find that someone called Peter York had run a piece on the
mod revival, and that somehow, we were the stars.

When I finally found a newsagent posh enough to sell *Harpers
& Queen* (in Dulwich Village, not surprisingly), there we were,
under the headline 'Mods: The Second Coming'. In a picture
captioned 'The new, post-punk mods, photographed for *Jamming*,
one of their fanzines', five teenagers stood posing against a brick
wall. Four were wearing green army parkas, at least three were
in Verge of Insanity, and one proudly sported the band's logo
– the group's name wrapped around a mod target. My mate
Richard Heard leaned over his cousins' shoulders from the back
of the gang, a black tie worn loosely round an unbuttoned
collar, his eyes betraying the effects either of speed, alcohol,
or just a youthful love of the flash lens. In front of them all,
staring down the camera with his own brand of cockiness, stood
a chubby kid with unkempt blond hair in a black vinyl jacket
and a pink and purple, button-down, hand-me-down shirt that
had, thanks to the Buzzcocks' single sleeves, recently become
fashionable – and that was me.

I'd never seen the picture before. Nor had Jeff, and he had
taken it. After doing so, it turned out, he had given the film
to a neighbouring kid from Tenison's who claimed access to a
dark room. That kid obviously had access to the world of
Harpers & Queen as well because he sold the magazine the
negatives, no questions asked, no permission (from me or Jeff)
granted. *Harpers & Queen* then captioned another of Jeff's
photos as 'an original mod' from the sixties when it was, in
fact, Huggy from the Teenbeats, walking on the Hastings beachfront just a few weeks earlier. You might have guessed as much
from the fashions and the cars and the storefronts around Huggy,

but then The Who hadn't worried about such matters either when they filmed *Quadrophenia*: spotting modern road signs and latter-era import Who LPs was part of the fun of watching the film a second or third time.

Jeff's mum, though, was not one to take such matters lightly, and she made phone calls all the way up the publishing chain until she reached Peter York himself, at which she gave him an earful for ripping off her son's photography. On top of that, she said, she couldn't understand the bloody story. She wasn't alone. York asserted that the *London Weekend Show* special hosted by Janet Street-Porter had condemned the mod revival to a short lifespan, a point I'd also made in *Jamming* (though it was the *Quadrophenia* film's high-street success that really signalled the movement's instant journey from underground to overdone). He also wrote how Street-Porter had studied architecture, which seemed totally irrelevant. But then we were coming at it from different angles. My rant about mod in the latest issue of *Jamming* was from the perspective of a kid who'd grown up on The Who and The Jam and hoped that the revival might have some creativity and unity to it. York focused relentlessly on class: 'the punk idea of working-class authenticity', 'the original mods (as) working-class suburbanites who rejected the factory wage-slave thing . . .' And so on. Eventually, because I remained genuinely pissed off about the whole thing, Jeff's mum got Peter York to call me at home and, just as I thought, he had a posh accent. I couldn't get over the feeling that he was looking down on us all from some ivory tower of high fashion, selling his theories to rich people who wouldn't dare attend the Wellington at lunchtime, let alone stand on the platform at West Kensington tube station after a gig at the Nashville while someone was getting their head kicked in alongside them. And nothing came along to change my mind.

My anger at *Harpers & Queen* was partly from being labelled in the photographs as a mod. I wasn't a mod. I wasn't a punk either. I wasn't a rude boy. And I certainly wasn't a skin. All

this labelling of cults, as far as I was concerned, was a joke.
But I was just as addicted to the idea of looking good as anyone
else my age who was going to gigs, and I needed to make my
own fashion statement. Back when I'd first met him, Joly had
been advertising, alongside his badges, 'teddy bear jumpers',
which he fashioned out of the material used to make cuddly
toys. Being Joly, he did so in Rastafarian colours – red, gold
and green – which made them especially lurid. I bartered one
from him around the time he printed the first *Jamming* for me,
and took to wearing it religiously. (Rastafarianism was, after
all, a genuine creed, one that viewed the Emperor Haile Selassie
of Ethiopia as the reincarnation of Christ on Earth, women as
second-class subjects, and ganja as an essential part of the daily
diet. I didn't buy into this any more than I thought Jesus had
risen from the dead in the first place, but I liked Rastafarians
all the same – the real ones at least, the ones with the dreadlocks grown from neither cutting nor washing their hair, the
ones who didn't eat meat or drink alcohol, the ones who were
genuinely peaceful types. You could usually tell them apart from
the violent wannabes on the Railton Road and Ladbroke Grove;
you just had to be quick about it.)

My red, gold and green teddy bear jumper was hard to ignore.
In fact, it stood out so brightly that I bought a pair of tight
red jeans on the King's Road just to take people's eyes off it.
And trusting in the assumption that anyone who looked this
outlandish couldn't possibly be worth fighting, I regularly took
to the streets dressed like this. Somehow, it worked. Punks
would be kicking each other to death on the tube platform,
skins would be ready to maim anyone who so much as looked
at them the wrong way, and the last bus home would be full
of drunk straights just aching for someone to kill, but this
flumpy fifteen-year-old in a kaleidoscope of colours. . . for some
reason, I wasn't even accused of being gay. In fact, strangers
regularly came up to me and asked me where I got the jumper.
My friends came up to me, though, and told me that the red
jeans were so tight you could make out my balls – but not my

willy. I decided I needed something else to identify myself by.

I found it at Camden Market early in the summer. One of the stalls was selling a genuine Chelsea Pensioner's tunic, bright red with a high black rounded collar and golden buttons. It was something straight out of the *Sgt. Peppers Lonely Hearts Club Band* cover. The mod revival was firmly rooted in 1965. The skinhead/rude boy scene was 1969. But *Sgt. Peppers* had come out in 1967, during the psychedelic era in between, and though I disliked hippies and their tie-dye clothes and kaftan coats and open-toed sandals and the like, the *Sgt. Peppers* look had never dated. I tried it on and it fitted me like a glove. It cost £5, as much as I'd ever spent on an item of clothing. But my money box at home was rattling with loose change from selling *Jamming* for full price at gigs; I had just about paid off the three different printers. I bought it. And the next time I stopped in to see The Jam at the Town House, I wore it with pride.

Number 15:
LITTLE BOY SOLDIERS

The Town House was a recording studio on the Goldhawk Road, just off Shepherd's Bush Green in West London. If The Jam had been trying to distance themselves from the mod revival, they couldn't have picked a worse location. The Goldhawk Road was well known as The Who's old stomping ground, and half the *Quadrophenia* film, it seemed, had been filmed on the very streets that surrounded the studio. Sure enough, if you stopped into the Town House to watch The Jam at work, you'd often bump into the Goldhawk Road mods, who'd be doing much the same thing.

The Jam never announced an open door policy in the studio; it only felt that way. Paul had invited me to come and watch the group at work on the new album before we conducted a fresh interview for *Jamming* (and this time with the whole band), and when I was there he let it be known I was welcome to come back, and on the occasions that I brought schoolfriends with me, I was never told off for it. My confidence had grown over the twelve months since I'd first met Paul Weller at RAK, thanks to the success of *Jamming* (in which Paul had played a major part), and I felt genuinely comfortable in The Jam's company. Besides, thanks to their own success with *All Mod Cons*, the mood in the studio was constantly cheerful – even though the control room was sometimes so crowded with Goldhawk Road mods that you couldn't see from the mixing board to the recording room. At that point, Paul might drop a hint, but nobody ever took it, so it would be left to John Weller and Kenny Wheeler, when they arrived late in the afternoon from the 'office', to banish everyone to the lounge in the hopes that they'd get bored and go home. The lounge had a full-sized pool table and an incredible new 'arcade' game called Space Invaders. It also had a kettle and a fridge. Why would anyone go home?

That summer, The Jam released another single, 'When You're Young', and as far as I was concerned, it was the best record in the world, *ever*. The music was part of it: The Jam were clearly on fire at this point, and there was something contagiously joyous about the song's vaguely off-beat mod-rock rhythm, especially the attempted dub breakdown towards the end. But it was the lyrics that were most of it. 'Life is timeless, days are long when you're young,' sang Weller in the opening line, as if he had climbed right inside my fifteen-year-old head. As the song ran on, it became clear that he was warning me my dreams would turn to shit, but frankly, I didn't give a damn. I preferred the lifeline he offered us on the other side, that 'you don't mind you got time on your side, and they're never gonna make you stand in line.'

A few months earlier, upon the release of 'Strange Town', Weller had given an interview insisting that, at twenty, he was too old to keep writing youth anthems, but even if 'When You're Young' was intended otherwise, he'd only gone and penned his best yet. I played the single night and day all summer long. My mates knew I was obsessed with it, in a way I hadn't been with any previous Jam single, and they all knew I had a right to be, what with my constant running round town like the world was about to end and I had to achieve everything I'd set out to do in life before it did. None of them tried to talk me down from my high. Besides, they all wanted to hang out at the Town House.

Richard Heard was my obvious companion, not so much because he was a mod, or that he worshipped the very fag ends that Weller routinely crushed under his Shelley's shoes on the carpet of the Town House control room, but because he was my best mate. Richard was a wannabe Weller, and Paul would have spotted that a mile off, but he was intelligent with it, damn good-looking and not bad at holding his own in the kind of verbal sparring that was routine in the studio. If I *am* going to influence a whole generation of kids, Paul might have said to himself, I could do worse than have them turn out like this one.

Jeff was another obvious companion, because he was my bandmate. *And* my best mate. (When you're young, you're allowed to have more than one.) With Jeff around things could be more dicey, because he hadn't outgrown his devotion to Sid Vicious, Paul's old nemesis, and he didn't even proclaim himself a Jam fan to begin with. When I sat down for the big interview with the whole group, Jeff came along to take pictures and ask the occasional question. (Richard came along to hang out and look good.) Yet the moment the tape recorder was turned on, the band clammed up, as if I was a total stranger, another cynical member of the music press. It could have been the same nervousness I'd sensed from Paul when I interviewed him a year ago, though I suspected something must have gone wrong in the studio that morning, because for the first twenty minutes Bruce Foxton was visibly sullen, unable to look Paul in the eye. Questions about The Jam's place in the grand scheme of things, their sense of purpose, met with almost complete silence. I'd have taken my tape and run if I didn't already know them better. So I persisted. Eventually, the conversation turned to Squire and Secret Affair, bands The Jam had known before they jumped on the mod revival. A few comparisons between Ian Page and Jimmy Pursey as youth 'spokesmen' loosened us up. By the time I raised the subject of the Boomtown Rats, who were regularly topping the charts now while The Jam were languishing in the back of the Top Twenty, they were raring to go.

'Why is it you love Bob Geldof so much?' I asked, in on the joke.

'Cos he's a wonderfully "fab" person,' said Paul.

'He's "hip", isn't he?' said Rick.

'He's "in",' said Bruce.

'He's "number one",' said Paul.

Jeff looked on, nonplussed. 'Is that sarcastic or what?' he asked.

Good old Jeff. Once the laughter subsided, there was no looking back.

'But what is it you actually hold against him?' I persisted about Bob Geldof.

'I'd like to hold an iron bar against him,' muttered Bruce, warming at last to the occasion.

'Moving on from the Boomtown Rats . . .' I said.

'Stepping over them, you mean,' said Bruce.

'. . . How are you getting on with Polydor at the moment?' I asked.

'Great, we've been going out for two years now,' said Bruce.

Rick couldn't help himself. 'Haven't you fingered it yet?'

Paul laughed as hard as any of us. 'I dare you to put that in,' he said to me, meaning the quote, and so I did.

The cult of Paul Weller constantly overshadowed the presence of Bruce Foxton and Rick Buckler in The Jam. Paul was conventionally pretty and thousands of girls – and boys – were totally in love with him. But Bruce evinced a rock star confidence of his own, a cockiness even, and that too served as an aphrodisiac. With his punked-up hair and his muscular build, his tight jeans and T-shirts, he ran Paul a close second in the icon stakes. Rick had neither the looks, the haircut, nor the advantage of being up front of the stage, and he didn't seem to give a shit. He could be found many afternoons at the Town House flicking through the latest issue of a *Mayfair* or *Playboy*, as if, like me and my mates, it was the closest he was coming to naked women. I wanted to look at the magazines myself, but I wasn't sure it was cool to do so any more, because everybody involved in anything that had descended from punk was, surely, anti-sexist, and it didn't get much more sexist than paying women to take off their clothes for a dirty magazine.

Still, if the interview that lunchtime displayed the playful side to The Jam, a follow-up session revealed the pressures they were under, especially Paul. When I observed how long it was taking to record the new album, he complained how much The Jam had been touring since *All Mod Cons'* release. (They hadn't played as many shows as he seemed to think they had, not that many at all really, but when there *had* been a break from the road, they'd used the time to write and record new singles that street credibility stated could not then be included on the next album.)

'What it all boils down to is the writing,' said Paul. 'Say we had twelve or fourteen songs when we came into the studio – they'd all have been down by now. I've got loads of ideas, but not enough time. I don't want to rush them, and them turn out like shit. I'd sooner not make an LP this year than do that – I'd wait till next year.'

But Paul couldn't wait till next year, because The Jam's end-of-year tour had already been announced, and it included no less than three nights at the Rainbow. And so, as the summer turned to autumn, and we went back to school – fifth years now, top dogs, and not about to let anyone forget it – The Jam's new LP finally took shape. Paul said the record had some kind of connecting story, though it was difficult to make out. I could, however, identify with the songs individually, most notably 'Thick as Thieves', which started with the most perfect of Rick's drum rolls, the most glorious of Bruce's bass lines and then threw a ton of reverb on Paul's vocals, rendering them instantly majestic. The song was about friendship, and I came to associate it with Richard and myself. So did Rich – in large part because he was in the studio with me the day they recorded it. We'd talk about the song incessantly, not just how great it was melodically – because if ever there was an archetypal Jam song, this was it – but about its poetry. 'We stole the love from young girls in ivory towers,' ran one line. How the fuck did Paul come up with something like that? He'd left school at sixteen, stopped caring about it long before that. Where did it come from, this gift?

We knew that 'Thick as Thieves', like 'When You're Young', was a double-edged sword, that the characters ultimately stole the friendship that bound them together, but we also knew that wasn't going to happen to us, to Richard and me. The prospect of the 'Burning Sky' was something else though. A letter from one mate to the other, years down the line – the same mates as were once thick as thieves, most likely – 'Burning Sky' laid out our futures like lambs to the slaughter. The narrator was only partly apologising for not writing more often, for not coming out to see the same old crowd on Friday nights. His life, after all, had moved on. Work came first these days. And in any case it wouldn't be the same. Throwing a nod to the current Jam single, Weller threw an additional wrench in the works: 'Ideals are fine when you are young.' Rich and I looked at that one and . . . well, we saw something of our futures in it, to be honest.

Every song was relevant in some way or another. 'Private Hell' told of an unhappy middle-aged marriage from the wife's perspective, a brave move for a lad of twenty and one that caused many of us – though not myself, under the circumstances – to wonder if our parents might recognise their own tempered misery in it. On 'Saturday's Kids', Paul came close to talking down to his audience, what with lines about checkout girls wearing cheap perfume 'cos it's all they can afford' and the assertion later that 'these are the real people that time has forgot'. But then Paul was one of the few rock stars who *could* write about Saturday's kids, because those lunchtimes when he'd take us to the pub, he *would* dip the silver paper from his fag packets into the pint, and it *did* seem to fizz the lager back up, just as the lyrics suggested. Wasn't often that the pints sat around long enough to go flat in the first place, though. The Jam could certainly drink.

The most distinctive song on the album was 'Little Boy Soldiers', which had the audacity to arrange itself in three distinct parts, like a mini-opera. It was sung by a conscript sent off to help colonise what sounded like Africa – foreseeing his return home in a 'pine overcoat', a letter to his mum noting, 'Find enclosed one son, one medal and a note to say he won.' To emphasise the song's final word, a piano chord was struck with a finality that echoed the Beatles' 'A Day in the Life'.

Paul knew he was on to something with this song, and so, for the middle section, he expanded the arrangement, adding timpani and cello. Rick had no problem with the big drums. Bruce did not find the cello quite so easy. Sure, it was another bass instrument, four strings and all that, but you had to sit down and thrust this one between your legs, and it was played with a bow, and there were no frets to help you out. A sixteenth of an inch was all it took to go horrendously out of tune.

I knew all this, from playing the cello myself all these years. But I had been finding the instrument an increasingly heavy burden to carry, in all senses, as my extracurricular life took on more and more challenges. Eventually, my cello teacher had given me an ultimatum: I would either need to buy my own concert-worthy cello, at a cost of several hundred pounds, and practise several hours a day, with the hope that I could eventually join a classical orchestra, or . . . I could give up. There didn't seem to be much middle ground for mere competence. And because nobody in rock music ever used a cello, I called the teacher's bluff and quit.

And now I found myself in a recording studio, with The Jam, staring at a cello that nobody else knew how to play. It was Jeff who dropped the hint on my behalf. His revelation was initially embarrassing, indisputable evidence that I was posher than I liked to pretend. But The Jam knew that already. And they did, after all, need some help. So Bruce let me into the recording room to show him how to play the instrument. I sat down, put the cello between my legs, and struck a long bowed note with some vibrato thrown in for good measure.

'Great,' I heard someone say from the control room. 'We should have you play it.'

'Great,' said Bruce, and he took the cello back from me. He was already suffering under Paul's increasingly long shadow without the need of a fifteen-year-old taking his additional credit from him. Bruce eventually recorded a handful of long, drawn-out notes and, once they were mixed in, they sounded just fine. I couldn't have done much better.

Later on, The Jam hired a full string quartet to record a new backing for the B-side to Foxton's own composition, 'Smithers-Jones'. I wasn't around for that session. School had a claim on me, for one thing. *Jamming* for another. My band for one more. Besides, it was getting down to the wire in terms of The Jam finishing the album on time, and invitations to the studio became increasingly infrequent. The nights had long drawn in by the time Paul called me at home one evening and invited me to stop by the Town House the next day.

'We're gonna listen to the final mix,' he said. 'You should come join us. Come on your own, though.'

I didn't need to be asked twice. I arrived the next evening, straight from school, to find a dozen or so people already in the control room. The Goldhawk Road mods were not among them. But Dennis Munday, The Jam's man at Polydor, was there. So was John Weller, Dave Liddle, Kenny Wheeler, Paul's girlfriend Gill, and producer Vic Coppersmith-Heaven. Plus all three of The Jam, of course, smoking nervously and drinking copious cups of tea.

Setting Sons, as Paul had eventually titled the album with what was now becoming a typical sly pun, started with the ringing of a telephone for 'Girl on the Phone', a nod to the groupies who had started stalking him. It ended with the Merton Parkas' Mick Talbot (or Merton Mick, as everyone now knew him) playing piano on a last-minute cover of Martha and the Vandellas' 'Heatwave'. This was the same song that The Who had covered on their LP *A Quick One*; again, The Jam were sailing perilously close to their influences. But who cared? At full volume, with a saxophone blaring through the instrumental section, it sounded every bit the match of Wilson Pickett's 'In the Midnight Hour', which had served similar duty on *This Is the Modern World*. As it blared from the speakers,

John Weller looked over to Paul, started imitating the piano and threw a thumbs-up. Paul nodded proudly.

Right before 'Heatwave' came 'The Eton Rifles'. It was the longest song on *Setting Sons*, the loudest too – or at least the most abrasive – and for those reasons, might not have seemed the most obvious choice of single. But it had a hell of a chorus: 'Hello! Hooray! It's such a nice day for the Eton Rifles!' with a 'hoi!' thrown in for good measure. You could understand why the record company had gone for it. (The album was so late being delivered that the single was already lined up for release.) 'The Eton Rifles' took a whole different approach to Sham 69's latest shout-along, the painfully immature 'Hersham Boys'. It included eloquent verses about class distinction and had one of those classic bridge sections that Jimmy Pursey couldn't have written in a month of Saturday nights down the pub.

'The Eton Rifles' announced, as much as any song on *Setting Sons*, the arrival of a grown-up Paul Weller. This, most certainly, was not the teenager who'd seethed that he'd be voting Conservative back in 1977, back when The Jam performed with Union Jacks all over the place. (And as he told me during our second interview that summer, 'I don't know what that was about really. It was partly stirring up a bit of controversy. Maybe I meant it at the time, foolish youth that I was.') This was a proudly working-class poet, one who had it in not just for the public schoolboys of Eton, but for anyone else that reeked of the establishment. He wasn't trying to set himself up as a spokesman for his generation, but as he listened back to *Setting Sons* in its entirety for the first time, knowing that it was a great album despite his earlier fears, aware that 'The Eton Rifles' was already getting more airplay than any other Jam single to date, he must have sensed that he was about to take on the role all the same.

A few days later, Weller called me at home and asked where I'd bought my Chelsea Pensioner's jacket. I'd worn it all summer long to the Town House and The Jam had become used to it;

they'd even expressed disappointment when I'd started showing back up in my black school blazer. Paul said they were thinking of using something similar to perform 'The Eton Rifles' on *Top of the Pops*; the single was expected to enter high in the charts. And when I watched the show that week there, indeed, was a group on stage wearing red tunics just like mine. They weren't The Jam, however, who were dressed in their own fanciful fashions (Weller sporting a cravat inside his jacket, as if imitating and simultaneously taking the piss out of the upper classes); they were members of a mod band called the Cards, mates of Paul's that he'd brought along to shout out the 'Hello! Hooray!' part. They looked good in their rented red tunics, and I felt flattered. Like I was a fashion leader.

That sensation lasted less than twenty-four hours, until I walked into the Marquee wearing my Pensioner's jacket.

'Fuck me, didn't take you long, did it?' Some mod in a suit, someone who thought himself the Ace Face, slagged me off the moment he saw me. I didn't bother telling him that I'd been wearing the jacket all summer long. I didn't need to. Paul was up at the bar, in the corner by the dressing-room doors, nursing a pint, the first of many he needed to settle pre-gig nerves. He had Kenny Wheeler by his side to keep what they called the 'muppets' at bay, but they invited me over to join them for a swift half. Paul had a newly minted set of *Setting Sons* badges (printed by Joly) and was happy to give me a set. Affixed instantly to the Pensioner's jacket, they put me right back on top of my game.

The Jam gig at the Marquee that night was meant to be a secret, a warm-up for the sold-out tour, a chance to try out the last of the new songs and have some fun in the process. It had been billed as John's Boys and I certainly hadn't told anyone otherwise. (Well, other than my schoolfriends, who'd told their friends . . .) But Mike Read, an afternoon DJ on Radio 1 who liked The Jam and was playing the hell out of 'The Eton Rifles', figured on making a name for himself. He spilled the beans, on air. Thousands descended on Wardour Street within minutes.

John Matthews only just got to the box office in time. Richard Heard did not.

The support band were the Nips – as Shane MacGowan's Nipple Erectors were now known. Shane and Paul were close friends and the Nips' new single, 'Gabrielle', was much better than almost anything out of the mod revival. The Jam opened with 'Girl on the Phone', a song that only a handful of people in the room knew already. An hour later, Paul came back out into the sauna-like conditions, for the final encore, bare-chested, which would have provoked screams from the girls if there had been more than a handful present. He invited Shane MacGowan to join him on stage for the last number. This was a serious honour; *nobody* got an invite to join The Jam on stage. But Shane was in the bar, next door, getting drunk, and when Paul saw him there and beckoned him to the stage through the window, Shane thought he was just waving hello. He waved back and carried on drinking.

It had been a night to remember, and it ended early enough that I was able to hang about for a while afterwards. The Jam emerged from the dressing room almost immediately to have a pint with their friends; I seemed to be one of them. Guy Pratt had snuck into the gig, passing himself off as a roadie at the back doors, and I introduced him to Paul; they seemed to hit it off immediately. I introduced Guy to John Matthews as well, and it turned out they lived near each other and figured they'd travel home together. After our swift pint, the three of us headed down the Marquee's narrow hallway to the front door, feeling pretty good about life . . .

And walked headlong into a gang of skinheads. They were so close we could see the whites of their eyes, and there was murderous intent visible in them. The announcement of the gig on Radio 1 had been too good an offer to turn down. Skinheads had rallied from all over the London suburbs and descended on Wardour Street to kill some mods.

But at this moment, they were still – just – the far side of the Marquee doors, which the bouncer Big John and other members of the management team were desperately trying to wedge shut with their bodies. Big John shouted at me and anyone else in earshot to get the fuck back inside the club. He was holding a two-by-four for protection as he did so.

As we ran back up the hallway, we heard the glass panes of the Marquee door smash to smithereens. Then we heard the sounds of wood against skull and boot against bone and the swearing and shouting that routinely accompanied such violence. It was terrifying, in a way that most football aggro, which took place on open terraces or in streets where there was always somewhere to run, was not. I fully expected us to get chased down and kicked to a pulp. But when we reached the club proper, everything was oddly serene. The Jam were hanging out at the back bar now, having one more drink for the road as their gear was loaded out back. Dr. Marten's apocalypse was taking place just a few yards away, but The Jam didn't seem bothered by our panicked description of it. They had security around them and private cars to take them home. '"A" Bomb in Wardour Street', like 'Down in the Tube Station at Midnight' before it, had been reduced to a series of chord changes.

Eventually, word came through that it was safe to leave by the front door. Guy, John and myself gingerly made our way. We found broken glass all over the hallway. Blood, too. And Wardour Street devoid of traffic; the police had cordoned it off. The desolation and quiet only made it that much more frightening. We reached Shaftesbury Avenue without encountering any marauding skins, and then we said our goodbyes, John and Guy heading to Waterloo Bridge and me to my usual bus stop at the top of Haymarket. I'd just attended one of the most exclusive – and best – gigs of 1979. I should have remembered the evening for The Jam. I recalled it, instead, as the night that Big John was officially 'retired', defending the likes of me from the likes of *them*. I never saw him at the Marquee again.

Number 14:
FEEL THE PAIN

D irection was all well and good for a band name back in
1978, but now it made us sound like just another bunch
of mod revivalists, as proven by a band called *the* Direction*s*
showing up in gig listings, especially around Shepherd's Bush,
and particularly on mod bills. They could keep the name, we
figured; we would come up with something better. It was John
Matthews who did so. He just blurted it out one day that
summer.

'You should call yourselves Apocalypse.'

It seemed an inspired suggestion. Not only was it the last
word of a Jam song, which suited me, but it was frequently
used in the last book of the Bible, Revelation, which Jeff was
busy studying in preparation for Judgement Day.

Now that we had a new name, and one that we agreed upon,
we could get on with promoting it. I found a picture of a
mushroom cloud from a nuclear test, and Jeff cut out letters in
a punkish style to spell 'THE APOCALYPSE' over the top of
it, and with that, we had a logo. We first distributed it to the
world on the inside cover of that summer's issue of *Jamming*,
the New Group special, for which we took out a full-page ad.
(For free, of course.) At the bottom of the page, we announced
two gigs we'd been promised. Within days of the fanzine being
printed, both shows were cancelled. I stripped the info off the
page, convinced Joly to press another plate, and carried on
running the ad without any explanation. It looked more
intriguing that way.

And then, at the very end of August, we took delivery of

1,800 stickers, a more effective way of spreading the word. They began showing up on bus stops and phone boxes all over South London, and I wasn't sure how. Then one day I rode a bus with Jeff, and as we reached our stop, he stood up, walked to the front of the bus, peeled off a sticker, placed it dead centre, so that everyone on the top deck would be duty-bound to notice him doing so, and then walked calmly past the other passengers, head held high. His self-confidence was alarming.

The next time I went up to the Town House, I handed Paul Weller a few stickers. It was the summer of mod and 2 Tone, and the Apocalypse mushroom cloud didn't fit in whatsoever. Paul, though, looked at the image, noted his approval, walked into the recording room, peeled a sticker from its backing and put it straight onto his favoured black Rickenbacker.

For much of the last two years, Weller had used a Rickenbacker with a Boys sticker placed prominently on its fore. The Boys had never made it big, but Weller's endorsement may have been the reason I went out and bought their second album *Brickfield Nights* anyway. Now his guitar featured an Apocalypse sticker. We were as one with the Boys. It didn't occur to me that we might be doomed to similar obscurity – especially when Weller used that black Rickenbacker on *Top of the Pops* for 'The Eton Rifles', the same show on which the Cards wore (my) red Chelsea Pensioner jackets while standing in front of him. He used the same guitar at the Marquee for the John's Boys gig the following night, and on *Top of the Pops* again, a couple of weeks later, by which time 'The Eton Rifles' had risen to number three in the charts, an unprecedented position not just for The Jam but for almost every single punk and new wave group around them. He was using that same guitar in Southampton the following Saturday, 24 November 1979, where I went to see The Jam with Richard and his older brother, and we were invited backstage before the show, to hang out and drink beer with the band. (We also hung out backstage afterwards. I was speeding. Weller laughed at me, it was so obvious. But he didn't pass judgement.) And though he had switched guitars by the time I went to Bath for the final night of the tour with my schoolfriend Mark Blakemore, and we were given a lift back to London on the tour bus because it was snowing and we'd made no other plans (and Paul got into a drunken fight with Gill on the bus and we were told not to mention it to anyone when we were dropped off at Victoria station at three in the morning), by that point a photograph of Paul sitting on the drum riser with the Rickenbacker in question, during a soundcheck, had appeared in one of the music papers. I cut it out, circled the Apocalypse sticker and stuck it in the scrapbook I'd already started up to record such momentous events.

All this unexpected and entirely free publicity posed a problem. Weller fans up and down the country would be asking each other about 'the Apocalypse', and we needed to start gigging to give them the answer.

It was Jeff who finally secured a venue: the Students Den at Hastings Polytechnic, on a Friday night at the end of November. The bill already featured Charlie and the Criminals, the Aardvarks, Anti-Art, the Gits and the Spikes. The Apocalypse would fit in perfectly. As confirmation of our credibility, we were halfway up the bill. Our first-ever gig would not even be an opener.

I was, of course, furious. Not only was Jeff writing songs already, not only was he singing some of them, not only did we have a new name that he liked as much as I did, not only was he affixing our stickers around town more courageously than I was, but now he had booked our first gig! Wasn't I the one with all the contacts in the music world, the one who was going to get us opening slots with trendy London bands if I could just be given enough time?

Hastings it was, then. And to prove that we were serious about it, we booked a rehearsal at Alaska Studios at the start of the month. Two nights before the gig, we rehearsed again – in Chris's front room in Brixton. There was only so much money to go around.

We did visit the headmaster's office, though: we needed permission to take the afternoon off school. We rarely saw the head outside of school assemblies; Coco, as we called him for his clown-like features, mostly hid away in his cubby-hole under the stairs, no doubt praying to reach retirement before he had to actually deal with the realities of his newly comprehensive intake. Now here was a trio of fifth years, among the last of the grammar boys, telling him that their rock band came above their schoolwork. He reminded us that our 'mock' O levels were right around the corner, that the real event would be following just a few months behind, that it was time to start thinking about what we'd be doing with our lives.

But we already knew what we'd be doing with our lives. We'd be doing *this*.

That caught Coco by surprise. He hadn't expected us to be so committed, so cocksure of ourselves. He wished us good luck anyway.

That Friday lunchtime, the three of us went to Jeff's house at the Elephant, where we changed out of our school uniforms and into our stage clothes; we were taking a train straight to the venue. (Jeff's parents would follow down to Hastings after work; we would all stay at their house overnight.) I had on my red Chelsea Pensioner's jacket, Jeff his black leather jacket, and Chris sported a Fred Perry shirt and Farrah trousers. Our clash of cultures was captured on camera by the two mates Jeff brought along for the journey: his next-door neighbour Paul, and a local lad called Jeremy. Both were, like us, just fifteen years old. How *they'd* got permission to take off school that afternoon was uncertain. I was more taken by the subtext: while our Tenison's mates missed out on our momentous debut, Jeff had brought his own entourage.

The Students Den was notably free of students by show time. It was equally devoid of mods; the flier for the gig had made it clear they weren't welcome. The room was filled, instead, with the local punks and skins. I liked most of this crew; even though a number of the skins couldn't help revealing their racist tendencies from time to time, it didn't seem to be a driving motivation for them. They tolerated me, my fanzine and my red Chelsea Pensioner's coat. They even bought me the occasional pint. I was Jeff's mate, after all.

We'd prepared a set list eight songs strong, and all of them our own, but by the time we took the stage, the night was running way behind schedule, and we had to drop a couple of numbers: somehow, they were both mine. One of Jeff's three songs was called 'Death Destruction Judgement Day' – or 'D.D.J.D.' for short. Anyone who'd heard his new heroes the Pack and their single 'King of Kings' knew where he'd got it from. But then anyone who'd heard 'I Can't Explain' knew where I'd got my song 'Superficial' from as well. Besides, 'D.D.J.D.' did have something going for it: the repetitive final line, 'Here Comes the Apocalypse'. Looked like Jeff had also written us a theme song.

We ended the night with Jeff's *other* obvious anthem, 'Case of Non Conformity'. It went down a storm. We were thrilled. We had been as professional as any other band on the bill. (The competition, admittedly, was thin.) In Chris, we had the best drummer of the night. In Jeff, we had a natural co-front man. In me, we had something of some sort; all I knew at the time was that there was nowhere else I would rather be, and preferably for the rest of my life. It felt so natural being on that stage that I couldn't remember anything about it afterwards. It was like I'd been high the whole time.

The headliners, Charlie and the Criminals, closed out the bill with some especially volatile punk rock, to an especially volatile audience. When it was obvious that it would shortly be time to lock up the Students Den for the night and for that audience to go home, then the skinheads among them, which was most of them, set about destroying the room.

I'd learned long ago from football violence that there were three ways to react to a riot breaking out around you. One was to actively participate, and another was to actively run, both of which indicated taking sides, and therefore opened up the possibility for a beating. The third choice, however, was to stand quite still and take on the role of neutral observer, something the perpetrators greatly needed to spread word of the violence (and hopefully to exaggerate it in the process). Because of this, spectators who clearly denoted themselves as such were generally considered off limits.

So I did what seemed natural under the circumstances: I stood on a chair to watch. And I was quite happy doing so until someone kicked it away from underneath me – at which I came crashing down to the floor, landing on my right wrist. Everyone around me laughed, and that might have included the skinhead who'd kicked the chair away – except that he wasn't paying attention. He was busy smashing the chair against the floor.

When there was little left to destroy, by which point the police had arrived anyway, we walked the couple of miles back to Jeff's parents' house. My right hand was hurting so much, I couldn't carry my guitar case, and though I was able to pause for a team photo back at the house – my arm hanging limply around Chris's shoulder, his hanging more firmly around Paul's, Jeremy leaning in on Jeff, all of us sporting enormous grins that were a combination of post-gig euphoria and post-gig beer – by the time I got to bed I was almost screaming with pain. We were bedded three to a room, and Jeff revelled in my discomfort as only a best friend and rival could. Every time I moaned or screamed in semi-drunken agony, he would encourage me to make the most of it.

'Feel the pain!' he'd say, quoting a song by the Damned, drawing out the words for maximum effect. I felt the pain all right. It felt like hell.

At breakfast, I was given a couple of aspirin, and there was a brief debate about whether I should see a doctor, but then we quickly returned to reviewing the previous night's triumphant debut. We hadn't told Jeff's parents how I'd *really* hurt my wrist: had they known that we were associating with rioting skinheads they'd probably have taken away Jeff's bass. They dropped us at the station – they were planning on driving back later that day – and we boarded a late-morning train back to London. By the time we pulled in at Waterloo I was almost crying in agony.

We were a band now. Tried, tested and true. And so we made a band decision to go to St Thomas' Hospital together. All for one and one for all and all that. The five of us, dishevelled and hungover, traipsed in together and took over a large chunk of the emergency waiting area. And as we sat there, waiting and waiting for me to be seen, in walked Chris's nineteen-year-old brother John, accompanied by a couple of his mates, a couple of girls, and, following a few steps behind them, Chris's parents.

I always got a cold shock of fear when I saw John Boyle. The incident in Ruskin Park had never been mentioned again, though at my end it had never been forgotten. But of course they weren't here on our behalf. It turned out that John had got his girlfriend – one of them, at least – pregnant, and now she'd just given birth. In the excitement of playing his first gig, Chris had forgotten all about becoming an uncle. He decided to follow his family upstairs and check out its latest addition. He came back with exciting news. When his brother and family had walked into the hospital, they'd looked across the waiting room and, just for a moment, until they recognised us, figured our gang for trouble. We'd given John Boyle pause for thought. That's what he told us.

A couple of hours and a few X-rays later, the doctors told *me* what by now was painfully obvious. I'd fractured my wrist. They put it under plaster immediately. They were nice enough to give me painkillers as well. At some point, an adult showed up to sign for them. It may even have been my mum. Most likely, it was Chris's.

The Apocalypse walked into Tenison's on Monday morning feeling every bit like rock stars. We'd played our first gig. We'd gone down great. There had been a riot. I'd fractured my wrist in the mayhem. As far as setting foot – or hand – on a myth-making journey, this was an impressive first step indeed. Better yet, because it was my right wrist – my writing wrist – that had been injured, I was let off homework for the next few weeks. Only the French teacher was smart enough to utter the word 'technology' and insist I do my homework on cassette. I had a minor scare that I might prove *completely* incapable of activity with my right arm in plaster, but as I quickly discovered, there were some things you could do with your left hand. I remained as big a wanker as ever.

Number 13:
IT'S THE NEW THING

The Gang of Four were from Leeds. They were male, they were white, there were four of them, and they played rock music using guitar, bass and drums. And yet the way they approached that music was almost entirely different from anything coming out of London. The guitarist slashed at his instrument as if at random, inventing new chords as he went, while the drummer and bass player frequently hinted that they might be incorporating disco rhythms into the music; verses would have some semblance of order until the choruses would erupt in a mass of repetitive shouted vocals and the listener would be left clueless.

The Gang of Four were unashamedly political. They were named after a breakaway faction of Chinese Communists. They sang not about Saturday's kids or the modern world but about capitalism and communism, and actually referenced the 'working classes' in one song, as if speaking of a distinct species. Their first EP included the song titles 'Armalite Rifles' and '(Love Like) Anthrax', words we barely understood. About the only bands you could compare them with were the Mekons – who also hailed from Leeds and had a lyrically confrontational single of their own entitled 'Never Been in a Riot' – and, at least for their scratchy guitars, political lyrics and attendance at Leeds University, Scritti Politti.

On the face of it, then, the Gang of Four did not seem commercial. But things quickly happened for them: an acclaimed single on indie label Damaged Goods; a popular session for John Peel. Paul Weller, an early fan, invited them to open for The Jam at the Music Machine (and urged me to get there in time to see them, which I did). And then, in the spring of '79, they signed to EMI. Immediately, there were letters in the *NME* noting that EMI was not just Britain's biggest record company but also one of its biggest weapons manufacturers and that a political band like the Gang of Four should think twice before signing with such a corporation. The Gang of Four, though, like Adam Ant before he left Decca with his tail between his legs after the dismal failure of 'Young Parisians', saw their deal – especially the *size* of their deal – as a victory for the oppressed masses over their corporate bosses. They even presented the precise terms of their lucrative contract to the British music press, right down to the compli- cated process of 'options', as if they were the first band from the north of England since punk happened to sign with a major record label – and who knows, perhaps they were.

But then they released their first EMI single, 'At Home He's a Tourist', and came abruptly up against reality. The original words to the song, as heard on their Peel session, referenced Durex 'in your top left pocket'. By the time it came out on vinyl, the specific brand had been replaced by the word 'rubbers', apparently at EMI's insistence. This still did not satisfy the *Top of the Pops* producers who, panicking at the potentially permissive effect of mentioning condoms to millions of pubescent wankers, insisted the Gang of Four change it, again, this time to 'rubbish'. The group, probably wondering if they might not be better off in totalitarian China after all, walked off the show rather than compromise further. They got tons of good press for doing so, but 'At Home He's a Tourist' stalled at number fifty-eight and the odds of them being invited back on *Top of the Pops* in the future were placed at zero. So much for changing the system from within.

That was one of the problems with *Top of the Pops* – it played such an important part in the hit-making process, largely because there was almost no other opportunity to see a decent band on television (other than *The Old Grey Whistle Test*, which appeared stuck in the year 1975). But then *Something Else* came along. Broadcast on BBC2, from a different city every Saturday night, *Something Else* claimed to be handing over the production reins to local youth. It didn't do anything of the sort, really – there was a reason the BBC was known as 'Auntie' – but still, it made a welcome change to have some spotty teenager stumbling over his or her cues than Janet Street-Porter or Whispering Bob Harris condescending to us. And *Something Else* did, indeed, have something else: live bands. Good ones. Great ones. Including, on the same night in September 1979, The Jam and Joy Division.

The Jam were the headline act, the one with the hit singles and the long-standing reputation. And they played like it, introducing 'The Eton Rifles' to the public that night alongside a cracking version of 'When You're Young' and, as much as anything, just *looking* like the best band in the world, Weller with hair perfectly pointed at top, meticulously flattened other-wise, dressed all in sharp black, apart from a 2 Tone guitar strap and conspicuous white socks. Foxton sported a fat silver tie knotted tight under a bright blue jacket; Buckler wore what looked like a cycling jersey, white with a single red and blue stripe. It was as far removed from army parkas and target T-shirts as could be while remaining indisputedly mod. It was also, come to think of it, very southern. Joy Division, by comparison, though they also wore long-sleeved shirts, proper trousers and the occasional tie, dressed in muted colours, greys and off-whites, as if deliberately declaring their northern roots.

Joy Division had not signed to EMI, or Polydor, or CBS, or even Rough Trade. They'd stuck with their Manchester home city's Factory Records, which had just released their debut album *Unknown Pleasures*. John Peel had been playing *Unknown Pleasures* relentlessly this last couple of months, just like he had the couple of singles that preceded it, and an incredibly popular Joy Division session recorded at the start of the year. And if this all sounded similar to the Gang of Four . . . well, yes, Joy Division were male, they were white, there were four of them, and they played rock music using guitar, bass and drums. And yes, the way they approached their music was almost entirely alien to anything coming out of London. Or elsewhere. Joy Division's drums were compressed so tightly that they sounded almost electronic, synthesisers were occasionally employed in a faintly sinister manner, and the lyrics were introspective to the point of depressing. And yet you had to be particularly cynical not to hear an incredibly powerful – and novel – emotion come charging through the middle of the music. There was something fresh about Joy Division. Something that pointed to the future. Something else.

On the TV show that night, broadcast from Oxford Road in Manchester itself, Joy Division performed their new single, 'Transmission'. The singer, Ian Curtis, began the song clutching the microphone so tightly you thought he'd never let go. A mere half-dozen teenagers – as if that was all the BBC could afford – stared on from in front of the stage, bemused, motionless. Then the chorus kicked in – 'Dance dance dance dance dance to the radio' – and there was a sudden twitch, a spastic gyration, the microphone appeared to leap out of its stand, and Curtis was running on the spot, his arms flailing, his voice rasping, his gaze at the camera so transfixing it was either the result of a serious speed habit or something much *much* more intense. Later, on 'She's Lost Control', a song we already knew from *Unknown Pleasures*, Curtis went a step further, losing himself completely in that insane dance of his, like a man possessed by demons, gyrating for so long that we weren't sure he'd ever return to normality.

His performance was all anyone could talk about at the Prince Of Wales Conference Centre that evening. Located beneath a YMCA close to the Centrepoint building, where Tottenham Court Road met Oxford Street, the Conference Centre had recently started hosting the cream of the flourishing independent label music scene. Those who had seen Joy Division appear there just the previous month luxuriated in their superiority as they sipped pints of warm lager at the bar.

The rest of us took comfort in the fact that the band on top of the bill that night were also from Manchester and that we might one day be able to claim that we'd seen *them* before they made it to national television.

That band, the Fall, were equally popular with John Peel, who had already invited them in for a couple of sessions. They were also much liked by the music press, in part because front man Mark E. Smith gave good quotes. But unlike those other bands, there was nothing remotely anthemic about the Fall. The nearest Smith and his crew came to a pop song on their debut album, *Live at the Witch Trials*, was the one that went 'Yeah, yeah, industrial estate' as if sending up the whole concept of a chorus line, while their first single 'It's the New Thing' had demonstrated a healthy cynicism about pop culture in general. Despite – or perhaps – because of all this, *Live at the Witch Trials* was selling at a furious rate: something about the Fall's straight-faced simplicity – and Smith's earnest, half-sung, half-spoken Mancunian drawl – had struck a nerve. Certainly, *Live at the Witch Trials* was refreshingly uncomplicated: all the instruments, including a cheap keyboard, seemed to play at once, and none of them appeared to have gone through a mixing board. (The LP had been recorded one day and mixed the next.) The Fall's dress code was equally unfussy: cardigans, open-collar shirts, V-neck sweaters. To cap it all, Mark E. Smith spent most of his time on stage with his back to the crowd. In comparison, Scritti Politti, who were also on the bill at the YMCA, might as well have been the Clash.

Live at the Witch Trials had been released by Step Forward, the same label that put out Alternative TV's records, which made it easy enough for *Jamming* to land an interview with Mark E. Smith. He was joined for it by his latest guitarist Marc Riley. Smith was known as a difficult interviewee but, and especially compared to Paul Weller once a microphone was thrust in his face, he proved perfectly talkative. Asked to define his ambitions for the Fall, he was clear-cut: 'To keep it going as long as I can.' Requested to explain his plain image, he was unapologetic yet polite: 'I'm just not into clothes,' he shrugged. Invited to define his relationship to punk, he admitted the debt. 'Before the Pistols, I thought, "If I get up on stage and start singing, people will just bottle me."' (They still did. At the Lyceum earlier in the year, the Fall had opened for both Generation X and Stiff Little Fingers. Their bravery in the face of flying pint glasses had earned them begrudging respect even from those who couldn't stomach their music.)

And, asked outright whether a key line from *Witch Trials* – 'I still believe in the R 'n' R dream' – was sarcastic or serious, he admitted that it was 'half and half', before opening up on the subject.

'My attitude is that we are rock 'n' roll and no other fucker is,' he said, lambasting those new wave bands that had re-embraced the dreaded sense of 'technique'. 'Audiences don't know who's a good musician, but they know *what's* good. They feel it and they know it's good. It's like me – I can't sing but I know what I'm doing is good. And I know that rock 'n' roll is not the *playing* of instruments – you don't *play* instruments in rock 'n' roll and bands that do are copping out in my estimation.'

As if to prove the point, I was given a test pressing of *Dragnet*, the band's second album. 'Produced' by the enigmatically named Grant Showbiz, *Dragnet* was so thin that you could barely hear it. I subsequently wrote in *Jamming* that 'it sounds like it's been recorded in a bathroom'. I had assumed that this was the Fall's intent, but after the piece was published, Smith wrote in to say that while 'we're into bad tribal sounds . . . most of side 2 sounds better without the original window-polish-ridden pressing'. His was a common complaint among the new independent label groups, who approached their craft rudimentarily perhaps, but with pride nonetheless, and were furious when mastering studios and pressing plants alike wouldn't afford them the courtesy of a professional service.

As he had with Alternative TV, Step Forward's Nick Jones was good enough to take out an ad for the new Fall album in

Jamming. Paul Weller was kind enough to do the same thing for his new publishing company, Riot Stories, which was putting out a book of poetry by his old Woking schoolmate, Dave Waller. I ran the Waller and Fall full-page ads opposite each other, not to dismiss them as such but because they both featured poems. Lyrics. It was like an extra editorial section.

I thought the ads complemented each other for other reasons too. The Fall and The Jam each exuded self-belief – self-righteousness, perhaps – that could be difficult to digest but was impossible not to respect. Though The Jam had some of Smith's derided 'technique', recorded for a major label, had spent three months on their new album (rather than the three days the Fall took for *Dragnet*), and were the very height of fashion, each band had an unequivocal, highly visible leader, someone who took his work seriously, who believed in his band, who spoke his mind clearly and took shit from no one. You could like both bands without appearing not to have made up your mind. (More so than you could, at this point, claim to love both The Jam and the Clash, at least in front of Paul Weller. Around election time, the Clash had released their *Cost of Living* EP, and Weller had openly scoffed at their cover of 'I Fought the Law'. He felt they had disappeared up their own arses in self-mythology. Plus, the Clash were obsessed with the USA, and Paul despised the place. He was obsessed with Britain, instead.) Perhaps that's why, in the letter he wrote to me after publication, Mark E. Smith not only paid the surprising compliment that 'your attitude is fucking great and I wish it was more prevalent', but that 'you've also made me seriously rethink my attitude to mod and a few other things'. At the same time they shared a *Jamming* front cover with four other groups, The Jam and the Fall also shared the top of our readers' charts – along with the Specials, Madness, the Chords, Secret Affair, the Purple Hearts, Stiff Little Fingers and, in case this all pointed to the Fall as the odd ones out, the Raincoats, Swell Maps, and an anarchist punk band called Crass who were selling copies of their controversial seventeen-track EP *The Feeding of the 5000* faster than Small Wonder could press them.

All in all, the ninth issue of *Jamming* was the epitome of eclecticism. At a time when everyone was taking sides on the style divide, *Jamming* embraced, seemingly, everything. Joining The Jam and the Fall was Jeff's long-standing idol, Shrink, along with his latest idols, the Pack, fronted by a handsome blond punk with a megaphone for a voice, Kirk Brandon. (Their single, 'King of Kings', was on Rough Trade.) And I was excited to feature the band Rudi from Belfast who had been the first-ever act on the Good Vibrations label, and with their long overdue follow-up, 'I-Spy', had now released what I thought was the best powerpop single of the year.

Plus, we finally got over the stigma of only featuring white acts. I'd been hoping to get to 2 Tone's Specials or Madness, given their popularity with the nation in general and the younger end of our readership in particular. Joly told me I should bypass both bands for the label's newest signing, the Selecter. With his help, I went to the Electric Ballroom, a few steps from Camden Town tube station, and interviewed them before their first big London headlining show.

All I knew about the Selecter was that a song of that name had appeared on the B-side to the Specials' 'Gangsters', that their first proper single on 2 Tone, the irrepressible 'On My Radio' backed by the irresistible 'Too Much Pressure', had just that week entered the Top Forty, and that, like the Specials, they hailed from Coventry. As it turned out, there wasn't that much more to know. Except that you couldn't sit still to them if your life depended on it.

Nobody sat still that night at the Electric Ballroom – especially not the skinheads. They danced their way enthusiastically through the opening band, a multi-racial act from Birmingham called the Beat. They put up with the middle act, an all-girl group called the Mo-dettes who made up in charm for what they lacked in polish. And they went ballistic to the Selecter. Throughout the headlining band's hour-long set, the core of the crowd was a sea of bobbing bald heads all doing the Skinhead Moonstomp – and Sieg Heiling while they were at it.

This, then, was where we'd found ourselves. At the end of a decade marked by muggings and Paki-bashings alike, a decade notable for the rise of the National Front, for the eventual fight back on the streets of Lewisham, for Rock Against Racism and the Anti-Nazi League and their successful festivals in Hackney and Herne Hill, for the election of Maggie Thatcher on an anti-immigrant platform, and the unfortunate rise and now, hopefully, the overdue fall of Sham 69, we finally had a musical movement whose very name, 2 Tone, proclaimed a desire to bring black and white kids together, a movement that celebrated Jamaican ska music and English fashion alike, a movement that didn't care about the colour of your skin as long as you didn't care either. And yet, as the six black and one white member of the Selecter flew the 2 Tone flag at a ballroom in Camden Town, a floor full of skinheads dancing in front of them offered the Nazi salute as a sign of appreciation. The Selecter had a song called 'They Make Me Mad'. It probably hadn't been written about the skinheads but as the band played it that night, it must surely have crossed their minds.

Number 12:
I WANNA BE YOUR BOYFRIEND

The Trafalgar was a pub that put on mod bands in the Shepherd's Bush shopping centre, across the Green from the Central Line tube station. It was hardly the most glamorous venue in the world, but when Speedball offered us a support slot there, at the beginning of a new decade that we were sure would have the name Apocalypse written all over it, we accepted, immediately.

We didn't even mind being bottom of a four-band bill; we figured it would give our schoolfriends plenty of time to get home. Unfortunately, they didn't show up. A gig in a shopping centre on the other side of London, on a Thursday night in January, didn't carry quite the same sense of importance for them as it did us. Freed recently from the plaster on my arm, I spent most of my time on stage – a space on the floor in between a couple of speaker stacks – berating the few mates who *had* made the trek for not dancing. Afterwards, the best of those mates, Richard, told me that I was a prat for doing so, that people would only dance when they felt like it. Jeff handled the crowd's lack of response in his own fashion: he took his bass with him into the middle of the 'dancefloor' and started pogoing merrily about on his own.

It was a dramatic comedown from our Hastings high, but it didn't last long. A couple of weeks later, Jeff and I went to see the Directions, opening for a band called the Soft Boys at South London's only rock venue, the 101 Club in Clapham Junction. Jeff, not normally given to spending Saturday nights on the mod scene, was curious because the Directions' single,

'Three Bands Tonight', had slagged off his mates the Teenbeats. Rather than a bunch of pilled-up teenage mods looking for aggro, the Directions turned out to be a group of grown-ups. Guitarist and band-leader Tony Burke was married with a kid. The drummer was married, too; the singer was Tony's brother. They had brought two *rented coaches* of fans across the river with them. By the end of the evening, in part perhaps because we interviewed them for *Jamming* there and then, they had offered us a support gig. At the Trafalgar. It was their home venue. *Their* gigs were on Saturdays.

When we got to the Trafalgar on the night in question, we found that there was another band on the bill: Riff-Raff, led by a friendly bloke with a big nose by the name of Billy Bragg, who agreed to go on before us. He recognised that, on this occasion, we were the ones with the pulling power – because the difference for our schoolfriends between a Thursday night and a Saturday night was the difference between being told by their parents to stay at home and do homework and being told to go out and get lost. About thirty mates showed up, at least half of them girls. Among them was Shona. She and Chris had gone out for a few months after Nantes, long enough for Chris to let on that he was seeing parts of her that her school uniform typically covered up, and then they broke up (with annoying amicability, as if they were adults already). She was, officially now, unattached.

The Trafalgar gig with the Directions was our best yet. Our schoolfriends, loaded up with lager or Bacardi that went straight to their heads, all got up and danced, quickly joined by the Directions' fans. We felt like we had played a real gig, as a real band. And so, in the afterglow of our popularity, before the Directions could take the stage and bring us down to earth with their professionalism, I asked Shona out.

I knew what I was doing. I knew that I really liked her, as a person as well as an object of beauty, and that I wanted to be her boyfriend. I knew too that if I waited for my adrenalin to settle down, I'd lose my bottle. So I blurted out the words before I could change my mind.

'Shona. Um, do you, um, want to come to see a film with me some time?'

Her face froze. She looked at Samantha, her faithful lieutenant by her side as always. Then she whispered in Sam's ear. Now Sam's face froze. Then Sam whispered in Shona's ear. Finally, Shona spoke.

'We need to go to the toilet,' she said, and she and Sam walked off, arm in arm.

Sam was Shona's best mate. She was duty-bound to speak honestly, like Richard always did to me. But what could Sam possibly tell Shona about me that Shona didn't already know? The fanzine and the band and the access to The Jam was all common knowledge. So was the fact that I got drunk a lot. At a Christmas birthday party held in the Kingsdale caretaker's bungalow by CEB fifth year Linda, I'd made a fool of myself jumping drunkenly through the French windows from outside, hoping to roll over the sofa like a stunt man. But the curtains didn't divide in the middle like I thought they did, and I brought the whole thing crashing down, complete with curtain rail, on top of the couple snogging on the sofa. They were furious and so was Linda – but when her parents got home from their own Christmas do in the school hall, a bunch of mates in tow, the broken curtain was the least of their concerns. A gang from the Kingswood Estate had already tried to gatecrash the party once and were now back for a second attempt.

'Leave it to us!' Linda's dad had roared, a mixture of alcohol and nostalgia in his voice. 'We grew up fighting.'

He and his mates kicked and punched the Kingswood lads all the way back to their council flats and then came in to have a drink with us. Linda didn't know whether to be impressed or embarrassed. Walking home together through Kingsdale's playground that night, Jeni and I snogged ferociously, but when I woke up the next morning, my Pensioner's jacket still clinging to my right wrist – in my drunken state I hadn't been able to get it over the plaster on my broken wrist – I immediately regretted doing so. Jeni and I were close friends already. Going out with each other was impossible.

With Shona it was different. It was all very nice to be good friends with her, but she was the trophy girl, our very own Leslie Ash/Steph, which meant that it was that much better to go out with her. So when she emerged from the toilets a couple of minutes later, Sam at her side, I was no longer just sweating from the gig; I was sweating in anticipation of her answer.

'Sure,' she said, all smiles. 'I'll go out with you.'

As with Kate a year earlier, word spread within minutes. My credibility soared. Unfortunately, I now had to embark on the actual process of dating. Other than my time with Kate, I had no experience to draw on. (And in that case, Kate had led the way.) Shona found this out soon enough, the night we went to the flicks, and on the way home, I put my arm around her on the bus as we sat down, but across her back, not her shoulders, so she couldn't sit properly, and she had to ask me to remove it. Or the time we spent a whole Sunday together in my bedroom – my bedroom! – and I couldn't work up the courage to touch her. It wasn't a night-time party, I wasn't drunk, I hadn't just played a gig, and it wasn't as easy as I thought it might be. I knew that she knew how to make a move if she wanted to. I was sure that when she and Chris had been in this situation, they'd have been snogging already. But she didn't do anything to initiate the closer contact, and the afternoon passed without as much as a kiss.

I took her to the Palace one time. She seemed up for it. So much so that she invited her younger brother, a twelve-year-old potential skinhead hooligan, to join us. I liked Shona's brother well enough, but his presence made me totally self-conscious, and despite the fact that it was cold that day (it was February, what else would it be?), I didn't dare put my arm around Shona the whole time we stood there on the terraces.

There were other times, though. One night, I dropped her home to Stockwell like I was meant to, and she said she wanted to wait at the bus stop with me, that it was all right, her dad wouldn't mind. So she came back out to the street, and she leaned against a railing, and I leaned in against her, and she kind of wrapped herself around me, and we nuzzled, and then we kissed, and it felt incredibly warm and cosy. So I had hope.

In the meantime the Directions, impressed by our ability to bring our friends across the river – without need for rented coaches – invited us to open for them at the famous Fulham Greyhound. But the gig was on a Sunday, which meant that nobody showed up, except for the couple of Jeff's mates who could be heard, on a cassette tape we made of the gig, asking us to play a song for the National Front. (They knew it would wind us up, and they were right.) Better we play the Trafalgar again, on a Saturday night. Sure enough, our friends made the journey again for this one – about forty of them this time. When they got there, they were told they couldn't come in. They were under-age.

We were under-age ourselves, but it was different for us: we were the musicians. So we took up the plight of our friends – our fans – like any good band would. It had been no problem two weeks earlier, we pointed out. Sorry, the landlord said, the police have been sniffing around. We begged and we pleaded, and we pleaded and we begged. We reminded the landlord that we'd all travelled on a minimum of two tube trains from South London. We promised that none of our friends would drink, that they just wanted to see us play our gig and then they'd go home. Eventually, about ten minutes after we were already due on stage, our friends were allowed in. A couple of the bigger lads went right up to the bar and bought pints for themselves and the other boys – and Bacardis for the girls. And while they were carrying the drinks from the bar, the Trafalgar was raided by uniformed police.

The cops didn't throw anyone out. But they did ask several of our younger friends their ages. Naturally, everyone lied, and understandably, the police confiscated their drinks to be on the safe side. We played our gig and it was subdued – and we found out a few days later that the landlord had been taken to court following the raid. We were now officially banned from the Trafalgar, for being under-age. This did wonders for our street cred – for the legend we were steadily building in our minds and my scrapbook – but it hardly helped us get known on the gig circuit.

There was only one solution: a gig without age restrictions. A gig at school. There hadn't been a rock concert the entire time we'd been there; to our knowledge, there hadn't been one at Tenison's, ever. So we set about making history. We secured the support of our form teacher, who had words with the higher-ups, and the school hall was reserved for a Friday afternoon in March. We were given permission to book a PA, to print up fliers and to charge at the door. We were just told to make sure we behaved and that we didn't play anything inappropriate.

As the date grew closer, excitement grew higher, and two other bands formed at school in time to open for us. One was called Thor: heavy metal had its own following at Tenison's. We didn't care and we gave them the gig. They could be as long-haired and loud as they liked. Nothing could take away from this being our event.

And nothing did – though Jeff called me the night before the gig, unnerving me with the news that he had a bad cold and was worried about his voice, before handling it like a true budding rock star: he took the morning off school, came in at lunchtime to soak up attention and further raise anticipation, and then went home again for the afternoon to 'rest'. All day, the classrooms buzzed with the prospect that the school hall was to be used for something other than a Gilbert and Sullivan opera or Speech Day. The arrival of a real PA during lunchtime only raised expectations higher. We secured permission to take the last lesson off school, and then started sound-checking before that lesson was over. Sure enough, teachers came running from every direction threatening to have the concert cancelled unless we stopped. We had only done it to provoke such a response in the first place.

By the time that lesson was over, we'd locked all the doors into the hall but one, which we had staffed with trusted friends demanding the advertised fifty pence from everyone, no exceptions. (Several of the teachers refused to pay anyway; they were the exceptions.) The girls from CEB journeyed up the Camberwell New Road in a pack, and the third and fourth years in our school grew even more excited as they realised they could rub shoulders – and maybe even something more – with girls of fifteen (sexually knowing).

The opening band – a couple of fourth years who used Thor's drummer and played covers – did their thing. It was OK. When they were done, we drew the stage curtain for dramatic effect – and then, unexpectedly, and without apparent forethought, Jeff grabbed the microphone, and embarked on a solo rendition of the school hymn.

'Tenison's Tenison's where'er we may wander, keep we in memory the deeds of today . . .'

There was a brief pause out front, on the other side of the curtain, presumably while everyone registered what was happening – and then a chorus of cheers went up. Jeff kept singing.

'Carrying onward the glorious tradition . . .'

Jeff wasn't abusing the hymn: he didn't change a word. And it was, as far as hymns went, a good one, with the kind of commanding melody that might once have led a man into war – or at least onto the rugby fields. But just the sound of a punk rocker, standing on the school stage, singing it uninvited, unaccompanied, unadorned, was enough to render it blasphemous. Jeff had entered school as such a nice boy: so mild, so polite, so obsequious and studious. The same, just possibly, could have been said of me. What had gone wrong? Nothing, really – except that during the five years we'd been trapped in Tenison's, the world around us had changed, irrevocably. The school's make-up had changed – from grammar to comprehensive, from mostly white to predominantly black. Pop music had changed, from glam to prog to punk to new wave to 2 Tone. Politics had changed – from the near socialism of the Labour governments to what was starting to feel like authoritarianism under Thatcher. Youth culture, in particular, had changed, what with all the skinheads, punks and mods out there. And, of course, our expectations had changed. We weren't interested in the kind of careers the grammar-school system had hoped to train us for – nor the ones that our newly converted comprehensive might substitute in its place. And that was assuming that there were any jobs to be had: Thatcher may have been elected on the back of 'Labour Isn't Working', but the number on the dole was steadily getting higher – and disproportionately younger. We were interested only in taking the band as far as it would go. This was our hour, the one that would make the previous five years all worthwhile.

And so, after Thor's thirty minutes of juvenile heavy metal, we pulled the curtain back across the stage again – but the audience rushed, as one, right in front of it, and pressed themselves up against the stage. There was nothing for it but to open back the curtain, and unveil the vast Apocalypse banner that Jeff had painted on a spare sheet or three, especially for the occasion. It looked like something you'd expect to see from Crass or one of the bands that was rapidly forming in their anarchist likeness. So did Jeff for that matter, in his leather jacket and peroxide hair. (He had dyed it gradually, hoping that our form teacher wouldn't notice until it was too late. He had succeeded.) I looked nothing of the sort: I was dressed in Eton Rifles T-shirt, red Chelsea Pensioner's jacket affixed with the badges Weller had given me back at the Marquee, and my hair was matted down in a floppy fringe. Chris, as ever, wore his Farrahs, a gold chain hanging from his open-collared neck.

We opened with a new song, 'Schizophrenic', that I had written about Jeff. Being his mate, I had told him as much. He disputed every word of the lyrics but sang along like he believed them all the same, and as far as I was concerned, this proved my point. 'Schizophrenic' was essentially 'Superficial' with a break-down dub section, like the part in The Jam's 'When You're Young'. The reggae influence was also apparent on 'Monday's Child', about a poor working-class woman who couldn't afford to feed her baby, my attempt at something Scritti Politti might do (better). That song sped up and slowed down in the chorus, and both Jeff's anthem 'D.D.J.D.' and my own 'Poser's Paradise' sped up at the end. 'Poser's Paradise' also included a section that, in tribute to the Gang of Four, involved slashing at my guitar at random, inventing new chords as I went.

Every one of these songs was received by our fellow pupils as if it was the greatest thing since free sex. They pogoed and kick-danced in front of the stage. They smoked, freely. At one point, a beer can flew through the air; it wasn't even empty. The teachers lined the sides of the hall and the organ loft like so many prison guards. We could sense some of all that was going on, but we were in our own little world, a bubble of perfection. My amp didn't pack up for once; I could hear myself properly. I had room to move around. The PA sounded superb; we had not been let down. Every time I looked at Jeff or Chris, they seemed to be as much in their element as I was; and every time I looked out front, I saw a sea of beaming faces.

We finished our eight songs, we went to the side of the stage and we waited all of about twenty seconds – and then we came running back to play 'Railway Station Love' again. And as we did, the audience invaded the stage. Stage invasions were going on all over Britain for the bands we liked – but that didn't mean we had it expected it to happen to us. In all the madness, someone pulled my guitar cord out from the amp. But I didn't mind. It was their moment as much as ours, and I danced alongside my fellow schoolkids as we ran through the chorus one last time, dozens of kids to each mike.

We ended the event as fully anointed rock stars. We had

not only survived our five years at school: we had conquered it. We could walk out the gates tonight, without looking back, and school would have been a triumph.

So we walked out the school gates, a small crew in attendance, without looking back. We wanted to celebrate our success. But where? The cafés closed at tea-time, and I didn't like them anyway; there you'd find the school bullies. We were hardly going to go to a kebab shop after such a moment of glory. And none of us ever went to restaurants without our parents. (And rarely even with them.) There was nowhere left, then, but the pub – and yet the memory of the Trafalgar was fresh in our minds as we headed off through the Kennington streets. If it was hard enough to get our fourteen- and fifteen-year-old mates into a gig when they had dressed up for the occasion, on a Saturday night, how were we going to get them into a pub when they were still in some sort of school uniform?

Jeff knew a place, though: the White Bear on Kennington Park Road. He'd been there with Shrink. It was surprisingly empty when we walked through the doors, but sure enough, Jeff introduced himself to the landlord, putting on his finest manners – the schizophrenic that I claimed him to be – and we were allowed to buy a round. Shona had already gone home, much to my disappointment; I wanted her by my side to complete the evening. But I settled for what I had: a high that no amount of speed could ever replicate. We were sitting there still soaking in our glory, getting ready for a second round, wondering who had pockets deep enough to spring for it, when the landlord came up.

'I don't mind you having the one drink,' he said. 'But you should know that the place will start filling up soon.'

'That's all right with us,' we said.

'No, but you might not like some of the people coming in here.'

'We like everybody,' I said. And I meant it.

'Well, you should probably still go now.'

'Why?'

'This is a gay pub, lads. Any minute now, there's going to be a lot of men here dressed as women.'

Some of our friends were out of there before we could stop them. The three of us in the band weren't so bothered – we had, genuinely, seen more of the world than them – but there was no point celebrating if we didn't have anyone to celebrate with. We, too, packed up and headed to the street. Outside, it was pissing down with rain: the reality of South London in winter. The long wait for a number 3 bus further sobered me up. When I got home, I realised just how exhausted I was from the day's activities and went straight to bed. It was only ten o'clock. So much for being a rock star.

I was the only member of the band to show up for school on Monday. This enabled me to take the full force of the entire school's compliments, including those of a fourth year, Sean Hogan, who handed me a three-page typed review of the concert. It was his only copy and he wanted me to have it. I felt honoured, and sat down eagerly to read what he had to say.

Sean noted that 'Schizophrenic' sounded like something by The Jam. I knew that already, though I wasn't quite so pleased to see it written down. He then observed, of the impromptu school hymn rendition, how 'Jeff doesn't realise how much power he's got . . . The more moronic fifth years and younger ones practically worship him.' I knew this as well, but only deep down, and it wasn't something I thought was public knowledge. And then Sean went further: he compared Jeff's dilemma with that of Jimmy Pursey and John Lydon. 'I don't know what I would do' in Jeff's position, he continued. 'But since I'm not blessed with such a marvellous personality as Jeff, I wouldn't get into the situation.'

Jeff Carrigan on a par with John Lydon? What the fuck was Hogan on about? I knew Jeff when he was still a four-eyed swot in the front row, not a potential working-class hero. And why didn't he talk about anyone worshipping *me*? It wasn't like I wasn't equally popular, was it? I mean, wasn't I going out with Shona?

Not for much longer I wasn't. I found her at the bus stop after school that day, and asked if I could take her home. She said that I could. We got on the bus together, and when we got off at Stockwell, I put my arm round her. She tensed up.

'I've been thinking,' she started, and I knew it was ominous. 'We've always been good mates, haven't we? Ever since back in Nantes?'

'Yeah, we have,' I said. How was it that I knew so clearly what was coming?

'Don't you think we're better off going back to that? You know, just being good friends?'

It was posed as a question, but it wasn't meant as one. What it meant was that she didn't want to go out with me. She'd been nice enough to wait until after the big gig, the one that confirmed my status at school, both as the band's front man (all right, co-front man) *and* as her boyfriend. Yet the fact remained that, even though she was a year younger, she was more grown-up than me, in so many ways. She was used to boys who were men – boys like Chris. Me and my sexual fumbling, my emotional insecurities, my public ego, my inability to know when and how to hold someone's hand and kiss them and cuddle them and slowly get inside their bra . . . she didn't need it. We said goodbye before we got to her house, and I did my best not to cry on the bus ride home.

I was pissed off, and I made sure she knew it. For the next week or two, I barely even acknowledged her at the bus stop. But then one of the CEB girls threw a Saturday-night party when their parents weren't around, as was increasingly the case, and I got drunk as always, and I got off with a girl, and I didn't know her as well as Shona or like her as much as Shona, which meant I wasn't frightened of her like I was with Shona. So, while we were kissing during a slow dance, I rubbed my hands all over her blouse and she didn't stop me. Later we went off to a bedroom and we laid on the floor and she let my hands wander inside that blouse and then inside her bra as well. When I got home that night, I had a wank on my bedroom floor. And in the moment of ejaculation, my sexual desire for Shona vanished. I made up with her on Monday and we became what she always wanted: best friends.

Number 11:
THE DREAMS OF CHILDREN

Paul was apologetic. 'Sorry couldn't make your gig,' he wrote of whichever support slot in the Shepherd's Bush shopping centre I'd invited him to, as if he'd genuinely liked to have been there, 'but we were recording that night (honest).' The results of that session, he now informed me, was a 'double A-side': 'Going Underground' and 'The Dreams of Children', complete with an unprecedented bonus package. 'First 100,000 with a live EP costs about £1.49.' This was more than the cost of a normal single, but not exactly double; the implication was that the live EP offered genuine value, yet was not being given away simply as some sort of promotional tool.

Late the previous year, a producer from BBC Schools TV had come to my house in West Dulwich to pick my brains. It was classic 'Auntie' behaviour: having no real idea what 'the kids' were into, the producer figured on asking one of 'the kids' themselves, one who was running a fanzine and had his finger, presumably, on the pulse. I mentioned Scritti Politti, the Raincoats, Spizz Energi, even the Homosexuals. But he was most interested when I talked about The Jam; he'd heard of them, at least. I explained to him that teenagers looked up to The Jam because they were energetic, melodic, relevant, smartly dressed, and put on the best live show in the country. In addition, Paul Weller was the greatest lyricist we had. He spoke to us without talking down to us, and kids respected him in a way they hadn't done for anyone else in a long time. They were the only original punk band that had stayed close to their ideals.

The producer seemed impressed. He left with an assurance about including me on whatever show he got together. I didn't hear from him again until I got a thank-you note letting me know that they'd acted on my recommendation and had already filmed The Jam at a secret show in Canterbury. (So secret that Paul Weller only told me after the event, at which he'd written to apologise for having a 'memory like a sieve', as if it was his responsibility to have invited me all along.) The TV show would be going out next week and maybe I could publicise it around my school.

I wrote this off, appropriately for education TV, as a learning experience. I learned that the mainstream media is only ever out for what it can get for itself, and if you want something in exchange, you have to lay out the ground rules early on. I had not done so. Oh well. The more good things happened for The Jam, the better, I figured. 'Going Underground' was starting to get played on the radio – continuously. In the space of 'The Eton Rifles', The Jam had gone from being Radio 1 outcasts to its prodigal sons. You could barely turn the dial to 1053 or 1089, the station's newer homes in the middle of the medium wave, without hearing the band, as if they were suddenly some sort of institution.

'Going Underground' was commercial, all right – it was like they'd fine-tuned everything that had worked for them over the last year and combined it into one massive readily identifiable anthem – but the odd thing about it getting so much airplay was that it was also their most explicitly political song to date. Over the course of the Christmas holidays – on Christmas Eve, to be precise – the Soviet Union had invaded Afghanistan. The 'Cold War' was not something we focused on much as fifth years, or even claimed to understand. And even if we did, some of us weren't sure which side to come down on. After all, a lot of the people I hung out with, around Rough Trade and Camden Town and, especially, the long-haired hippie who worked at Honest Jon's Records a couple of doors up from Better Badges, were far more inclined to vote Communist than

Labour. (And others I knew back south of the river were, equally, more inclined to vote National Front than Tory.) But we knew, instinctively, the potential consequences of the Soviet invasion. The super-powers had stocked up on nuclear weapons over recent years like some of us had been collecting 45s. They had more than enough to blow up the world many times over. And the leaders of these super-powers – especially now that Ronald Reagan had just been voted in as president of the USA – seemed crazy enough to use them. The prospect of nuclear war was all over the newspapers throughout the school holidays, and through much of the subsequent winter term, too. Older teachers tried to tell us it was nothing compared to the Cuban missile crisis, which they'd lived through in the early 1960s – but try telling us that.

Weller, who'd shown no interest in global politics until now, seized on the looming dark clouds of destruction. 'Going Underground' was full of references to 'nuclear textbooks' and 'atomic crimes', and how 'the public gets what the public wants', though whether the title referred to a fall-out shelter or some sort of alternative culture wasn't immediately clear. Ultimately, it was just non-explicit enough for the BBC to get behind it in a way they had never done with, for example, the Gang of Four.

Yet it hadn't occurred to me just *how* much they – and Polydor Records – had got behind it until the Tuesday after it was released. I was walking back up the Oval to school, after a visit to the chip shop, when I was approached by a third year. I only knew him as someone who lived locally and, perhaps because of that, went home for his lunch. He knew me perfectly well – as did everyone at school – for knowing The Jam. And that's why he approached me.

'Guess what's number one in the charts?' he asked.

The charts were revealed on Tuesday lunchtimes. Once upon a time, back when I was ten, I used to go home for lunch myself, from Langbourne, and tune in to Radio 1 to be the first to hear that week's rundown. But most of the bands I was listening to rarely made the Top Thirty, and I was no longer obsessed by the ups and downs and highest climbers. All of which meant that I hadn't given much thought about this week's number one and I told the kid as much.

'The Jam!' he exclaimed. 'The Jam!'

The Jam? *Our* Jam? Was he kidding me? Five months ago, The Jam had never had a Top Ten hit. And now they had a number one single? That of itself was miraculous. But the fact that it had happened on the week of release . . . Christ, the last act to have a single come straight in the charts at number one had been Slade, five or six years ago. (This statistic was set to be repeated frequently over the next few days in the press. The sad fact was that I already knew it.)

I was elated. I went running up to the classroom and shared the information with my class as we assembled for afternoon registration. A massive roar went up. We found ourselves jumping up and down together, like we all supported the same football team and they'd just won the Cup. A number of us had met The Jam, hung out with The Jam – in the studio, backstage, on the tour bus – and we felt like we knew them, as mates. Certainly, we loved them, as family. We believed in them. We trusted them. Many of us had been buying their records since 1978, and some – like me – since 1977. Back then, I'd felt as if I'd come to the band late. But now, I understood, I was among the elite. We all were. We'd been Jam fans since before the rest of the country had been Jam fans. And now they were at number one. Our band. Top of the charts.

And with that, it sank in. They were no longer our band.

Number 10:
CUT MY HAIR

I was now firmly established in two different music scenes. One was based around The Jam, the major labels, the charts, and the big concerts that went with it; the other involved the thriving world of DIY records, independent labels, self-published fanzines and back-room gigs. I had succeeded in the goals I'd set for myself back when I was thirteen, when I fell for The Jam and started feeling different from the other kids at school: I had broken away from the numbers. Yet instead of capitalising on this, instead of moving further into an adult world where I already had respect, I headed in the opposite direction. My balls having finally dropped, my voice having finally broken, I starting spending my spare time with Jeff and his mates from round the Elephant. Having earned my street credibility the hard way, I felt compelled to hang out on the streets and act hard.

I even bought the clothing to go with it. At the start of the New Year, despite the fact that I had just established my own distinct uniform (the Chelsea Pensioner's coat, the teddy bear jumper), and despite having steadfastly avoided ever owning a leather jacket (as favoured by Jeff Carrigan), a parka (John Matthews) or a Carnaby Cavern suit (Richard Heard), I went up to Camden Town with my Christmas money and I bought myself a beige Harrington jacket with tartan lining, and a red and white Ben Sherman button-down shirt to go with it. Skinheads wore Harringtons. I knew that. But so did mods, I figured – and most of the 2 Tone bands, including the black guys. The Harrington was, perhaps, the only truly universal item of working-class clothing – except for the Ben Sherman. I was Mr Universal. I finally fitted in.

A couple of weeks later, I went a step further. I walked into a hairdresser's (not a barber's, mind, a hairdresser's) and told the lady to cut my hair short.

'But your hair will stick straight up if you cut it short,' she protested.

'I know,' I said in return, congratulating myself for finally speaking up. 'That's how I want it.'

I came home with short spiky hair. Not quite as spiky as Billy Idol or Bruce Foxton, and thankfully not as short as a skinhead crop, but short and spiky all the same. My mother took one look at me and said that I looked 'horrible'. I could feel a generation gap coming on. Good. It was about bloody time.

So developed a routine. Me, Jeff, his next-door neighbour Paul, and Paul's cousin 'Bim', who lived in the same house (both slight, waifish, barely passing for fourteen, but solidly working class, and funny with it), would meet up on weekend mornings, usually at Brixton tube station. Jeremy, who'd come to the first Apocalypse gig, often joined us; we called him Jel, now. And there was Stevo, a skinhead mate of Jeff's of dubious racial tolerance. If we were lucky, some of the girls from CEB would join us, including, during the time I went out with her, Shona. Once we'd finally waited for everyone who'd said they were coming – or not, as the case might eventually prove – we generally just went 'into town', into the West End, where we'd roam the arcades (I was getting ever better at, and ever more addicted to, Space Invaders), the record shops, and the clothing stores, spending what little money we had on our way.

One Sunday, we ventured up to Speakers' Corner, planning on some good-natured heckling. Instead, some dirty old man flashed at one of the girls like we thought only happened on the Benny Hill show, and when we reported him to the nearby police and they shrugged it off – because they took one look at us and figured we were making it up – we followed him all across Hyde Park and took matters into our own hands . . . That is, we shouted at him and bad-mouthed him and called him a 'dirty bastard'; we weren't nearly tough enough, or violent enough, to actually hit him.

Another Sunday, though, we stayed close to home – and left the girls behind. The National Front were marching from Camberwell, and I wore my Harrington to meet my mates at the end point, the Elephant and Castle, where it was my fervent hope that mobs of anti-Nazis would break up the march and beat up the fascists, like they had done so famously, down the road in Lewisham, in 1977. What I found, instead, was that the march had been re-routed at the last minute to prevent exactly this kind of violence, and that the area – the vast Elephant roundabout, big enough for several football grounds and a couple of comprehensive schools and still with enough subway space left over for random attacks out of sight and earshot – was mainly full of police. They looked at us, with our Harringtons, leather jackets and short haircuts, and drew their own conclusions.

'You might want to make yourself scarce,' said one of them. 'There's a lot of those anti-Nazis around looking for trouble.'

'We're not NF!' I shouted.

'Speak for yourself,' said Bim.

Do what? I turned to my new mate. This was a kid totally into The Jam, who liked Madness and the Specials, the whole 2 Tone sound . . . and yet he was telling me that if it came down to choosing sides that day, he was choosing the National Front?

It turned out he wasn't the only one. Now that it was in the open, our gang split right down the middle.

I could have walked away. I should have walked away. But I didn't. I hung out with my friends throughout the afternoon, trying to argue my cause. And they tried to argue theirs. It was the same old story: I was a middle-class kid from Dulwich who hadn't even been born in London. They were from working-class families who'd lived in the area since forever, and now they were besieged by immigrants on all sides. Unemployment was through the roof; surely if the blacks and the Pakis just went home, there'd be plenty of jobs for all of us, right? And there wouldn't be no muggings, neither. I knew it didn't work like that, that the world was never that simple, but for all that I could string impressive sentences together in print, I couldn't seem to win a simple argument like this in person.

Later that evening I went to see the Directions, in Clapham – and I invited Stevo along with me. By bringing a skinhead to a mod gig, having him hang out with the grown-ups around the Directions, I hoped I could show him the error of his ways. Instead, the following Saturday, we took one of our regular trips 'up to town', and while Shona and Sam bought tickets to see The Jam at the Rainbow, Stevo bought the debut LP by the Cockney Rejects. And so did I.

I'd hated Sham 69 from the beginning. I could see right through them. Could predict, even at the age of fourteen, what was going to become of them and their following. But the Cockney Rejects were the *real* East End deal; their hit single, 'The Greatest Cockney Rip-Off', was aimed directly at the Hersham Boy himself. They had the endorsement of John Peel, too, who had brought them in for a session the previous summer, airing the unapologetically titled 'Are You Ready to Ruck?' alongside his usual extreme experimental art music and Rastafarian dub reggae. He must have liked what he heard, because he had the Rejects back for another session a few months later, by which point they'd signed to EMI (*always* EMI!), and were ready to unleash the album I now owned.

I couldn't claim to identify with their songs 'Police Car', 'They're Gonna Put Me Away' and 'Fighting in the Streets'. (If any of the tracks on the album had my name on it, it was 'Shitter'.) And although I genuinely believed that the Rejects weren't racist, it was hard to look at a title like 'Where the Hell Is Babylon?' and not suspect that many of the National

Front members around the Rejects in the East End – and especially at their gigs – wouldn't take it as such. Still, I found plenty to like in the group's simplicity, its honesty and its total lack of pretension, and so I played *Greatest Hits Volume 1* at the volume I believed it justified. Full volume.

It was the only LP, all this time, my mum complained about.

'I've never complained about any of the music you listen to, all this time,' she said. 'But this is just rubbish. In a year you'll regret ever buying it.'

Number 9:
NOISE NOISE NOISE

T he Damned were the first British punk band to put out a 7-inch single, the first to put out an LP, the first to get a member of Pink Floyd in to produce its follow-up, the first to endure a backlash from their fans as a result – and they would have been the first to break up, too, if the Sex Pistols hadn't beaten them to it by barely a month. Then, at the end of 1978, the Damned became the first British punk band to re-form already – and within a year, they had their first hit singles. One was 'Love Song', as joyously fast and furious as anything that had come out of punk since, well, probably the Damned's debut single 'New Rose'. (Jeff Carrigan learned the bass intro by trial and error and was soon playing it at rehearsal and on stage as his party piece.) The other was 'Smash It Up', a merry old pop tune propelled by, of all things, a Farfisa organ straight out of the sixties. Despite its blatant pop appeal, Radio 1 took one look at the title and refused to play it.

By the time we went to see them at the Electric Ballroom the Saturday night before Christmas '79, the Damned were back in the charts with an almost equally cheerful number entitled 'I Just Can't Be Happy Today'. Being the Damned and not The Jam, the 'we' in question meant Paul and Bim and Stevo and Jel (and Jeff of course). Outside Camden Town tube station, we had to run a bigger-than-usual gauntlet of skinheads 'asking' for a 'spare 10p', but the show was everything we hoped for. Captain Sensible played naked, his privates hidden by his guitar; Dave Vanian looked frightening (to us at least) in regulation Dracula cape and slicked-back black hair while sounding equally sinister thanks to his resonant deep voice; Rat Scabies hit the drums harder and faster than anyone I could think of since Keith Moon; and the band's new bass player rounded out the line-up as best he could given the over-sized personalities around him.

Machine Gun Etiquette, the Damned's third album, was just as much a delight. It contained all three singles, and the segues were full of innuendoes and asides, with the occasional shout of 'bollocks', and an 'I saw ya' in direct imitation of Pete Townshend's famous aside to Keith Moon at the end of 'Happy Jack'. But the Damned never forgot their sense of melody. Or harmony. Or musicianship. In Captain Sensible and Rat Scabies, the Damned had probably the most talented lead guitarist and drummer to have come out of punk rock, and yet on 'Noise Noise Noise', they insisted that it was irrelevant:

'Noise is for heroes (heroes!)/Leave the music for zeroes (zeroes!)'

So many contradictions. So much fun. I had to interview them for the next issue of *Jamming*.

We got our chance when we went to see the support band from their Electric Ballroom show in Clapham and ran into the Captain himself. You couldn't exactly miss him: he was over six foot tall, with an unruly mass of curly peroxide hair, a permanent grin such as Jeff Carrigan had perfected long ago, and loud, colourful clothing that celebrated his refusal to play by any and all rules of fashion. We approached him with the confidence that came from being 'mob-handed', and after some quick repartee – Paul's diminutive size enabled him to get away with all kinds of cheek – the Captain told us that the Damned were recording demos at a studio, RMS, opposite Selhurst Park, and that we might be able to stop in that Friday. He took my number and promised to call me to confirm. And when he didn't, we descended on the studio anyway.

RMS was a (shit)hole in the wall, a bare bones sixteen-track studio in the back of a former shop at the end of a row of other crappy shops on a run-down street in the depths of Thornton Heath. It was more than a journey across London from The Jam's luxurious abode at the Town House; it was a million miles away. Still, the Captain greeted us as if he'd rather expected we might show up, sat us down, offered us all a cup of tea, encouraged us to feel at home as best we could given the studio's general squalor – and then, as soon as we started in on the interview, promptly resorted to image, abusing us and just about everyone else whose name came up over the course of the long evening.

Algy Ward, the bass player we'd seen at the Electric Ballroom, who had subsequently left the group? 'A fat ignorant cunt,' said the Captain. 'Next question?'

The Sex Pistols? 'Their music sounds like old Deep Purple, with some cunt screaming over the top of it. Really turgid old heavy metal.'

The Jam, at number one in the singles charts as we sat there? 'Nice suburban lads. The drummer came up to me once and said, "I wish I could dye my hair like you but my mum won't let me." Don't *you* think they're really suburban boring wankers?'

The Clash? 'Just the same as all the groups they tried to replace. They're exactly the same as the Stones. They're just rock stars.'

The Clash had ended 1979 with *London Calling*, a double album that had restored their pride, and significantly boosted their following. Strategically titled, perhaps, to make up for the American focus of *Give 'Em Enough Rope*, it travelled through almost every style of music known to man, not just the punk and reggae and Mott-the-Hoople-style rock for which they were already known, but funk, soul, dub, rockabilly, even strains of jazz and country. It had been acclaimed on both sides of the Atlantic. Surely the Damned didn't think that poorly of the Clash, did they?

The Captain did. 'We made our album in the same studio as them. They were so stoned all the time that they couldn't play their instruments. They were just sitting there, Strummer at the piano and Mick Jones, fucking joints hanging out their mouths. The stench was appalling and the sound was appalling. Absolutely disgraceful. Then the tapes went away, and next time we heard them, they were really professionally mixed.' He left the insinuation there.

And yet he reserved most of his ire for us, the Damned's audience. The Captain was well known for slagging off fans from on stage, and now he explained why. 'I think the whole gig situation is so ludicrous – all these people standing there, and there's a group up there, and they're all going, "Ooooh, that's good, I must go out and buy their records . . . ooh here's £2.50, I'm going to see my favourite group, hurray . . ." It's all rubbish, right? I think they should get their own stinking groups together, so there's no more playing records. It's all crap.'

The Captain said all this with such joy and enthusiasm that it seemed shameful to argue; even when he was slagging off The Jam, I couldn't help but laugh along. (Besides, we *did* have our own stinking group together.) The mood changed, though, when Dave Vanian emerged from the booth, where he was recording vocals to the Jefferson Airplane's 'White Rabbit', of all unlikely cover versions. Having ascertained that we hadn't brought any booze (the idea had occurred to us, it being a Friday night, but we'd thought it presumptuous – and besides, we were broke, as always), he quickly removed the cassette from my tape recorder, stuck a fag end in the device – it seemed vaguely amusing at the time – and then, while I was busy trying to remove it, seized my sheet of handwritten questions and began reading them aloud.

'Now this looks quite good,' he said. '"Anarchy? Violence? Do you vote?" What's "Do you vote?" got to do with "anarchy" and "violence"?'

Quite a lot, I tried to say. Thanks to Crass, the word 'anarchy' was being bandied about much more now than back when the Sex Pistols had first made the word fashionable among punks, and there were competing camps about its true meaning. One, promoted by Crass themselves, was that it represented a peaceful refusal to engage in the political system; the other, as the Captain now put it, was that it stood for 'wanton destruction and chaos'. Given that Stevo had recently decided to label himself an anarchist – perhaps to avoid the more familiar accusation of 'racist' – I invited the members of the Damned to ask him for further clarification. They took one look at him, with his short haircut and Harrington jacket and hapless grin, and almost fell over laughing.

'Kick him!' enthused Vanian.

'Let's throw him out and see how bloody anarchistic he is then!' roared the Captain.

Stevo winced. Certainly he didn't try and explain himself. Like the rest of us, he was too busy enjoying the show. For this was, in every sense, a Damned performance. Better even than being at one of their gigs. It was cheaper, for one thing. It was exclusive, for another. And it was safer, for sure: it was Friday night in South London and for all that the Damned were dismantling my tape player and threatening to jump up and down on Stevo, we were much better off in that room than we were on the streets of Camden Town, being harassed by skinheads for spare 10ps, or the Elephant and Castle, or, for that matter, Thornton Heath.

So Vanian and Sensible kept up their double act, insulting not just Stevo, not just their various punk peers, but newly emergent pop star Gary Numan, Adolf Hitler, people with beards, and the Queen ('She should have her bloody head chopped off,' roared the Captain), and we kept laughing, and the evening passed by, and soon enough it was time to go home, and we emerged back onto that cold and depressing Thornton Heath street with a new understanding of our pop idols. We could look up to The Jam as fashion icons and social spokesmen. We could rely on the Fall to keep us down to earth. We could hope for the Specials to unite black and white. We could expect the Clash to attempt all this and more. But the Damned wanted no such place in our scheme of things. They offered no explanations, asked for no expectations. They left not just the music to what they called 'zeroes', but all the politics, posturing and posing that went with it. That made them the most honest group out there. It also guaranteed that they would never become any more popular than they already were.

Number 8:
MAYBE TOMORROW

We were at a party in Streatham. Again. It seemed to be the routine now for Saturday nights: a fifth year from Tenison's would host a sixteenth birthday party and he'd invite everyone he liked from our school and every girl he could muster from CEB. Chances of copping off were good under those circumstances, but they typically involved the same old faces, the same musical chairs, the same embarrassed looks at the bus stop on Monday afternoon. Better, then, to be at *this* party, hosted by one of the vast Heard clan, a mate of Richard's older brother, turning eighteen or nineteen. Older teens threw *real* parties.

And here we all were – me, Richard, Mark Blakemore, Keith Percival and a couple more from Tenison's' Streatham and Norwood contingent – trying desperately not to look out of our depth. Oh, we acted tough enough; we stood in a circle near the record player, which we did our best to commandeer, and we moved our feet to the beat, and we drank a lot, and we cracked jokes, and we laughed loudly at them, and if any of the older Heards came over and cracked jokes *for* us, we laughed even louder. But our circle faced inwards all night long; surrounded by so many elders, we didn't have the confidence to look out.

I couldn't help checking this one girl, though. I placed myself at a point in our circle where I could drink my lukewarm beer, laugh at Richard's jokes, keep an eye on the record player, and still admire this strangely strong beauty. She wasn't what I thought was 'my type'. She had short brown hair not styled in any particular fashion, and she wore a baggy jumper and army fatigues. It was the look of the tomboy, yet to balance it out, she had this gorgeous smile that she flashed frequently – but only at her mates, six of them in their own little group. They were all older than us, by a couple of years I figured, and they seemed so much more worldly wise, the way they held their drinks, the way they smoked their cigarettes. As the night wore on, I thought the tomboy sensed my staring at her a couple of times, and I turned away quickly in case she returned my gaze. For what would I say to her if she asked why I was staring? I'm sorry? I like you? What's your name? What's it like being a grown-up? Is sex as good as they say it is? She was less than ten feet away all night and it felt like a universe. I kept my distance.

The hour got late. Our little group got drunk; it was how we protected ourselves. Soon, it was time to go home. The party had not been a roaring success. I decided on one last piss in case I was caught waiting thirty minutes for a last bus.

Only when I opened the bathroom door did I notice the tomboy behind me. I assumed we must have had the same idea at the same moment, and I tried to think of something to say about it that would be funny and yet mature – a chat-up line that didn't sound like a chat-up line. I couldn't think of a single word.

She spoke instead.

'I've been watching you,' she said. That was all. She followed me in, closed the door behind her with her shoe, pushed me straight up against the wall – and kissed me.

What was going on here? Had I been that obvious? Surely she couldn't actually fancy me, could she? I rubbed my hand across her back to test the theory, and she pulled me away from the wall, down to the floor alongside the bath, our lips still locked as she did so. I was drunk, and I realised that she was drunk as well, but given how I'd been lusting after her for the last few hours, I wasn't going to complain. Emboldened, I slipped a hand inside her sweater, tentatively sent it northwards . . . and she responded by lifting it up all the way over her head, removing it entirely – taking her T-shirt and bra with it – and bringing me back down on top of her.

This was a first: I'd never found myself confronted with a topless girl like this. (Well, not in the flesh.) Hers was an unbelievably athletic body and, pausing to admire it but still seizing the moment, I sent my right hand down the front of her jeans. She lifted up her bum, as if inviting me to remove the rest of her clothes. I had them halfway down her legs in seconds.

That was when the door opened. It was Darren, the party host.

'Fuck me,' he said, clearly surprised at the sight. (He wasn't the only one.) But instead of acting like Jimmy in *Quadrophenia*, giving it a 'go on my son', and leaving us to it, he came on all aggrieved, like we'd broken some sort of unspoken trust. 'This is a toilet, not a bleedin' knocking shop,' he said before slamming the door shut, and it was enough to ruin the moment. Immediately, she was up on her feet, pulling up her jeans, quickly putting her T-shirt back on and her sweater over it. (The bra, apparently, could wait; she stuffed it down a back pocket.) Flush-faced, she ran out of the bathroom without another kiss. She left the party moments later, before I could even explain to a quizzical Richard what had transpired.

But she was with me in my bed that night. I could hardly sleep for playing with myself to the image of her body. Perhaps I wasn't such a flump after all. She would have gone all the way, I was certain, if only we hadn't left the door unlocked. Fuck.

I decided to find her.

It wasn't going to be easy. Not only because I didn't know her name, but because of what it entailed: tracking down and then talking to an older girl, and on the phone, while sober. Still, I had my fanzine experience, proof that I could get to someone when I needed, and it was really about time I showed that I could cut it with girls, so I set about the task. Sunday evening, when the hangover had just about subsided, I called Richard and asked for Darren's number.

'Good luck, mate,' he said when we hung up. Rich had long ago put the embarrassing episode with Shona behind him, scored a beautiful French modette at some party I'd missed, and together they'd been steadily fumbling their way towards the final act. Now there was a chance I might beat him to it.

When I got hold of Darren and told him why I was calling, he was all right about it, too. 'Her name's Monica,' he said. 'I don't know her that well. I just know the mates she came with. I'll give you Gary's number.'

I thanked him.

'Oh, and one thing before you go.'

'Yeah?'

'Look for a bedroom next time' He sounded almost disappointed that he'd stopped me from having my way with her.

I thanked Darren, and I stared at the number I'd written down. Insanity. No way. Not on a Sunday evening. Not that soon after the party. Not with the hangover still retreating. I went to bed, instead.

It took until Tuesday to work up the courage. Richard had kept on at me about it.

'If she was all over you like that, she's got to be *into* you,' he said. 'You'd be stupid not to give it a try.'

He was right. I had nothing to lose, except my virginity. I called Gary that evening. He seemed to remember me. Like Darren, he laughed about it. I didn't know if he knew what had gone on in the bathroom during the one or two minutes we'd been in there, but he played along. He gave me Monica's number.

'It's for work,' he said, implying that he had her home number as well but that he wasn't about to give it out to me. 'Just don't tell her where you got it.'

The next day, I was home from school swiftly. Thankfully, no one else was in; there was no way I could make the call if my mother or my brother were about.

But then, I could barely make the call anyway. First time I tried, my finger started shaking and wouldn't dial properly. Second time, I dialled all seven digits, but then panicked when I heard the phone ring, and promptly put it down again.

What the hell was I thinking? If she was working in an office, that made her a year older than me. At least. I was still a schoolboy.

Then I remembered Kate. She'd been a year older than me, as well. She'd assured me age didn't matter. And to prove it, she'd done all the pursuing. I dialled again.

Yes, but Kate didn't want to go all the way with me, did she? She was only after a companion. I stopped dialling.

Ah, but Monica *did* want to go all the way with me. She wanted *me*. So, I dialled again and before I knew it a receptionist had answered. I heard a voice ask to speak to Monica, and then I heard the receptionist say, 'Putting you through,' and then I heard a third voice.

'Hello, this is Monica,' it said. I didn't recognise it from Saturday night. After all, we'd barely said a word.

'Monica?' I needed to hear my own voice again before I went any further.

'Yeah, who's this?'

'It's um . . . it's um, the boy you met at the party.'

'Who?'

'Well, we didn't really introduce ourselves. We um . . .'

'Oh. Yeah, I remember. How did you get my number?'

'I um . . . I asked around.'

'Good for you.' Her voice was flat and firm, like her stomach. I couldn't tell whether she was intrigued or insulted by the fact that I had called her. I had no choice but to push on to find out.

'I um . . . I wanted to know if you wanted to see me again,' I said, surprising myself that I'd managed to get the words out.

'That's very sweet of you,' she said, and she laughed. It was the first sign of emotion in the voice. But it wasn't the right kind of laugh. 'You didn't plan on just forgetting about it?'

Panic-stricken, I tried playing for time. 'About what?'

'About *it*.'

'Why?' I asked, and I knew even as I spoke that my words were redundant, that they were only postponing the moment. 'Did you?'

'Oh, most definitely,' she said. And suddenly her voice sounded almost cheerful. 'Thanks for calling, though. That was sweet of you.'

And she hung up.

Number 7:
TOO MUCH TOO YOUNG

Paul was proving eager to help in ways I had never anticipated. The week I turned sixteen – the same week that six newly re-released singles by The Jam entered the Top Seventy-Five, giving them the most songs in one week's chart since the Beatles' heyday – he wrote to tell me about a new monthly magazine called *The Face*. It had been founded by Nick Logan, whose name I vaguely remembered as the *NME*'s editor during that paper's conversion to punk, before he went on to found *Smash Hits*, the modern-day equivalent of *Disco 45*. According to Paul, *The Face* was looking to hire young writers and 'would be a good break for you I reckon'.

Paul knew about *The Face* because he was due to appear on its second front cover, the honour for the inaugural issue having gone to Jerry Dammers of the Specials. This made sense. The Specials had had a number one hit in February, just ahead of The Jam, with a live EP of classic ska songs led off by their own 'Too Much Too Young', a rapid-paced diatribe against teen pregnancy that, in slower fashion (and with a classic dub section tagged on afterwards) had been the highlight of their best-selling debut LP. The EP's contagious energy was reflected in its cover shot, a black and white photograph taken from the front of the stage at one of their gigs – but facing outwards to the crowd. That audience was shown to comprise skins and rude boys down to every last teenager: there were no mods, and there was only one non-white face out of the fifty or so who crowded the camera lens. But what could the Specials do about this any more? At least there was no hint of nastiness, of violence, of outward racism or antagonism. At least at this gig, the Specials hadn't had to chase those crazy baldheads out of the hall, as they'd recently (and courageously) started doing when the sight of Sieg Heiling skins terrifying the rest of their audience had become too much to accept. No, this audience radiated a sense of unadulterated joy, one that came from being crushed up at the front of a gig watching a favourite band in its prime, in their own prime of youth. You'd have seen something similar at a Jam show – but it was to the Specials' credit that they put a picture of their audience on the front while The Jam kept using images of themselves.

It had never been my ambition to 'join' the music press, not least because I'd finally witnessed for myself, with the mod revival, its habit of building bands (and movements) up only to knock them back down again. (Admittedly, the quality of singles by the Merton Parkas, Secret Affair and, frustratingly, even the Chords – who had signed to Polydor but somehow couldn't balance their vitality and melody in the studio – had not helped the cause.) *Jamming* had just been prominently featured in a major *NME* round-up of fanzines by its new star writer, Paul Morley, who concluded that 'in its chummy, concerned, exhaustive way it's the definitive contemporary popzine'. If that was the case – and I wasn't going to dispute it – then why did I need to write for any other publication?

I didn't. But *The Face* was different. It was new and unproven, not yet part of the 'establishment'. It was promising a fresh approach to music, *and* film, *and*, intriguingly, fashion, too; it was eager to sign up some new young writers alongside the proven old guard; and it was a monthly. (The only other monthly was hippie fanzine turned punk semi-professional magazine *Zigzag*.) Nor was it any kind of competition. The print run on my latest issue, though enormous by fanzine standards, had been all of 2,000; *The Face* would be distributing 50,000 or more, mostly to newsagents. Plus, *The Face* would pay me. Money, I had come to discover, had its uses.

I went knocking on the magazine's door – located on Carnaby

Street (The Jam had been right about that one; it was mainly now a tourist trap) – and Nick Logan agreed to see me. He didn't look like a music journalist, the way Ian Penman, for example, looked like a music journalist. He wasn't scraggly, for one thing. He dressed properly. He was trim and healthy, too. A little stressed out perhaps, but I knew that feeling from setting myself too many impossible deadlines. I told Logan about *Jamming*, he told me he'd heard of it, and without more than a cursory glance at the copies I'd brought him, he asked if there was anyone I wanted to write about. Sure, I said, I'd just interviewed the Damned, and though I didn't want to give him *that* story (it was too funny not to save for *Jamming*), I'd be happy to go back and talk to the Captain again. I also liked this band Speedball – they would outlast the mod revival, honestly – and there were all these interesting independent compilations coming out, centred on local scenes, like *Made in Coventry*, and *Bouquet of Steel* from Sheffield, that I'd be happy to review. Logan said yes. To everything.

I had the Captain's home number now, though technically it wasn't *his* home; he still lived with his mum and dad, in a terraced street in Croydon. (Rick Buckler, the Captain's idea of a 'suburban wanker', also lived in Croydon, having finally moved up from Woking. He'd given me his address there and I'd decided to drop round the last issue of *Jamming* in person. I'd been staggered to find that he was living on the top floor of a crappy semi-detached in what was, my own loyalties to Crystal Palace FC aside, one of the shittier of London's suburbs. Wasn't he a rock star? Weren't The Jam making money? Or was Paul getting it all as songwriter?) The Captain was always happy to supply a few quotes for the music press, and I came back to Logan with a Damned feature that detailed their run-in with the Mafia on a recent tour of Italy and their fall-out with record label Chiswick upon their return; apparently, the Damned were unhappy with their version of 'White Rabbit', but Chiswick released it regardless. (It was not a hit.) My piece ended with a quote that I thought embodied the Captain's lifestyle:

'In twenty years' time I still want to be going on stage. I'd like to come on in a wheelchair and still be insulting the crowd, saying, "You ought to cut your tits off and stick them up your bum." I think that would be really fantastic.'

Perhaps you had to have been there, because when Logan ran the story, in the third issue of *The Face*, by which time pretty much everyone in London was buzzing about the magazine, he added the final word. In brackets: '(Yeah, great – Ed.)' I couldn't complain about his sarcasm; I'd done the same thing with my own writers – Lawrence Weaver, Christopher Modica, Jeff Carrigan – and pissed them all off in the process. I'd probably got the idea from the *NME* to begin with.

But Logan must have seen something in my enthusiasm – or, perhaps, just my Harrington – that gave him an idea. Because shortly after accepting my first assignments, he called to ask if I'd be interested in writing a longer story for him. A full-length feature. He thought I'd be perfect to interview Madness.

Signed to 2 Tone by the Specials as kindred spirits after meeting at a London gig all of a year ago, Madness had been an overnight phenomenon. Their take on ska exuded a childlike wonder and musical simplicity that allowed them to reach the parts of pre-pubescents that political bands like the Specials, The Jam and the Clash could not. The sight of them grinning like nine-year-olds and dancing like drunken teenagers to tunes such as 'My Girl' and 'The Prince' on *Top of the Pops* didn't harm either, and the inclusion on their LP *One Step Beyond* of titles like 'Night Boat to Cairo', 'Mummy's Boy' (ouch) and 'Tarzan's Nuts' had all further helped it become an unprecedented success, producing no less than four Top Twenty hits.

I knew from Tenison's that Madness were popular with younger kids – with people like Shona's wannabe skinhead younger brother David. And that led directly to the other main point about them: that all seven of them were white, which meant that they had been adopted by the *truly* racist skinheads, who figured they now had a ska band they could root for without apology. Madness were portrayed as authentically working-class boys from Camden, a neighbourhood not unlike the Elephant and Castle (singer Suggs's graffiti from his days as a Chelsea hooligan skinhead could still be found on many a London brick wall), and that made it difficult for them to disassociate themselves from their more disreputable followers. So, even as they'd been livening up the pop charts, even as their 'cheeky chappy' persona had begun finding a new format via instantly classic videos – which were themselves becoming a regular part of the promotional game for major acts – the press had been painting them as something more sinister. The relationship had recently reached rock bottom when Deanne Pearson, the *NME*'s newest muck-raker, had quoted Chas Smash, the Madness MC famed for inventing their 'Nutty Dance', as saying, 'We don't care if people are in the NF as long as they're having a good time.'

It was a stupid thing to say. Assuming that he said it. Or that he meant it the way it came across. (Though, knowing my own white working-class mates, I suspected that he did.) Either way, Madness had been forced into a corner, and now they had their guard up, and they weren't about to let it down for anyone, including *The Face*. As Logan explained it to me, the best way to get a good piece on Madness, a *true* piece on Madness, perhaps the *only* piece on Madness, would be to assign someone who understood their audience. Someone who *was* their audience. That would be me: the sixteen-year-old Londoner with the Harrington jacket and the short hair. To that end, how did I feel about flying down to Cornwall to join them on tour? It would mean staying overnight in a hotel. The record company – they were on Stiff now – would be paying for it. I'd even have my own room.

The only hotel I'd stayed in 'on tour' so far had been the previous summer, with Speedball. They'd played Brighton Polytechnic and, late at night, after we'd emptied out the student bar, 'bunked' me through the back door into one of the town's larger guest houses. While I tried to sleep on the sofa, Robin rebuffed a bald-headed girl who had followed them back from the gig, even when she went down on him under the covers. I couldn't understand his disinterest; I found her shaved head sexy. I also didn't understand why she didn't just come and give me one; my virginity was driving me crazy. But Robin kicked her into Guy's bed instead, where Guy eventually appeased her and allowed us all to get some sleep.

The thought, then, of travelling to see one of Britain's biggest bands, of staying in a proper hotel, and of getting paid for it in the process, was almost beyond comprehension. The fact that I wasn't sure how much I liked Madness, that I didn't own their LP, and had been suspicious of them for all the reasons the NME had stated, suddenly didn't matter. I asked Nick Logan what dates we were talking about. He told me, and I had to inform him in turn that I couldn't do it. They clashed with my O levels. That's what he got for hiring a schoolboy writer: a schoolboy's schedule.

Number 6:
THIS IS POP?

S treet Level was the name of a new recording studio in Maida Vale. It was only an eight-track, and barely more glamorous than RMS in Thornton Heath, but unlike most small studios in London, it was run by actual musicians . . . of sorts. The people behind Street Level were the Here and Now, the hippie band that Alternative TV had toured with before making their unlistenable second album, *Vibing Up the Senile Man*. Undeterred, perhaps even enthralled, by the fact that he had alienated his original punk rock audience, Mark Perry had subsequently renamed Alternative TV as the Good Missionaries, and had thrown himself wholeheartedly into his brave new world of free-association hippie jazz rock poetry. The Good Missionaries recorded at Street Level. So did the Fall, who didn't appear to need anything bigger or better despite their popularity; besides, their 'producer' Grant Showbiz was a co-owner of Street Level and presumably could cut the Fall a good deal. Along with the Here and Now's Kif-Kif and Twink, Showbiz also ran a cassette label, entitled Fuck Off Records, which initially put out album-length tapes with humorous titles like *Music for Pressure* and *Folk in Hell*, before succumbing to the thriving DIY vinyl scene and releasing a series of 7-inch, 12-inch and probably 10-inch records too, complete with hand-drawn/photocopied/typed sleeves and hand-stamped labels, featuring the likes of Danny and the Dressmakers, the Sell Outs and the Instant Automatons.

I didn't always care for the music of these bands, who seemed to revel in their rank amateurism, but I liked the scene itself for that same reason. And so, despite the fact that the Street Level culture was alien to my intended future as a rock star, I brought Jeff up to North London with me one day to check out the studio; he approved, and we booked Apocalypse in for a full day's recording at the end of May.

We needed the boost. After being banned from the Trafalgar, none of the bigger bands we knew and liked would risk booking us as opening act in case we brought our under-age fans with us. Offers would occasionally come in for dates in places like Oxford or Colchester by people who'd heard about us if not necessarily heard our music, and we'd agree, without having seriously thought about how we'd get out there, but invariably the gig would be cancelled anyway. Paul Weller had mentioned the possibility of Polydor paying for studio time, but nothing came of that, either. The pressure of our impending O levels hardly helped.

The O levels had already claimed one casualty: *Jamming*. After the phenomenal success of the previous two issues, and despite the handicap of the broken wrist and the temporary distraction in January of our mock exams, I'd continued lining up and conducting interviews, had chaired a 'DIY Records Discussion' featuring various musicians doubling up as their own record company bosses (held, of course, at Rough Trade), had kept up with the correspondence that came in from increasingly far-flung corners of the globe, and continued the regular circuit of record and book stores at weekends and after school, stocking up shops from Croydon to Camden with back issues as regularly as I could collate them. (Thanks to The Jam's newly acquired status as Britain's biggest band, the additional 500 copies of the 'Paul Weller' issue that first put me in debt had all but disappeared off the bedroom floor.) I just hadn't got round to finishing off the layout. For that, I needed Jeff.

I assumed it was just a matter of time until we got it taken care of. But one evening during the late winter, Jeff told me he wouldn't be able to work on *Jamming* until the end of June. He intended to focus on his O levels first.

'I didn't go to Tenison's for five years to fuck them up,' he said.

Jeff was the school rebel, the punk rocker with the dyed hair, the one that Sean Hogan compared to Johnny Rotten and Jimmy Pursey. He wasn't even staying on for sixth form: he planned on attending the London College of Printing instead, at the end of his street, where he could enjoy the freedoms of adulthood without any of its real responsibilities. But to get accepted, he needed at least a handful of O levels. And so his original swot instincts had kicked back in.

Now that he mentioned it, *I* didn't go to school for five years to fuck up my exams either. I was too smart for that, in all senses. I wanted to prove to the school, especially those 'teachers who said I'd be nothing' (both of them), that I could run my fanzine, be in a band – *and* pass their stupid exams. I wanted to show them who was boss.

We decided to put off the tenth issue until the summer. I printed up an A5 flier announcing as much, took it round town with me on my restocking ventures and pinned it to the wall of every record store and book shop that allowed me to do so. I sent it out to the subscribers as well. I didn't want them to think I'd absconded with their money – although it was becoming increasingly difficult to just leave the cash in the tin can on my desk, the way it had been before I'd started drinking and smoking.

This decision made, it soon became evident that Jeff was not quitting all extracurricular activities. He was merely prioritising – hoping, I concluded, that I'd continue to focus on *Jamming* alone, leaving him free to take charge of the Apocalypse. I couldn't do that. The fanzine, after all, was but a trial run for my real purpose in life. So, with neither of our egos allowing the other any room for freedom, we *both* focused on Apocalypse to the exclusion of *Jamming* – and with such unrelenting energy that before we knew it, we'd booked Street Level on the very eve of our O levels: the time we didn't have for the magazine we had easily found for the band.

Jeff, Chris and myself were up bright and early for the Saturday session – so early, in fact, that there was nobody at the studio to let us in when we got there. We did what any aspiring fifteen- and sixteen-year-old rock musicians would do at 11.30 a.m. on the day of their first big recording session: went to the local pub. There I ran into Jackie Levan, singer with a group called Doll by Doll, who had acquired a reputation with the music press for being somewhat 'difficult'. Levan, living up to form, gave us just one piece of advice: never trust a journalist. I didn't tell him that I had just started writing for *The Face*.

By the time we returned to the studio, Twink was waiting for us. In the spirit of the Here and Now's approach to music-making, he spent approximately thirty minutes 'getting a sound' and then told us we should start recording. We played 'Schizophrenic'. He pronounced the backing track perfect and suggested we move on. Not much later, we had another two backing tracks 'in the can'. We decided to delay work on the fourth song, 'Summer Holiday', given that it would feature acoustic guitars, and we honed in on the overdubs.

We were not complete novices: Jeff and I had always been sure to make the most of our time at recording studios, from the Town House to RMS, watching and, so we thought, learning. We knew what most of the knobs were for, we understood the concept of mixing, we'd even pre-allocated our 'eight' tracks per song. We just hadn't realised that the process of overdubbing could be so mentally taxing, so emotionally draining, so physically challenging. As the afternoon wore on into evening, we found ourselves struggling to sing our harmonies in tune with the lead vocals, to play overdubbed guitar lines in time with rhythm guitar parts. The fact that both 'D.D.J.D.' and 'Monday's Child' purposefully sped up and slowed down didn't make things any easier.

Fortunately, just at the point that we were starting to lose the plot, Kif-Kif came in to relieve Twink, Grant Showbiz came along to hang out, and, with it, the mood changed. As we finally switched to 'Summer Holiday', Kif-Kif taught us the most important studio lesson of them all: enjoy yourselves. He encouraged us to come up with seaside banter (much like the Undertones had with 'Here Comes the Summer' for their Peel session, not that we realised how blatantly we were copying them), he had us perform hand-claps, he stressed the importance of emotion over perfection, and by the time we were finished with it, the hippies in the room, like everyone else who had heard us play it this past year, thought that 'Summer Holiday' had the makings of a hit single. The fact that 'hippies' and 'hit singles' had, like chalk and cheese, no more in common than shared first letters, didn't strike us as odd; as we packed up our gear and prepared for the long journey back to South London, the Radio 1 playlist seemed quite within our reach.

Number 5:
THICK AS THIEVES

Marco was an Italian college student who'd come to London to improve his English. He did so by enrolling with a company in Crystal Palace called Anglo School. Over the years, my mother had regularly placed these foreign students with families around the area, earning a useful commission in the process. Every now and then, we took one of the students in ourselves, for two, three, four weeks at a time. They came from all over the world, as far away as Thailand, but it never seemed too much of a hardship.

Until now. My brother had taken his A levels a year earlier and got disappointing results. Unable to attend the universities he'd planned for, he'd opted to join the workforce instead – with the new American restaurant franchise that was all the rage: McDonald's. The standard of employees couldn't have been that high, though, because within months, Nic was promoted to store manager, at the age of eighteen. The only catch, and it was a big one, was that his store was out in Ilford, the other side of London and then some. The daily commute was such that, after the best part of a year, he decided to move closer to it. Finally, I would be the undisputed man of the house. The *only* man of the house. Except that, the very day I helped speed up the process by carrying boxes laden with clothes and books and, possibly, those treasured old copies of *Men Only* and *Mayfair*, out to a waiting van, my mother got a call from Anglo School. One of the host families had encountered an emergency. Could my mother put someone up at impossibly short notice? Taking into account the impending loss of the rental income she'd been charging my brother this past year, she said yes. Marco moved in as Nic moved out.

But Marco was all right. He wasn't much older than my brother, and he didn't have authority in the house. He liked rock music. He claimed to be a Communist. And he was a massive football fan, too. This was useful, given that the European Championship was starting up the week he moved in; it would give me someone to watch the games with. And it created an instant rivalry between us – because not only were the games being held in Marco's native country, but England and Italy had been placed in the same group.

The tournament, though, was a disaster all around. During England's opening game, a number of fans went on a routine terrace rampage after the team let in a goal to Belgium, at which point the Italian riot police acted according to their own script – unleashing multiple rounds of tear gas, so much that it drifted onto the pitch and into the eyes of the players, causing the game to be stopped and the international media to once again condemn English fans as the scum of the earth.

This was becoming hard to dispute. Palace had just ended their first year back in the top flight, and a couple of months before the European Championship, I'd attended three games in a row with Jeffries. The rest of the Dulwich crew had largely stopped attending, despite our return to the top division. They'd all left school the previous summer. They no longer saw each other in the corridors of their posh schools to vibe each other up about the next away game, to incite each other to aggro. They barely saw each other in the pub any more, either. Some of them, like my brother, had got jobs and left home; others had gone to university. Most of them had girlfriends. And girls had a way of splitting up boys.

Jeffries had left school and taken a job, and a girlfriend, but continued living at home. Unlike the others, he stayed with the Palace, and his reputation on the terraces had grown along the way. At Tottenham, he'd refused to vacate his spot on the terraces even after a home crew had vacated the rest of it by force, and the Tottenham fans were so impressed that they agreed to leave him alone for the afternoon if he'd join them for an upcoming bout against Millwall. He came back from that match with tales of fighting that seemed beyond common reason.

So when he and I went to an away match at Arsenal in March and some Palace fans made an attempt to 'take' the home end, Jeffries was furious not to have been a part of it, and compensated by scrapping in the tube station afterwards. And the following Saturday, when we were at home to Manchester United and the 'Cockney Reds' attempted to take *our* home end, he steamed into them single-handed. I didn't see him again until the following Tuesday, when I got out of school early for some reason, and I called him and he seconded my impulse decision to go to West Bromwich Albion, up in Birmingham, by train that night, even though he was still nursing the bruises from running the gauntlet of Cockney Reds.

We lost 3–0 at West Brom that night. The evening cost us £7.50, which meant I couldn't afford to see Joy Division at the Moonlight Club the next night (though there'd always be another chance). And on the train home, Jeffries got into a heated exchange with some of the other Palace hard nuts, who wanted to graffiti the train with the NF logo. Jeffries' girlfriend was black, and he had already taken a lot of stick from the Dulwich crew as a result. I knew it was part of the reason he didn't hang out with them much any more. He wasn't about to take it from anyone else, Palace hard nuts or not. He vowed to graffiti SWP if the others wrote NF. He stared them down as he said it, and the train was left unscathed (for once).

Jeffries didn't come to the big Palace–Brighton derby the next week. He enjoyed a good ruck, a fair scrap between those who were looking for it, and he wouldn't normally have missed the confrontation against our south-coast rivals for the world. But with all the racist fans, it wasn't worth fighting for any more. And it was hard not to believe that the England fans now rioting out in Italy weren't exactly the same kind of people who put the colour of their skin ahead of the colour of their team.

For England's next European Championship game, I sat with Marco on our family sofa, as the Italian team played what I insisted to our unfailingly polite house-guest was a 'dirty' and 'cynical' form of football, one that involved defending for seventy-nine minutes, scoring a goal against the run of play in the eightieth minute, and then putting eleven men behind the ball for the remaining ten minutes. Marco's English was somewhat limited, but it was good enough to know the power of the phrase 'one-nil'. I couldn't afford to be too despondent; I had an O level to sit the next day.

Until now, I had always been able to pass my exams; something in my brain allowed me to focus when it really mattered, and the fact that I was good at English meant I could generally bluff my way through essays even when I wasn't certain of the subject at hand. But I hadn't expected the O levels to be quite this hard. Or for there to be quite so many of them. Every subject had multiple tests, which meant that my nine O levels required over twenty exams. We were sixteen, damn it (my best mates Richard and Jeff were still only fifteen) and the world was meant to be our oyster. The O levels were turning it into a clam.

The European Championship, then, provided one distraction. Writing reviews and small features for *The Face* offered another. The Bob Marley concert at the Crystal Palace Bowl yet one more. (I didn't attend. I sat out in our small back garden, listening to the music as it wafted down the hill. I tried to convince myself that I didn't need to be at the show, that I'd seen Steel Pulse, Aswad and Misty in Roots all in concert and that Bob Marley was far too popular for reggae's own good. But earlier in the day I'd ridden the bus home from Brixton; it was full of Jamaicans in joyous anticipation of seeing their prophet play, right here in the heart of Babylon. I kicked myself for not getting a ticket after all.) Playing book cricket – a pointless game that awarded runs according to the order of printed letters – offered entirely meaningless escapism.

Yet none of these distractions occupied my mind quite like the quality of our demo tape. I'd learned much from the day at Street Level, but the most valuable lesson was this: that which sounds brilliant at the end of a long day's work, with a couple of lagers inside you, on a studio sound system, in the company of your bandmates and friends, never sounds so good in the cold light of day, on a home stereo, with only yourself and your doubts for company. Every time I put the tape on to assure myself that it had been time and money well spent, I'd hear a fresh mistake, another missed opportunity, and I'd go to sleep convinced I was a failure. I'd wake up in the morning, persuade myself that it was a new day, go into school all bright and cheerful, and then, in between O levels, provoked (I suspected) by his own frustrations with exams, Jeff would criticise my singing voice and assure me that it had made us unmarketable. Falling back into a flunk, I'd come home, and listen to the tape again, knowing that Jeff was right while refusing to admit it to anyone but myself.

Still, it was all we had. And it had cost us £75. So I called Street Level and put in an order for twenty-five cassette copies. Jeff designed an insert despite his misgivings. And on one of the few days when there were no O levels on the calendar, I went up to Carnaby Street, dropped in my latest review for *The Face*, took a tube up to Maida Vale, picked up our box of tapes from the studio, and came straight back down to the West End, to the Polydor Records building opposite Bond Street tube station, where The Jam were recording at the label's in-house studio and where, as always, I had an open invitation to stop by.

Revolver was on the turntable when I got there, and Weller was eager to play it for me. This was something I really liked about him – that, even as he had become Britain's biggest rock star, admired, envied and worshipped by hundreds of thousands of teenagers and young adults, he was still a fan at heart, contagiously enthusiastic about his own musical discoveries. Certainly, he was handling his new-found fame better than had Ian Curtis, who, unable to rid himself of whatever demons inspired that crazed dance of his, had hanged himself a couple of weeks earlier, on the eve of Joy Division's first American tour. And perhaps because Joy Division had been on the road to greatness, his death became a moment of shared consciousness. Everyone on the independent music scene felt it – especially John Peel, who took to playing the group's new single, the mournfully melodic 'Love Will Tear Us Apart', far in advance of its release. The remaining members of Joy Division, meanwhile, handled Ian Curtis's death in exactly the opposite way than The Who handled the death of Keith Moon. They broke up immediately.

Weller had been greatly upset by Curtis's suicide. He'd only turned twenty-two the week we recorded our demo tape, which made him a full two years younger than Ian Curtis, and younger than two of the Beatles when they'd had their first British number one. Perhaps that's why he was currently obsessed with the music of the world's most popular band, to see what steps they had taken to avoid creative stagnation at such a young age. He was expertly placed, then, to point out to me that the Beatles' transition from a singles-based pop band to an albums-oriented rock group had not really taken place, as conventional wisdom (and my dad's own record-buying habits) had it, with *Sgt. Peppers* in 1967; it had occurred a year earlier with *Revolver*. All right, so it wasn't exactly a concept album, but any LP that started with George Harrison's defiant 'Taxman', continued with Paul McCartney's majestic 'Eleanor Rigby', found time to detour into every little kid's favourite Beatles song, the Ringo-sung 'Yellow Submarine', and still ended up with John Lennon's masterpiece 'Tomorrow Never Knows' was obviously something special.

I was keen to hear more of it. I was especially keen to hear how The Jam were being influenced by it. But when I handed him an Apocalypse demo tape, Paul downed tools so that we could go into the office of A&R man Dennis Munday and listen together. The next thing I knew, we were lining it up on *truly* state-of-the-art equipment, the kind that the Street Level engineers would probably refuse to use on principle. I had as my audience not only the spokesman of my generation, and his A&R man – who, presumably, knew good music when he heard it – but The Jam's bass player too, Bruce Foxton seeming no more committed to a day's work in the studio than Paul. We sat back in leather armchairs and couches, our feet up on glass coffee tables . . .

And when 'Schizophrenic' announced itself with a pair of drumsticks counting off the beat followed by the sound of a Gibson copy lamely emulating one of Paul's Rickenbacker riffs, I sensed Weller's face tense up. Bruce, typically, was more vocal in his reaction. Halfway through the first chorus, he said something dismissive about our influences – our lack of originality, that is, not the influence itself – and Paul stared daggers at him; whatever his own impression, he clearly thought Bruce's response to be rude. Only when 'Schizophrenic' finally emerged into its dub section did I feel some relief. Sure, it was a rip-off of 'Thick as Thieves' and 'When You're Young', but it showed that we had *some* imagination. Besides, we did the reggae stuff pretty well, and there were brief compliments all around. Then the track ended with a squeal of feedback and the sound of me toggling the pick-up switch on the guitar. If it was a trick originated by Pete Townshend back in the sixties, it was one that Weller had perfected as far back as The Jam's first LP, and it just about occurred to me how it must have felt for *him*, listening to a poor imitation of The Jam imitating The Who and wondering what disease he'd unleashed on the world.

Weller stuck it out for all four songs. And when they were done, he mentioned something about a support slot with The Jam some time, as if we'd passed a test just by proving we could save up our money, hire a studio and go through the process of recording a demo tape, and that the overall quality of it wasn't really the issue. Admittedly The Jam had no dates lined up at the moment, and none planned in London until Christmas, which was half a lifetime away as far as I was concerned, but still . . . It was exactly the kind of carrot that would help get me through the rest of my exams.

I came home with something else that day: a copy of Dave Waller's *Notes from Hostile Street*, hot off the presses, finally. (Paul Weller, it turned out, wasn't much more punctual with his publishing enterprises than I was.) *Notes* fell somewhere between a fanzine and a songbook, and it suggested that there might be a new kind of lyricism that, likewise, could fill the large gap that existed between the written essay and the pop lyric. Waller wasn't big on rhyming couplets, or punctuation for that matter, and some of his titles ('Subway', 'Slumlands', 'Warpoem') seemed like they might have originated back in his own schooldays, but when I showed the book to my mum that evening, she was immediately impressed.

My mother didn't really know what to make of my friendship with Paul Weller, any more than she really knew what to make of everything else that I was doing with the fanzine and the band – and at the same time, all that I was not doing with my O levels. It was hard for her to know whether the people I was hanging out with were punk rockers or pop stars (or both), whether they were mentors or menaces (or both), and she was bound to be worried that, if my short haircut, Harrington jacket and Ben Sherman were anything to go by, I was no more likely to attend university than my brother. But bringing home books of poetry, that was a different matter. And for all that she was a student of Shakespeare and Thomas Hardy, she was also a teacher in a tough inner-London school. She understood the importance of offering her pupils material that was relevant to their own lives. In fact, she was so immediately taken by Waller's words that she asked if he might want to come in to Stockwell and read to one of her English classes. I didn't have Waller's phone number, but I suspected The Jam would still be at the studio; like any band, they didn't get in the groove until mid-afternoon at best. I called up, got through to Weller, he gave me Waller's number in Woking, I called it, Waller was home, I put him on to my mum, and the school visit was arranged, there and then. For a rare day without O levels, it had been a good one all around. And in the process, whatever generation gap had been opening up between me and my mum appeared to have closed just as rapidly again.

Besides, my mum had been right about something else. After they'd allied themselves with the fortunes of their local team West Ham United, recording a version of the terrace song 'I'm Forever Blowing Bubbles' to coincide with the Hammers' appearance in the FA Cup Final against Arsenal, it became apparent that the Cockney Rejects had signed their own death warrant, that they wouldn't be able to play a gig anywhere else in the country now without facing down the local football crew, often on the stage itself. Just like Sham 69, who had similarly overestimated their ability to control their audience, their days were numbered, and already their fans numbered one less. Because the more that I listened to it, the more I realised that *Greatest Hits Volume I* was, indeed, rubbish. Especially in a world that included *Revolver*.

Number 4:
REALITY ASYLUM

C rass were Britain's biggest punk band. This was almost funny, considering that their first release, the 1978 12-inch *The Feeding of the 5000*, had included a track entitled 'Punk Is Dead'. But then the EP had also included perfectly punkish song titles like 'Fight War, Not Wars' and 'They've Got a Bomb', and it had opened with the question 'Do they owe us a living?' to which they had shouted their own answer, 'Of course they fucking do.' (Actually, the initial pressings of *Feeding* opened with a track entitled 'The Sound of Free Speech', two minutes of silence that replaced the *intended* opening cut, 'Reality Asylum', which the pressing plant had refused to handle because of its apparently blasphemous lyrics.) *The Feeding of the 5000* came in a black and white sleeve with stencilled lettering, and a collage that depicted mankind in all its misery, and it carried the insistence that the consumer should pay no more than £2.00, half the price of a normal LP. Punk is dead? Not bleedin' likely.

As the record took off, it became apparent that Crass had hit a raw nerve. For tens of thousands of (mostly) teenagers, upset at missing out on the original rebellion of 1976–77, far from swayed by the 'new wave' in all its varieties of DayGlo, cynical about the mod and ska revivals, and disgusted by the Sham 69 school of back-to-punk basics, Crass were the real deal, a chance to press the rewind button and then press punk forward in the direction they felt it should have gone all along. Crass helped matters along by occasionally circling the A on their name to intimate that they were anarchists, and any number of kids, my mate Jeff Carrigan among them, followed suit, applying it to exercise books, leather jackets and train station walls alike with such frequency that there was the danger of it becoming just another fashion symbol, no more vested with meaning than the mod target.

Still, when Crass left Small Wonder to start their own label, found a pressing plant (in France) that would handle 'Reality Asylum' and then not only restored it to their own pressing of *Feeding* but released it as a 7-inch single as well, they demonstrated a commitment, beyond any other so-called 'punk' band, to put their money where their mouths were. They also confirmed why 'Reality Asylum' had caused so much controversy to begin with. It called Christ a 'Suicide visionary. Death reveller. Rake. Rapist. Gravedigger. Earthmover. Lifefucker'. It then added, for good measure, that he 'scooped the pits of Auschwitz'. This was so far *beyond* blasphemy that few people even had a word for it.

Crass wore black clothing, and their logo was suspiciously similar to a swastika, but nobody mistook them for fascists – least of all the stormtroopers of the National Front and the more blatantly aggressive British Movement, who took it upon themselves to disrupt Crass gigs, hoping through sheer force of intimidation to prevent the group from spreading their message. After a couple of Crass shows were ruined by a display of mass Sieg Heiling and the cracking of several skulls, the hardest of London's hard-core leftist thugs, many of them veterans of the attack on the NF march in Lewisham in 1977, came together at a Crass concert at London's Conway Hall in 1979, where they locked the doors, convinced the hapless organisers (it being a benefit, as were most Crass gigs) not to call the police, and pounded the Nazis with every weapon in their arsenal. It was a battle the likes of which, according to those unfortunate Crass fans who were caught in the middle, had never been seen before at anything claiming to be a rock gig. Ever.

It was partly – though not solely – the subsequent infamy of that Conway Hall battle that found me criticising Crass's music for being 'so harsh it just encourages violence', in an editorial I wrote for the late '79 issue of *Jamming*. The piece was called 'Tribalism' and in it I also had a go at the *NME* for labelling *Jamming* a 'mod fanzine', and, especially, at *Sounds* writer Garry Bushell for a piece that glorified a new wave of beachfront bank holiday mod riots on the south coast. When laid out in black type over bright red photographs of violent altercations (including the beer-can-throwing skinhead from the previous year's Reading Festival), surrounded by a hand-drawn brick wall of graffiti by Jeff, the piece seemed to touch a nerve of its own. Almost as soon as the issue was published, the post starting arriving through my letterbox. Among those to respond were Garry Bushell – and Penny Rimbaud, Crass's leader.

Anarchists were not meant to have leaders, of course, but anyone who knew anything about Crass knew that Rimbaud was the brains behind the musical brawn. Like several other members of the band, he was an unrepentant hippie, having been politically active since the turbulent late 1960s. He was, come to that, older than Keith Moon would have been, and all of this made me inherently wary of him, as it did others who believed that punk was meant to be a youth movement – a valid concern that Crass countered perfectly with their main male singer, Steve Ignorant, who was barely twenty years old, looked like Sid Vicious might have done had the Pistols' bassist laid off the drugs, and was occasionally joined on vocals by the youthful Joy de Vivre and Eve Libertine, two women who refused to distinguish themselves from the men in the band in any manner of attire or hair styling and who, in the process, created a new, feminist fashion. The suspicion that Crass were attempting to unite the hippie and punk movements was perhaps best proven by their new single, entitled 'Bloody Revolutions'. A comment of sorts on the Conway Hall night(mare), directed every bit as much at the leftists as the Nazis, it announced that 'Freedom has no value if violence is the price/I don't want your revolution, I want anarchy and peace.'

Anarchy and peace. For many, the two words were incompatible together, a little like 'Millwall' and 'peace'. And so, to get to the bottom of it, I finally accepted Rimbaud's invitation to visit Crass at their home base, a place called Dial House in North Weald, Ongar – at the far, Essex end of the Central Line. The intent, nominally, was to conduct an interview for the next *Jamming*, but the invitation was always about something much wider: come see how we live, wrote Rimbaud, come get a sense of what we're all about.

Jeff, naturally, was thrilled to join me. Though he favoured the anarchy symbol himself and had designed the Apocalypse banner in Crass's image, his family's politics were sufficiently Conservative that he had his own misgivings about their way of life. He took it upon himself to invite Stevo along for the ride too, no doubt hoping that Crass might steer his mate around through conversation in a way the Damned had failed to do by means of insult. The three of us took the train out to North Weald together, and we called Crass from the station as they'd told us to, and they gave us directions to their farmhouse and, after pausing for refreshment at a country pub, the novelty of which seemed too good to pass up, we eventually found Dial House at the end of a long cul-de-sac, seemingly in the middle of nowhere.

The house dated back to the 1500s, though its age was somewhat obscured by the number of rooms that had been added on over the years – and by the abundance of musical equipment, records, books, fanzines and the like. Something called *The Agricultural Notebook* had been written here a hundred years earlier, and an organic vegetable garden on the premises suggested that the author's spirit had lived on. Prior to forming Crass, Penny Rimbaud and other long-term residents had hosted avant-garde musical festivals here and, it turned out, they had launched the Stonehenge Festival from the very same premises. It had been easy to snicker about it all in advance, this idea of a hippie punk band living in a commune all the way out in Essex, but now that we were here, we could understand it. Dial House offered tranquillity and harmony. Here they could, truly, practise anarchy and peace.

Much of our time was spent just hanging out, as we had presumed it would: like Scritti Politti's confined space in Camden, the residents enjoyed debate for its own sake, over and above the desire to make music. (Our hopes of watching Crass rehearse went unrealised.) There was one almost predictably farcical incident – when I went to use the toilet, and one of the women was in there taking a bath, and she told me not to worry about her, just go ahead and pee or shit or whatever it was I planned to do, we were all just humans, weren't we, and I stood there at the toilet trying to shield my willy from her, totally unused to the experience. And naturally we were invited to share in a vegetable stew that had been cooking all day long – ingredients presumably grown in their Garden of Eden. I lived on a diet of chips, saveloys, sausages, kebabs, chocolate, lager and cigarettes. The idea of healthy food – of vegetarian food, especially – scared me.

And then there was a moment that had me genuinely worried – when Jeff played our Apocalypse demo, and they reacted to the blatantly Crass-influenced 'D.D.J.D.' so enthusiastically (and so unlike The Jam upon hearing 'Schizophrenic') that they suggested including it on a compilation of like-minded bands that they were putting together, entitled *Bullshit Detector*. Jeff was thrilled at the notion. I was less keen. When we'd named our group after the last line of a Jam single, I'd had no idea that there would soon be a movement afoot featuring bands called Discharge, Crisis and UK Decay, a movement to which the name 'Apocalypse' would so easily fit. But it was too late now. We'd played gigs, we'd made a demo, and our stickers, like the Crass stencilled logo, were visible all over London. If we decided on a less explosive name, we'd be back at the beginning.

At some point in the afternoon, we sat down to conduct an interview. It was my firm intention to catch Crass out somehow, or at least to challenge them, to prove that I was no easy convert to their sloganeering, but the group were, by now, past masters at justifying their beliefs – especially to young fanzine writers like ourselves. To our opening demand that they define anarchy, they suggested that it was a 'rejection of social control', and then elaborated. 'Through refusing to recognise something, it effectively ceases to exist.' This was somewhat deeper than the politics we had been discussing among ourselves in recent months – we had never considered the notion that school, for example, might cease to exist if we simply refused to recognise it – so we pressed the issue. Could anarchy work?

'If everyone was like us it would work,' they responded. (Penny, as I'd suspected, did most of the talking, but I had such a hard time distinguishing different voices on the cassette tape that I chose not to credit anyone individually, figuring that Crass, of all bands, could speak with one voice.) 'If everyone respected each other obviously it would work. We see anarchy as basically just respecting each other as individuals.'

Foiled in that regard, we followed up with a question that offered our underlying assumption that in a world of anarchy, there would be less of their own preferred 'respect' and more of Captain Sensible's presumed 'wanton destruction and chaos'. To which end: what do you do when someone's murdered?

'You do whatever you feel you should do,' came the initial reply, playing into our fears, perhaps. But right behind it came the clarification. 'The police force don't catch most of the wild psychopaths. There's very few loonies and they don't catch them. On the one hand, society is training people to kill as an everyday event, like soldiers, and on the other hand it's so malicious to anyone who actually kills someone else.'

So we turned to religion, and Crass paid Jesus lip service as a motivational speaker, but one who ultimately copped out of his responsibilities. Elaborating on the confrontational words of 'Reality Asylum', they explained that 'Christ shouldn't have humbly sat there in the garden waiting for them to come – he should have buggered off and done a gig somewhere else. If you look at the grizzly bearded figure on the cross with this tortured idea . . . It's just bad theatre. It's a tasteless, over-the-top production. Look at a figure of Buddha, who represents joy, life and religion, a beautiful happy little soul, sitting there, grinning away, and it makes you feel happy. But if I look at this tormented soul, who said all the same sort of things, but ended up doing that – it's depressing, it's desperate.'

This was a novel argument for people like Jeff and me, who attended a church school, complete with stained-glass windows in the assembly hall that included precisely that image of Christ on the cross. We had, to be honest, never stopped to consider the idea that it was sending out a message of violence to the world, let alone that the smiling Buddha of some far-off religion might be a better alternative. Fortunately, Crass had not just done so for us, but they had evidence to back up their (non) belief system, in the shape of guitarist Phil Free's children, a girl and two boys, all between the ages of about eight and twelve, and all full-time residents at Dial House. I was so used to the kids of my native South London: tense, trouble-some, turbulent little things. But Phil's children clearly were not like that; living out here, in the British countryside, in a communal/anarchic/pacifist homestead, they had been spared all the conditioning that had permeated our own upbringing. They appeared to be leading a charmed existence, totally at peace with the world. They were, I wrote when I got home that night, 'beautiful', a word that rarely passed my lips or my pen. They were little Buddhas.

The one issue we did not press Crass on was that of their hippie roots. It would have been hard to deny them, besides which, they had already endured great amounts of grief on this score from the music press's self-appointed champions of the working class, Tony Parsons and, in particular, Garry Bushell. Not being the types to take such criticisms lying down, they had responded in kind with a Sham 69 piss-take on their recent *Stations of the Cross* double LP ('Pay no more than £3'), entitled

'Hurry Up Garry'. For this they now apologised: personal vendettas, they had come to realise, looked petty, pathetic even, when placed on (the) record for all posterity.

But it was too late: battle lines had been drawn. Just as Crass had inspired an ever-growing number of openly anarchist and proudly tuneless bands in their own image, Bushell was single-handedly building a movement of short-haired, loud-mouthed, football fanatic, defiantly working-class bands in the mould of the Cockney Rejects and their northern peers, the Angelic Upstarts. He'd even come up with a name for it: Oi!, as simplistic as could be. Unlike Crass, the Oi! bands were perfectly willing to embrace violence as a means to an end – though quite what end they had in mind nobody, not even Bushell, ever seemed able to articulate.

There was a depressing sense of foreboding about all of this, a dark realisation that, as if we hadn't been through the wars enough already, things were about to get *really* ugly. For someone like me whose musical tastes lay elsewhere entirely (my brief fondness for the Cockney Rejects notwithstanding), I didn't necessarily have to worry about being caught in the middle of this impending showdown. I could, if I wanted, walk away from it all, return to the welcoming bosom of The Jam and co., where old-fashioned socialism manifested itself in the shape of sharp suits and even sharper tunes. But all the same, I came away from Dial House aware that I had been shown another path in life, one that didn't distinguish between Labour and Conservative, and barely saw the lesser of two evils in the SWP and NF; one that didn't celebrate rucking on the terraces under the misguided belief that it was codified and honourable and ultimately all good fun; that didn't involve smashing up abandoned buildings as an excuse that it was letting off steam; that didn't justify attacks on fascists by left-ists any more than attacks on immigrants by fascists; that didn't place any value in profits; and that kept a distinct distance from the revival of old fashions, be they mod, rude boy, skinhead or, for that matter, punk. That path originated in a fifteenth-century Garden of Eden out in Epping. Whether it could be routed through the streets of South-East London, however, was up to each and every one of us. As individuals.

Number 3:
IT'S DIFFERENT FOR GIRLS

Denise was a girl from West Dulwich with a reputation for sexual promiscuity. If I could have developed such a reputation, I might have been known as a stud. But because Denise was a girl, she was a slut. Nobody said it to her face, because she was, frankly, too much fun. But we all said it behind her back. It was the way of the world. Boys were *meant* to put it about. Girls were not. And yet boys like me, who so badly wanted to put it about, needed girls like Denise – and her mate Brenda – to do so.

All my closest schoolfriends had now lost their virginity. Chris had come first. I'd arrived at school one Monday morning early in the fifth year to find a group gathered around his desk, listening to him in awe. The way he described it was quite matter of fact. He'd been out with this girl on Saturday night and she'd asked him back to her place, and there they'd done it, on her bed, at her invitation. He told us that he'd kept his socks on, and that they'd laughed about it even as they started getting down to it. It was the kind of detail that you wouldn't think of making up.

Jeff followed not long after. He'd long turned into a magnet for punkettes – as I'd witnessed that night at the Marquee when he was still fourteen. Along the way, while hanging out with all the other youth tribes in Hastings, he'd met a girl his own age, all dyed hair and exotic make-up, they'd started going steady, and he had offered us all blow-by-blow reports on their progress. Inevitably, he came into school himself one Monday morning over winter and announced that he, too, had joined the club.

To make matters worse, Richard had lost it as well. After breaking up with the French modette, he'd met a nice girl somewhere, and they were properly in love. So much so that they even started meeting up at her place in Clapham during lunch hour. Seemed to me he barely had time to get there before he had to turn round and return to school. But, given that Jeff was constantly (and shamelessly) admitting to anyone within earshot that he couldn't last longer than two minutes, it seemed to be enough time to shag. I'd have liked to believe it was pointless, chasing something so brief, but until I could experience those two minutes for myself, it seemed like the most important race on earth.

Then Jeni threw her sixteenth birthday party, on a Saturday night near the end of June. Another week of O levels beckoned come Monday, but it would be the final week, and there was a sense that we were over the worst of it, that the finish line was in sight, that soon we'd be free for the summer. We could leave school behind for good if we so wanted, get jobs if we could find them, even get married. The thought that we were almost at the point that society would proclaim us as 'adults' (not that it yet trusted us with the right to vote) inspired an atmosphere of abandon.

Certainly, I was feeling good about myself as I got ready that evening. A few weeks earlier, I'd gone to Johnson's, the famous rock clothing store on the King's Road, and treated myself to a pair of lurid red and black leather shoes; in the store right next door, I'd found a matching black buttoned shirt with red stripes down the middle. The Harrington and Ben Sherman still had their place in the scheme of things, but I was returning to some statement of individuality – and without the pronounced 'look at me' aspect of the teddy bear jumper and the Chelsea Pensioner's tunic. I took a shower before setting off on the mile-long walk down South Croxted Road to Jen's. And when Denise, who was going steady now with a boy from Alleyn Road, Joseph Tomlins, told me early on that her mate Brenda 'fancied' me, I decided to act on it immediately. I went straight across the room to where Brenda was standing. With straight dark hair, and a round face, she was big in all the right places, and she had a look about her that suggested that she was experienced.

'Denise says you fancy me.'

'So?'

'So, you wanna come back to my place?' My mother had gone to her brother's house in Wembley for the evening. I really wanted to make the most of her absence.

Brenda laughed. 'The party's just started,' she said.

'So?' I said, imitating her own response from a moment earlier.

'So, don't you think we should get to know each other first?'

'You mean you might come back with me later?'

'I didn't say that.'

'You didn't say you didn't.'

She didn't say anything. I took a swig of whatever drink I had in hand, and she did likewise. I put my arm round her back, and she didn't object. I knew all along – always had done – that confidence was everything, that girls could sense it a mile away and generally reacted favourably to it. I just rarely had that confidence around girls the way I did, for example, around musicians. Tonight, though, I had it. I'd arrived with it. Denise had bolstered it. Brenda had bolstered it further. I gave her a peck on the cheek. She didn't object. I tried to kiss her on the lips. She didn't quite open them, but she didn't push me away either. I gave her a look, meant to signify that we were partners for the night, and she gave me a look that suggested the same thing. Then I went across the room to greet my mates from Tenison's who'd just arrived together from various points around the Borough and the Elephant: John, Keith and Ian. It had taken them half the evening to get here. In fact, it was 9 p.m. already, and if they were going to get back to the Elephant by bus, they'd need to leave in little over an hour. I told them they could stay at my place: what were friends for if not to host other friends when their mum had gone away for the night? We poured drinks. Threw them down our necks. It was 21 June, the longest day of the year. Why not draw it out as long as possible?

Denise came over to where we were standing, and pulled me aside.

'Did you just ask Brenda to go home with you?' There was a look on her face, and I couldn't tell if it was incredulity or admiration.

'Yeah,' I admitted.

'You *slut.*' She drew out the word so that it sounded like several syllables.

I shrugged.

'She fancies you,' Denise said again. And she walked off, wearing that conspiratorial smile of hers, leaving my imagination to sort out the rest.

Within minutes, Brenda and I were snogging. It just seemed natural. And only an hour or so later, we left the party together, alongside Denise and Joseph. Jeni's mother was coming home soon and she wouldn't put up with all the kissing. We walked up Alleyn Road to Joseph's house, but when we got there, his parents were home, and though they all knew Denise well enough and liked her, they didn't seem so sure about me and Brenda. The chance of us being left alone to act on any impulses was slim to none. So, again, I suggested we go back to mine, and this time everyone agreed.

There, we found Marco on the sofa, watching the late-night highlights of Italy's third-place play-off game in the European Championship. (England hadn't even made it out of the group stage.) Denise and Joseph sat down to join him as I led a willing Brenda upstairs. As soon as I got up to my room, I put an LP on to block out any noise: *Meaty Beaty Big and Bouncy* would do the job. Then Brenda and I fell on the bed together.

It was as easy as it was sudden. All these months of little and lean action, opportunities seeming to fade away as rapidly as they'd arisen, and here I was, with a minimum of discussion and debate, with no pretence to my ambitions and no protest either, alone with what I took to be a willing woman in my bedroom. Would she be the one? Experience was much more important to me right now than emotion, eagerness a far greater asset than finesse, and Brenda passed both requirements with ease. We locked lips and went for it, kissing furiously as we rolled on the bed. There were none of the usual tentative forays around the outside of each other's clothing; our sharp conversation and snogging had already rendered that unnecessary. My hands wandered instinctively up the front of her chest, and she did nothing to stop them. They headed in between the buttons on her blouse and again, she didn't object. They found their way straight inside her bra and rather than complain that I was moving too fast, she angled her body around so that I could reach behind her back and unclip it. I did so, though not too artfully, I knew. Her breathing grew heavier. I suspected that mine did as well.

All this was good, but it wasn't good enough. I'd been here a couple of times already. I needed to go further. So I removed my right hand and set it back down, between her denimed thighs. Typically, such a move was met by the closing of the legs, sometimes even the crossing of them. No girl wanted it spread around town that she hadn't put up a fight. Brenda, though, seemed – initially – to have no such compunction. She let my hand run freely between her legs, until it settled at the point where the foot of her zipper met the seam of her jeans. I pushed hard inwards, her breathing grew heavier in my mouth, and she pulled so hard on my short hair that it hurt. Hoping to seize the momentum, I tried to undo the button on her jeans with my one free hand – and I couldn't manage it. While I fumbled in frustration, she brought her hand down from the back of my head and placed it upon my own.

Well, I could hardly be blamed for trying. No pain, no gain, and all that. I was still cursing her convictions, her protection of a reputation, when Brenda nestled her fingers in among my own and, to my surprise, not only helped me undo the button at the top of her jeans, but attached our entwined hands to the fly – and had me unzip her.

It was only a minor adjustment to her clothing; it was but a small display of flesh and underwear revealed by the newly created V-shaped gap at the top of her jeans. But it was enough to suggest that a door had been opened, and I wasn't about to waste time asking if I could enter. I sent my hand underneath, seeking out my long-awaited prize. I found it wet with anticipation.

I leaned into her ear. 'I want to screw you,' I whispered between deep breaths. My bold talk had worked well for me so far.

'Not tonight,' she responded, equally breathlessly and just as forcefully. 'But don't stop what you're doing.'

I didn't. Several minutes later, with my arm aching and eager to quit but hers keeping it firmly in place, her vocal utterances rose an octave in scale and to fortissimo in volume, and her spare hand gripped the bed sheet as if in terror, while the other maintained its hold on mine to keep command of my actions. She emitted a long and only slightly muffled scream, followed by violent shudders. I watched in fascination as waves of relaxation proceeded to wash over her, and then – and only then – did she remove her hand, still attached to my own, from her crotch.

I smiled as I looked down on her. It was not a smile of love, or even, necessarily, of passion, but one of success and satisfaction. Of pride. We stayed that way for a few moments as she recovered. Then, suddenly, as if remembering an urgent appointment, she pulled her jeans and knickers back up, pushed me onto my back and, as I lay there bemused, in an impressively deft manner she undid my trouser button with a single hand that she promptly threw inside my underpants – forcing my zipper down in the process, and grabbed my aching cock. The entire move took all of a second.

'That's how it's done,' she whispered with an air of superiority, and her head descended between my legs.

How long had I dreamed of this moment? Probably since the first time I'd borrowed one of my brother's magazines, and read about the blow job as the ultimate male fantasy. Now here I was, finally on the receiving end, and it was every bit as good as I imagined. Brenda was only sixteen, my age, but there was an expertise to her actions, an athleticism, an artistry. She knew how to squeeze me, how to please me; in the words of the old Slade song, she was making it easy. And she was in the middle of doing so when my bedroom door opened – and in barged John, Keith and Ian.

Not again! Hadn't Denise and Joseph thought to warn them? Hadn't they thought to knock? How drunk could they possibly be that they wouldn't have suspected I might finally be getting the action that they too were surely desperate for?

'Fuck off!' I screamed. And, after taking in the scene, they duly scrammed, laughing loudly as they galloped downstairs while I hurled unrepeatable insults in their general direction. I felt like crying; after my experience with Monica, there was no way Brenda wouldn't act likewise, throw on her clothes and run out of my life in embarrassment.

But she didn't. 'What am I meant to do?' she laughed. 'Deny it?' And she went back to pleasing me.

When it was all over, I lay there for a while, ecstatic and exhausted, and somewhat in awe of her talents and pride in them, and when I sensed that we were both spent, and we weren't going to go any further tonight, I got dressed. We went downstairs together to find Denise and Joseph, Ian, John and Keith – and of course Marco – sat around half-heartedly watching the penalty shoot-out between Italy and Czechoslovakia. Knowing smirks were exchanged all around. Nobody would be able to accuse me of fabrication or exaggeration. I had witnesses. The only person who seemed embarrassed was poor Marco.

I told my friends to behave themselves and left them there, with the resident Italian, while Joseph and I walked Denise and Brenda home. In the morning, I made my mates breakfast, though not before one of them puked up his guts in the sink. It had been that kind of night. In the afternoon, I tried revising for my maths exam the following morning, but my heart wasn't in it. Nor was my head. It had been that kind of night. When Joseph called me later to say Brenda wanted to see me at Denise's house, I gladly put away the textbooks and set off on the mile-long walk towards the Rosendale area.

I was half-heartedly hoping for more action – conclusive action – but it was a Sunday evening, and it wasn't to be. Brenda, it seemed, wanted to hang out with me, to cement our relationship as a couple. And yet, in the cold light of day, I just didn't fancy her deeply enough to be her boyfriend. So we hung out, and we kissed when I said goodbye, and then I came home and watched the European Championship Final with Marco. West Germany beat Belgium. Neither of us really cared.

I was excruciatingly tired the next morning. I could barely keep my eyes open, let alone focus on the exam at hand. The advanced maths O level proved almost impossible. About the only sum I could figure out was the number of answers I didn't know – and it was enough to ensure that I would fail. Why did our O levels have to coincide with our period of sexual exploration? Why did Jeni have to turn sixteen in the middle of them, and not at the very end of them? Why did I have to sit the hardest of exams this Monday morning, not the easiest of them?

Ah, but was it worth failing an O level for what I'd scored on Saturday night? Even a fool knew the answer to that one.

Number 2:
BOY ABOUT TOWN

G uy was two years older than me, a better musician than me,
a better dresser, better looking, played better gigs and got
off with better girls. But the fact was, he'd still never visited a
state-of-the-art recording studio like the Town House. And so,
the day of my final O levels, in the space between a written
technical drawing paper in the morning and a French oral in
the afternoon, rather than follow the 'sensible' course of action
– going home to study or relax, for example – I invited
Speedball's bass player to join me on a trip out to Shepherd's
Bush. He could come and meet The Jam.

The previous Saturday night, at more or less exactly the
same moment I was receiving my first blow job, The Jam had
been on stage at the Loch Lomond Festival, their biggest
headlining gig in the UK since Reading almost two years earlier.
Not much had changed in all that time: the promoters still
threw mod bands (the Chords), skinhead bands (Bad Manners,
an all-white group with a monstrously large bald-headed front
man named Buster Bloodvessel), punk bands (Stiff Little
Fingers) and any number of new wave misfits (e.g. the Tourists
from Edinburgh) together on the same bill and hoped for the
best. The results were still much the same, too: fans got drunk,
and they fought. I had no regrets at missing it. (Especially
considering what I had gained in the process.)

Paul had hated the gig. It was, perhaps, a lone (though no
doubt lucrative) misstep in what was otherwise his determined
and admirable refusal to abide by the write-record-tour syndrome
that had found The Jam struggling to finish *Setting Sons* in

time. They had begun lining up relatively small shows, in different parts of the country, and announcing the dates just far enough in advance to ensure they'd sell out without turning into a circus. On stage they'd then introduce a new song or two before returning to the Town House or Polydor studios to knock those songs into shape.

The first fruits of this new approach – the follow-up to 'Going Underground' – were about to be unveiled to the public. And they were exciting in that the A-side, 'Start!', was different from anything The Jam had released before. It was not, however, different from anything anyone *else* had released before. 'Start!' was an obvious rip-off of *Revolver*'s opening cut, 'Taxman'. The bass line behind each song's verse was essentially identical, and the sharp sound of a Rickenbacker playing a major seventh chord on the off-beat during The Jam's instrumental bridge was highly similar to that of George Harrison's riff during the Beatles' verses. On one hand, it was refreshing to hear The Jam freed from the power chords that had reached a crescendo on 'Going Underground': the production on 'Start!' was pleasingly spare, the lyrics withdrew from the political back to the subtly personal, there was a marvellous middle eight that highlighted the more delicate and generally underplayed side of Paul's voice, and a wonderfully psychedelic guitar solo to round things off. As long as George Harrison didn't sue for copyright infringement, Paul could surely rely on another hefty bout of songwriting royalties of his own. Perhaps even another number one hit. Under the circumstances, it felt almost churlish to point out that the B-side, a ballad called 'Liza Radley', had plenty of its own in common with the ballad that followed 'Taxman' on *Revolver*, 'Eleanor Rigby'. I comforted myself instead with the fact that, on this evidence, even the most talented young songwriter in the world could be reduced to imitation.

Besides, I was equally taken by the other new material I was hearing in the studio, much of it on a cassette of demos and rough mixes Paul played for Guy and myself in the lounge over lunchtime. A few of these songs had already been introduced live: 'But I'm Different Now', loud and abrasive; 'Pretty Green', sufficiently familiar and anthemic that there'd been a push from Polydor to release it as the new single instead of 'Start!'; and 'That's Entertainment', a semi-acoustic poem about everyday working-class life – a follow-on, of sorts, to 'Saturday's Kids'. Paul had fretted how 'That's Entertainment' would inspire a Jam 'backlash', but after my experience misreading 'English Rose', and with its references to 'days of speed and slow time Mondays' and other perfectly articulated aspects of my own teenage existence, I was none so sure it wouldn't be proclaimed, instead, as the best thing he'd ever written.

Then again, I felt much the same way about 'Man in the Corner Shop', which used a circular melody to connect the self-employed shopkeeper to the factory owner to the factory worker, all of them figuring that the grass was surely greener elsewhere (and Paul reminding us that, in theory at least, 'God created all men equal'). 'Dream Time' and 'Monday' were unquestionably influenced by psychedelia: The Jam's journey through the sixties was moving irrefutably towards some sort of endpoint. And there were two numbers, 'Set the House Ablaze' and 'Scrape Away', that owed much to the influence of the Gang of Four, creating space for Bruce and Rick to stretch out, to open up and prove themselves as much more than merely Paul's rhythm section. Lyrically, too, they formed a pair. On 'Set the House Ablaze', Paul lamented the loss of a friend to the rising tide of jackbooted fascism; on 'Scrape Away', he accused another former acquaintance, self-centred in a manner that made the 'Burning Sky' protagonist seem positively sympathetic, 'of talking like some fucking hardened MP'. The me-first spirit of Thatcherism was starting to do that to some people.

Given all the quality competition, I didn't initially pay much attention to 'Boy About Town'. It was so short and simple, it seemed almost throwaway. It didn't even bother with an introduction, just launched straight into a chorus. But had I stopped to consider it, I might have seen myself in the lyrics, especially my tendency to float, as Paul put it, 'up street down street like paper caught in wind', whizzing as I did from printers to record stores to book shops, from Croydon to Camden, Shepherd's Bush to Soho, Ladbroke Grove to Leicester Square, Wimbledon to Walthamstow, taking in regular night-time gigs in any of London's four corners, and breezing into whatever twenty-four-track studio The Jam might be recording at on any given day as if I owned the place, my sports bag laden with fanzines to sell, records to review, and a tape-recorder in case of an interview opportunity, wearing either my Chelsea Pensioner's coat, my teddy bear jumper, the latest in Johnson's fashions or perhaps, as today, the remnants of the same school uniform I'd worn when it was brand new, two full school years ago, the day I met Paul at RAK.

I guess it must have looked like a fun way to get by in life, being a boy about town, because after playing the new songs, Paul told me he wanted to start his own fanzine, full of poems and prose and illustrations and cut-out graphics. He asked me if I could help him get it printed and I happily pointed him towards Joly; I liked the idea of the best-dressed man in Britain hanging out with my favourite hippie. Paul talked enthusiastically, too, about the poetry compendium he was putting together as Riot Stories' next publication; since issuing a public call for contributions, he'd been inundated with post from all over the country. His interest in the medium had even extended to the live format: when I'd been to see The Jam at Guildford in April, his favourite new young poet, Aidan Cant, had taken to the stage as an unaccompanied support act – which was ironic given that the night before I had seen one of the original punk poets, Patrick Fitzgerald, opening for the Fall, but weighed down now by a backing band that was surely his kiss of death.

In the twenty-two months since I had first met Weller, an inordinate amount had happened in my life – but it paled in comparison to his. Paul appeared, instinctively, to recognise that he might never experience this moment again, having the undivided attention of a significant number of the nation's youth and the opportunity to use it for some form of good. Because producing his own fanzine and putting out poetry books – as well as writing and recording a new Jam LP and playing the usual rota of live shows – was *still* not enough. As we sat there in the Town House lounge, over tea and cigarettes, Paul asked if I'd thought of starting a record label.

Of course I had. I was cursed with the entrepreneurial spirit, and secretly envisaged myself building an empire that would put Richard Branson's Virgin to shame. At the same time, my life was already so busy that I'd had to put the magazine on hold for the time being just to take care of my exams. I summarised all this to Paul. He nodded, as if he'd expected such an answer.

'What about if I was to finance it?' he continued. 'Would you be interested in running a record label then? We could call it Jamming. You could put out your own band. Put out a record by Speedball. You know, we could put out any number of these great bands that don't get a look-in with the record companies.'

Guy's eyes, bright enough at the quietest of times, widened to the size of saucers. He'd been jocular and amiable this past couple of hours, knowing the importance of making a good impression, but considerably more reserved than his usual outgoing self: he was in the presence of greatness, after all. Now Paul Weller was offering to put out a single for Speedball, offering them a lifeline before the mod revival *completely* capsized: he was almost on his knees in gratitude.

I was equally overwhelmed. I was barely an hour away from my final O level, and I hadn't figured out what would come next – other than six or seven well-earned weeks of school holiday. I couldn't afford to live off *Jamming*, and Apocalypse was still a long way from coming good, that much I knew. But I didn't want anything to interfere with either of those careers – not the hassle of a real job, and not, when I thought about it, the prospect of two more years at Tenison's, studying for A levels. On 'Boy About Town', Paul sang, 'I want to do what I want to do and I want to live how I want to live.' That pretty much summed me up.

But running an independent record label? Like Rough Trade, Small Wonder, Fast, Cherry Red, Good Vibrations, Mute and the dozens of others who were regularly stocking me up with their wares in hopes of a good review in *Jamming*? An independent record label like those in the brand-new Independent Charts, as published in the trade weekly *Record Business* since the start of the year, official recognition that, three years after punk first hit, there was now a whole new distribution system at work in the land? An independent label like Factory, which was in the process of taking Joy Division into the Top Thirty (though under tragic circumstances)? I expressed my enthusiasm, and Paul told me to go off and 'suss out' the details, get back to him, and we'd take it from there. In the two years I'd known him, he had always been good to his word. I had no reason to doubt him now. I told him I'd better get back to school in the meantime, and he wished me luck on the last of my O levels – even though I knew he had barely a couple of them to his own name.

The exam was, fortunately, a doddle. The same way that I knew I'd failed my advanced maths the previous Monday morning, I was certain I'd passed the French oral exam the moment it was finished. This was in no small part because of those two trips to Nantes, living with French families, hanging out with French kids – and my own good friends – eating the food, drinking the drink, speaking the language. They'd been the best days I'd spent at Tenison's. Which just about said it all.

Jeff took his French oral almost directly after me. And because I hadn't had a chance to corner my bandmate on the way in – naturally, I'd barely made it back to school on time – I waited around to grab him on our way out of the school, for our last time as fifth years. He listened to my breathless description of what I thought must be the most exciting news of the world – a Jamming record label, a chance to release an Apocalypse single – and then he offered his opinion.

'Let *you* put out *my* records? No fucking way.'

Number 1:
START!

S chool was out for summer. For those of us so inclined, school was out forever. There had been no ceremony at Tenison's, no grand farewell for the two-thirds of the fifth years who would not return to the sixth form. In fact, due to exceptionally bad behaviour in the final week of lessons at the end of May – I was witness to flour bombs in the hallways, water bombs from the roof, the tearing down of the female dwarf German teacher's bookcase in front of her very eyes – the entire fifth year had been suspended from its last full day of school. With all the overlapping exams, some of us never got to see each other again. We didn't even get to say goodbye. But that was OK: there were plenty of people I had no desire to keep in my life, and those that I did . . . well, I would.

Like Jeff. His negative reaction to my news about a possible Jamming label hurt me deeply, and we had spent an hour on the phone that same evening patching things up. His fear was that if I was put in charge of a record label, I'd most likely choose my own Apocalypse songs for release. My fear was that if he really feared as much, he might leave the group and start his own. But Jeff wasn't crazy enough to quit; we'd played six gigs after all, just recorded a 'professional' demo tape. We were stuck with each other, like a married couple with a kid on the way.

So the following night, the Friday night, we'd celebrated the end of exams by attending the CEB disco together. (At least they had one.) I hadn't bought a ticket; increasingly these days, I expected to be on the guest list. But the CEB disco didn't have a guest list, and worse yet, to prevent unexpected intruders (a valid concern given the neighbourhood), it was an all-ticket event, and I was forced to hang around outside the school for what seemed like an eternity, until I found a first year looking to offload a spare ticket. (A first year? I was going to discos with *first years*?) I truly wouldn't have bothered but for the fact that my *other* best mate was going as well. Jeff, the School Punk, and Richard, its Ace Face, rarely saw eye to eye on music or fashion, but they had in common this weekend that their steady, sexually permissive girlfriends were elsewhere – Jeff's in Hastings, and Richard's on holiday already. Being equally despondent about their lack of imminent love-making prospects, they bonded in a way they rarely had in class. One of them even smuggled in a bottle of vodka and we had the final school-time satisfaction of getting drunk on CEB premises, myself convinced that the female fifth years were all eyeing me up, but that I was far too cool to respond – let alone set foot on the dancefloor. Rich and I rode the bus back to Brixton together, laughing incessantly all the way. It may have been relief at having our exams behind us. It may also have been the vodka.

Now, twenty-four hours later, Saturday night, and Jeff and I were off to see my new favourite new band, Delta 5, at the London School of Economics in Covent Garden. Delta 5 were regularly compared to the Gang of Four, and it was true that their guitarist slashed away at his instrument just like that band's Andy Gill. It was also common knowledge that the two groups were friends from Leeds University. The Gang of Four had even given Delta 5 their first studio time, letting them record at night during their sessions for the *Entertainment* LP. (Rough Trade released the results, recorded at EMI's expense.)

But there the similarities ended. The Gang of Four's line-up was that of the standard male quartet. Delta 5's most certainly was not. For starters, they had *two* bass guitars going at any one time. And they had not a token girl in the group, or even a couple of them, but three women in all, each of whom took turns on the bass, and two of whom sang the vocals. The group's debut single opened with the two bass guitars overlapping each other in a delightfully amateur imitation of disco; similarly, when the girls' vocals came in, the timbre and intonation was not that of the professional singer, but the archetype of the British independent label scene, where nothing was ever quite in tune or in time and nobody really gave a shit.

And that opening line: 'Can I have a taste of your ice cream?' The follow-up: 'Can I lick the crumbs from your table?' The eventual chorus, and song title: 'Mind your own Business.' Who cared whether this was intended to mean anything, the way 'To Hell with Poverty' or 'Skank Bloc Bologna' were so evidently invested with meaning. It had a tune, and you could dance to it, and after two years or more of endless experimentation on the fringes of Britain's new wave music scene, this was something of a revolution. Or a revelation: take your pick.

I'd seen Delta 5 live a few months back, on their first trip to London, when Rough Trade had them open for the Raincoats. It had been no contest. The Raincoats that night had appeared dreary in comparison to Delta 5 and their twin basses, cool guitarist and equally enthusiastic drummer, and then those three gorgeous girls. Bethan, Julz and Ros weren't gorgeous in the way that Fay Fife, Siouxsie Sioux and Penetration's Pauline Murray were unequivocally gorgeous; they were gorgeous in the sense that they carried themselves with style and grace, they were confident in their figures, their clothing and their haircuts, and they sang with enthusiasm and charisma. Best of all, they had a sense of humour about themselves, the instinct not to take everything so damn seriously. They were feminists, but they were *fun* feminists, and that too was something new.

Now Delta 5 had a new single. Like 'Mind your own Business', 'You' threw out a series of apparently random questions for its lyrics – and when sung by girls rather than boys, at least one of those questions, 'Who likes sex only on Sundays?' carried with it a further sense of feminist mischief, the notion that a girl could complain about a boy's sexual frigidity and not come off as a slut. The chorus to the other side, meanwhile,

'Anticipation is so much better', suggested that sex with a new partner was never quite as good as you had hoped it might be during the pursuit. I wouldn't have known, my pursuit of Brenda having taken all of about fifteen minutes.

I had the prospect of seeing Brenda again this Saturday night. Joseph had called me earlier in the day to let me know of a party in West Dulwich, that Brenda would be there and was hoping to see me. But I'd stopped in to a Speedball rehearsal at Alaska Studios as well, and Guy had told me about another party in Camberwell. I'd also been considering going to see the Chords, and Jeff wanted to go and see a new punk band called Splodgenessabounds. So many choices. It wasn't until someone from Delta 5 called me at home (and I was in!) and told me I'd be on the guest list for the show tonight, and we could finally get an interview done, that a decision was made. Jeff agreed to come along and take photographs. He seemed interested in the idea of a party afterwards, as well. He might not have been able to get laid this weekend, but he had no intent of sitting around the house and moping about it.

The Delta 5 concert was everything the CEB disco was not. There was a guest list; we were on it. There was a legitimate bar; we were served at it. There were adults and teenagers, of all shapes and sizes, not merely teachers and kids. The music between bands sounded more like a John Peel show than a Top Fifty countdown. And left-wing politics resonated through the air: the gig, it turned out, was a benefit for Irish Nationalist political prisoners. This sat poorly with Jeff, and it didn't sit too comfortably with me, either; though I didn't think Britain had any business being in Ireland, nor was I in love with the IRA. As Stiff Little Fingers had said, however much to Bill Nelson's annoyance, killing wasn't my idea of fun.

When it came time to interview Delta 5, they seemed equally put out. 'It's the first benefit we've played in ages,' they offered as some sort of apology. And who could blame them? At their last one, for Rock Against Sexism (which had been founded in the wake of Rock Against Racism as surely as night followed day), they had opened up the event's pamphlet to read, 'Delta 5 claim their lyrics can be sung by a man *or* a woman,' which was true: the band was proud that, like the Buzzcocks, they avoided gender references in song. But the Rock Against Sexism organisers had added an editorial comment: 'We don't agree.' That just about said it all.

Politics aside, Delta 5 seemed quite content with their lot in life, especially their label, Rough Trade. They denied that they had any intention of looking for a major label deal, the way that Stiff Little Fingers, the Mo-dettes and the newly renamed Athletico Spizz 80 had all recently deserted the Ladbroke Grove indie for what were assumed to be more profitable pastures. 'It seems to be a bit trendy to slag off Rough Trade after you've signed to a major,' said Julz. 'I think that's really pathetic.'

Delta 5 took the stage soon after, and Jeff saw for himself what I had seen in them all along – that they were a party band, a dance band, and yet that they managed to be so without abandoning any loyalty to their DIY/left-wing roots, and as such, they represented a major shift on the independent music scene. But we left the gig early all the same, literally running across the Waterloo Bridge to get to the Wellington pub and pick up some off-sales before the dreaded last bell. We had parties to attend, after all. The anticipation of further sex with Brenda had been on my mind all evening, as had the inexplicable certainty that I had no desire to go out with her. But it wasn't fear of commitment that made up my mind; it was the expectation that the Camberwell party would be full of adults and therefore still raging, while the Dulwich one, populated by fellow sixteen-year-olds, would surely be winding up by now. So Jeff and I jumped on a bus heading due south, our testosterone running high, our cockiness even higher. We had a band. We had a sponsor. We had finished our O levels. Our entire adult lives lay ahead of us. We were free. We were sex machines. We were unstoppable.

We needed to be. When we got to Camberwell, the party

was considerably less than expected. It wasn't so much the numbers: there were about thirty people there, all of them older than us. Only half were mods. (The rest were all straights: so many young people had devoted themselves to a form of fashion that those who did not formed a fashion cult all of their own.) But the music was winding down, the booze was running out. The energy, most definitely, was on the wane. This would not do! I had not foregone the opportunity of further carnal activity with Brenda to grab an early night. I commandeered the record player; Jeff, with his impeccable bravado, got everyone going – including the mods – and we led an hour of manic dancing. We even shared what little alcohol we'd brought. It seemed a small price to pay for preserving the party.

Still, even we could only keep dancing like that for so long, and around one in the morning, as the booze dried up completely, so the music wound down, and those who had wheels made plans to use them. The rest of us made the usual sudden claim for various scraps of furniture and floor space. And it was then that I determined to make it with Madeleine.

Madeleine was tall and rake thin, she had inviting lips painted an alluring shade of dark red, and she had a head of neatly cut, short dark hair. She looked like the really good-looking girl in Delta 5 might have looked had she been born in the USA – because Madeleine also had the distinction of an American accent. I'd brought her into our dance circle a couple of times during the previous hectic hour, to join me and Jeff and Guy and whoever else was declaring themselves single and available, and she'd flirted with me, though only slightly; it was evident that she was carrying some baggage, that she had some problems. Now, as the party wound down, her male companions – none of whom appeared to be her boyfriend, nor remotely interested in such status – were to be found calming her down from some sort of personal crisis that appeared only marginally drink-induced.

I didn't pay much thought to the possible causes of her paranoia. I merely noted her friends' insistence that she lie down in the corridor there and then to get some sleep. I promptly lay down alongside her. The schoolkid who didn't know how to go out with Shona properly four months earlier, the boy who'd been scared to make a move on Monica two months back, didn't exist any more. He'd been replaced by the school leaver who'd so casually seduced Brenda, the boy about town with the prospect of a record label in his pocket. And so, uninvited but not uninhibited, I began caressing Madeleine.

Though we hadn't introduced ourselves all night, she responded as if she'd been expecting this – or better yet, anticipating it. Her touch was kind and it was soft and when I put my lips to hers, they opened and met my tongue warmly. I ran my hand under her shirt and was surprised to find no resistance, and no bra. Suitably encouraged, and without totally abandoning her upper body, I lifted her skirt and ran my hand up between her legs. Still there was no protest, just a deep sigh and a shift in position. It wasn't anywhere near as dramatic an invitation as Brenda's had been a week earlier; this shift was lazier, sleepier. But I wasn't going to question it. Spurred on, I undid my button, unzipped my jeans, pulled them down, dragging my underwear with it, praying that I had sufficient time before somebody inevitably interrupted us and . . . seconds later, found myself on top of her and inside her, vividly aware that, any moment now, I would no longer be a virgin.

That moment came, all too literally, sooner rather than later. I lasted five strokes at most. I knew I must have been a lousy lay, but Madeleine was kind enough not to comment. In fact, she didn't say anything. Searching for an appropriate gesture, I slowly withdrew and reached for a cigarette from my shirt pocket; I offered one to Madeleine, she accepted, and she finally took me in. And then, only then, after she had given herself to me, did she address me for the first time.

'Oh my God,' she said, in her exotic drawl. 'I don't even know your name.'

I told her. She seemed happy enough with the answer and

I threw a similar question her way. I knew her name already, but not where she was from, what she was about.

So it began. Madeleine was one-third English, one-third French, and, as I suspected, one-third American. She was some sort of model. And she was nineteen. I grinned upon hearing that, and she checked herself. How old was I, she wanted to know.

'Er, sixteen,' I replied.

'Oh my God!' she cried. And again. 'Oh my God! I don't believe it! Sixteen! Now I've done it all!'

But she was laughing as she said it. She rose from the rough carpet, pulled up her pants, fixed her skirt and opened the nearest door. It led into a bedroom. There was no one there. Oh well, I told myself as I followed her under the covers, if you're going to have sex with a stranger for your first time, you may as well have it in a corridor. Besides, if she'd found her way to the bed to begin with, I'd never have had the arrogance to climb in alongside her. It was all meant to be.

We lay there in that single bed together, our faces touching as they rested on the pillow, and Madeleine proceeded to tell me her life story. Or at least the part that mattered, the part that explained why she was so mixed up. She had fallen madly in love, just over a year ago, she said. The kind of love where you want nothing more than to sit in a park all day holding hands, gazing into your partner's eyes. I looked at her curiously and again she checked herself.

'You're very young,' she said, with almost maternal benevolence. 'But one day, you'll fall madly in love with someone, they will fall madly in love with you, and you'll understand what I'm talking about.'

I took her at her word. What I had experienced with Madeleine, out there in the corridor, was not the act of making love, I knew that much. It was just casual sex, between two young people who'd been turned on to each other at a party. But still, that unique warmth of feeling my body inside her – to paraphrase 'Tonight At Noon' – had felt right. So did this, now, lying in bed with her, learning about her.

Madeleine and her lover, she told me, had done what came naturally upon discovering each other. They'd got married. Committed to a lifetime together, because there was nobody else they could ever imagine wanting to spend their time with. Four months into wedded bliss, they'd gone out shopping together; her husband had crossed the road without looking and was knocked down by an oncoming car. He was killed instantly, in front of her eyes. Madeleine was a widow at eighteen.

There was no way to respond to such a profound tale of calamity, so I didn't even try. I understood why her friends had all been worried about her behaviour, and why she had chosen to give her body to a sixteen-year-old before she even knew his name. (Or age.) She told me she had given up on love now, that she didn't believe she'd ever find it again and that she would die by the age of thirty-three. I believed her.

We went to sleep after that, Madeleine and me, fully clothed, under the covers. There was no way I was going to try for a second, longer stint between her legs after the tale she had just told. In the morning, one of us must have woken the other, because we found ourselves looking into each other's eyes for a moment. Then we gave each other a nervous kiss, a polite smile, and climbed out of bed together. We meandered into the living room to find the host making coffee. He didn't give us a second glance. Nor, for that matter, did Madeleine's friends. If they suspected we'd had sex, they weren't bothered; I wasn't their idea of bad news. Madeleine took a cup of coffee, handed it to me, and began rummaging through the fridge for breakfast items. I didn't feel sheepish. Not the slightest bit embarrassed. The sex had been nothing to warrant the anticipation, but *sleeping* together, that had been perfect.

Jeff soon emerged from the toilet, where he had spent the night curled around the cistern – it had appeared, at the time, the only available space left to get his head down – and took me aside, asked how I'd got on. I confirmed that I'd now joined the club. I was back in the band. I'd *done it*.

'Did you use a Durex?' he asked, immediately. Not: was it good, was it bad, was it anything like you expected, did you last longer than two minutes, and, isn't she fucking gorgeous? But: did you use a Durex?

It was a stupid question. I didn't carry packets of Durex around with me. Jeff knew that. And I certainly hadn't considered losing out on my first-ever lay by asking *her* for one.

'You idiot!' he whispered noisily when I told him as much in a single word. 'You don't know what you're risking.'

He warned me not to give Madeleine my phone number. I could have got her pregnant, didn't I know that? Did I want to become a dad at sixteen and ruin everything we had going for us? The band, the label, the fanzine? He set about dragging me away from the inviting morning-after scene before I could challenge him and change my mind.

Madeleine was hovering over a pan of sizzling bacon and eggs when I told her I had to leave. She looked surprised, as if she'd expected me to stick around. We kissed briefly, on the lips. She didn't offer her phone number, and I didn't ask for it either. We had served each other's purposes for the night. I'd come to the party as a boy about town. I left it as a man, thanks to her. Still, we had met each other travelling in different directions; we would leave each other the same way. We would never meet again. But what we had would always remain. And that was, at least, a start.